Organization&
Management
Problem Solving

Organization&
Management
Problem Solving

A Systems and Consulting Approach

James T. Ziegenfuss, Jr.
Pennsylvania State University, Harrisburg

Sage Publications
International Educational and Professional Publisher
Thousand Oaks ▪ London ▪ New Delhi

11-14-7

For information:

Sage Publications, Inc.
2455 Teller Road
Thousand Oaks, California 91320
E-mail: order@sagepub.com

Sage Publications Ltd.
6 Bonhill Street
London EC2A 4PU
United Kingdom

Sage Publications India Pvt. Ltd.
M-32 Market
Greater Kailash I
New Delhi 110 048 India

Printed in the United States of America

Library of Congress Cataloging-in-Publication Data

Ziegenfuss, James T.
  Organization and management problem solving: A systems and consulting approach / by James T. Ziegenfuss, Jr.
      p. cm.
Includes bibliographical references and index.
  ISBN 0-7619-1915-5 (c)—ISBN 0-7619-1916-3 (p)
  1. Problem solving—Case studies. 2. Management—Case studies. I. Title.
  HD30.29 .Z53 2001
  658.4'03—dc21   2001002911

01   02   03   04   05   10   9   8   7   6   5   4   3   2   1

Acquiring Editor:	Marquita Flemming
Editorial Assistant:	MaryAnn Vail
Production Editor:	Diane S. Foster
Editorial Assistant:	Cindy Bear
Copy Editor:	D. J. Peck
Typesetter:	Marion Warren
Proofreader:	Joyce Kuhn
Cover Designer:	Michelle Lee

Contents

Preface and Acknowledgments

This book was developed as a result of consulting engagements over a 20-year period. Materials from the organization and management consultation course offered at Pennsylvania State University have gradually evolved into this text. The model used for case analysis and for learning about consultation and problem-solving philosophy and methods integrates the thinking of many writers on organization and problem solving including Ackoff, Blake and Mouton, Schein, Kast and Rosenzweig, Trist, Mitroff, and Lippitt. The cases have been "tested" by students over the past 10 years with the result that some additions and deletions mark this edition.

The reader will find that the cases include both more and less information than is "required" for successful problem solving. I have found this to be the situation in actual problem solving. It seems that we often must begin to search for answers with only a small fraction of the necessary data. Or, we are confronted by the output of "manic performance" by information analysts; a few cases have an excess of tables and interview data. Quality problem solving occurs when we add to or delete from this "database." Interestingly, the classes examining cases with limited data often have generated the most controversy, although sometimes "heat without light."

The cases are composites of real experiences—familiar but fictitious. They are all imperfect, and in each case much more and many different things could have been done. Applied problem solving is quick and messy.

Identifying names of the cases have been changed, and some data have been altered to preserve confidentiality. Learning can be accomplished without identification of the organizations and clients. The reader can "expand" the case material with local versions of the organization types (e.g., a community bank), with Web sites, and with personal visits.

Thanks are due to a number of colleagues and students who have generously read earlier drafts including Chris McKenna and Rupert Chisholm at Penn State, Cindi Teeter at Deloitte Touche, and graduate students from the seminars at Penn State. I am grateful for the systems thinking education and for the encouragement over the years of Wharton School professors Russ Ackoff and the late Eric Trist. Their ideas are well represented here. I also thank Katherine Ziegenfuss for editing and Ruth Brinck for the patient word processing. Penn State's graduate education fund helped with expenses.

James T. Ziegenfuss, Jr.
Pennsylvania State University

1

Organizational Systems Thinking and Problem Solving

*Synergy means behavior of whole
systems unpredicted by the behavior of their parts.*
—Robert F. Fuller, *What I Have Learned*

Work teams collapse into conflict. New software products fail to meet delivery dates. Some executives quit, while whole departments are "downsized" out of existence. Morale and job satisfaction are at an all-time low. At various times, we could be talking about hospitals, Internet companies, steel producers, computer manufacturers, or schools. These situations represent only a few of the organization and management problems sometimes facing leaders at all levels of our public and private organizations. Problem-solving teams and consultants are at work in North America and Europe (Kipping, 1999) as well as in Asia (Vieira, 1997). In the public sector, subjects include Utah's personnel

1

management department (Burrington, 1985), university admissions (Gose, 1999), and professional practices such as law (Dennis, 1999). Because *no* organization is perfect, we all become problem solvers—as "insider managers" or "outsider consultants."

Two questions are the focus of this book:

- How can academics, professional managers, and consultants use organization theory and systems thinking in teaching and practicing problem solving?
- Can a view of the nature of organization enhance our ability to teach and practice problem solving and consultation?

This book presents one organization and management problem-solving model used in a graduate management program and in a variety of field projects where the concepts were tested by public and private sector cases. The model and the cases have proved to be quite helpful to both managers and students, some of whom have had "McKinsey 101" experiences in learning consulting and problem solving in real projects (Hayes & Setton, 1998).

Introduction

This first chapter defines the philosophy, concepts, and analytical tools needed to attack organization and management problems from a systems point of view. The model is integrationist in approach, using the thinking and methods of many researchers and problem solvers. The model is a unique combination of diverse viewpoints that, as a whole, contribute to a new perspective on organization and management problem solving. In short, problems are viewed as systems design and redesign challenges.

In graduate schools of business and public administration, as well as in day-to-day management activities, we often forget that assumptions about the nature of organization form the basis of our thinking about organizational problem solving. Academics, executives, and practicing consultants continually search for methodologies and concepts that will help to develop their organizations. When managers engage consultants, they seldom talk directly about their own mental models of the organization, nor do they ask about the consultants' models. This often is the case when we teach students in M.B.A. programs as well. Managers, academics, and consultants need to respond to these shortfalls in two ways:

- Underlying assumptions that guide our organization and management problem solving must be surfaced.
- Practical models useful to managers, consultants, and students must be presented and field-tested.

Organizational problem solving and consultation often are presented in business school courses as a part of strategic management, management policy, organizational behavior, and organizational development. In schools of public administration, problem solving and policy analysis and development appear in courses in public management, program planning and evaluation, and public policy. In too few of these courses do we spend time considering our conceptual starting point. Senior managers only rarely engage in dialogue that clearly surfaces the assumptions of their organizational views of the world—a habit that, unfortunately, began in their primary education.

To understand this systems and consulting approach to organization and management problem solving (Figure 1.1), we must have answers to three questions:

1. *What* is the architecture of the organization we propose to fix?
2. *Who* are the problem solving consultants?
3. *How* do the consultants work?

The first question leads us to a systems view of the organization. The second requires us to understand the consultant's role, skill, and preparation. The third is about the problem-solving process itself.

In this first chapter, I introduce the elements of a systems approach to organization and management problem solving. The approach can be used both to teach students and to assist practicing managers. The following topics comprise the approach to problems and their solutions:

- Needs
- Nature of problems
- Organizational and sociotechnical systems concepts
- Action research and organization development
- Stakeholders
- Organizational model and development process
- Consultation and problem-solving phases
- Problem-solving intervention concepts

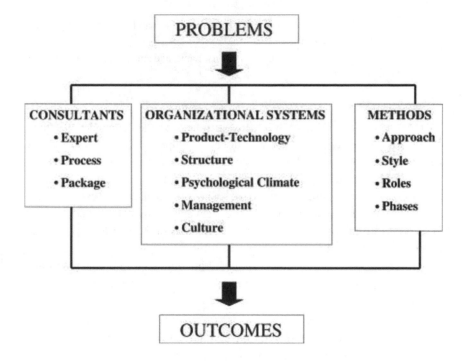

Figure 1.1.   Problem Solving: The Systems and Consulting Approach

- Problem solvers: Consultant types and roles
- Problem-solving outcomes
- Engagement analysis: Case reports

To help us understand the many diverse parts of this approach, we use the case of the "problems" at the Internal Revenue Service (IRS) in Washington, D.C. We all have "experienced" taxes, and many of us complain about the inadequacies of the IRS. In a recent *Fortune* article, the author opened the discussion with this comment on technology currency:

> However badly you think the IRS is, it is worse. The agency that processes 209 million of the most complicated forms known to humankind uses computer systems mostly designed in the 1950s, built in the 1960s, and jury-rigged ever since. . . . Charles Rossotti, the new commissioner, told *Fortune* that upgrading his vacuum tube era technology "will be like rebuilding Manhattan while we're still living in it." (Birnbaum, 1998)

The article came on top of many public media reports of taxpayer abuse (e.g., auditors threatening and abusing taxpayers [Bovard, 1998]), poor service, and congressional hearings on the troubled state of this federal agency. We use these problems to illustrate our approach because of the multiple dimensions of organization involved—technical, attitudinal, structural, and managerial.

With all the public commentary, it seems that the IRS is a problem-laden organization. A composite of some of the outstanding issues includes the following:

- Inadequate taxpayer assistance
- Undone revisions of forms and publications to reflect new tax law
- Telephone response problems, such as hours of availability
- Audit demeanor of IRS staff
- Internal quotas for revenue collection
- Inadequate staffing for high-demand periods
- Unfinished electronic filing capability
- Lack of currency in computer technology
- Bar code misprints on address labels
- Incomplete Web site development
- Fragmented authority structure

With 100,000 employees, as well as many millions of forms and telephone transactions, this is a very large organizational problem.

There have long been calls for reinventing the IRS (Lear, 1993). We have the option of continuing to criticize, or we can attempt to continuously improve the agency (Lear, 1996). Efforts have been directed toward restructuring (Laffie, 1997; National Commission on Restructuring the IRS, 1997). In addition, there is renewed attention to customer service (Bigelow, 1994).

Many times, the first solutions proposed are one-dimensional. We could fire the IRS commissioner. Or, we could reorganize—a favorite of many public leaders. For example, structural changes such as eliminating districts have been proposed for the IRS (Phillips, 1999). Commissioner Rossotti would create separate divisions for individual taxpayers, big business, tax-exempt entities, and small business. Changing the structure is the "quick-fix" focus; this "redesign of the order" is only one of many changes needed to fully dissolve the IRS problems. A systemic approach would help create an enriched view of the diagnosis, planning, and actions needed for an IRS turnaround.

To successfully attack the organization and management problems at the IRS, we should (a) know more about their nature and root causes in a diagnostic sense, (b) approach the problems of organization development and learning with experience in mind, (c) identify and use stakeholder opinions, (d) employ a process with phases and steps, (e) be aware of our multiple roles in problem solving, and (f) seek outcomes that demonstrate positive impact. We will continue to work on the IRS case, but let us begin our presentation of this approach with a discussion of some of the reasons why executives and managers need both inside and outside help.

Needs for Problem Solving and Consulting

We sometimes hear company executives say "We never use outside consultants; we have no need for them." Implied in this statement are both positive and negative assumptions. On the positive side, executives are expressing confidence in their internal problem-solving teams, even as they sometimes work on the wrong systems (Ackoff, 1993). Certainly, large corporations have both the range and the depth of talent to tackle many problems.

On the negative side, the statement can imply the following: "The company is so strong that all the managerial ideas and skills are in-house now and forever. We rarely have the need for problem solving because we are so well managed." On closer examination, this reveals a misunderstanding of the dynamic complex organization. No organization runs perfectly—or even close to it. Recognizing the ongoing need for problem solving is a throwing off of denial and an acceptance of the never-ending search for better harmony and continuous improvement. Too often, the failure stems from an inability to act (Sull, 1999).

At Southwest Airlines, consultants are thought to be helpful in adding capability, managing workload and risk, adapting to change, and providing influence and power (Sartain, 1998). Some years ago, Blake and Mouton (1982) listed some reasons for using consulting help, such as morale, change, conflict, missing competencies, "taking the heat," and disposing of funds. A survey listed two top reasons as providing expertise and providing an external detached viewpoint (Oakley, 1994). On occasion, an engagement begins as follows: "We are not sure what the problem is." The client has not self-diagnosed but instead is asking for help in defining the problem (e.g., "Why is morale low?"; "Why have we lost market share?"; "Why do we have a shortage of new product ideas?"). But consultants often are asked to go beyond specific problems, contributing to permanent skills through coaching and teaching (Bergholz, 1999).

Internal teams of problem solvers and outside consulting groups are engaged for two reasons: in *reaction* to problems and/or in an effort to be *proactive*. For example, "How can we reduce and better manage our production and transaction costs?" (Canback, 1999) is a reaction to cost problems and can be a preventive strike. We solve existing problems, or we confront the never-ending question of how to continuously improve. Leaders must respond to problems, and they also should address the question of how to be more effective next year than they were this year (no matter how good they currently are). This sounds reasonable enough, but throughout the process they must manage resistance to change (Lipton, 1996)—only one of the barriers to smooth and quick resolutions.

The Nature of Problems

What exactly is a problem? A dictionary definition may offer us a starting point. A problem can be one of the following:

- A question proposed for solution or consideration
- A question, matter, situation, or person that is perplexing or difficult

We are addressing organization and management problem solving, so we are interested in tackling the difficult questions, situations, and persons in public and private organizations. Problems include the never-ending quest for quality products, the development and maintenance of teamwork, and the adjustment of the company's traditional mission to an ever-changing environment.

Because the organization is a complex set of interlocking social and technical systems, we face not just isolated problems but also connected ones. Ackoff (1981) defined these organization and management problems as follows:

> A set of two or more interdependent problems constitutes a *system*. The French call such a system a *problematique;* for lack of a corresponding word in English, I call it a *mess*. (It seems appropriate to think of planning as mess management.)
>
> A mess, like any system, has properties that none of its parts ha[s]. These properties are lost when the system is taken apart. In addition, each part of a system has properties that are lost when it is considered separately. The solution

to a mess depends on how the solutions to the parts *interact.* Therefore, a plan should be more than an aggregation of independently obtained solutions to the parts of a mess. It should deal with messes as wholes, systematically.

In brief, planning is here conceptualized as a participative way of dealing with a set of interrelated problems when it is believed that unless something is done, a desirable future is not likely to occur, and that if appropriate action is taken, the likelihood of such a future can be increased. (p. 52)

How do we typically address problems in organization and management? We try to make them go away—quickly. But there are several options available, even though we rarely consider them directly.

There are three ways of dealing with these or any other problems; they can be resolved, solved, or dissolved. To *resolve* a problem is to find a means that does well enough that satisfies. To *solve* a problem is to find a means that performs as well as possible that optimizes. To *dissolve* a problem is to redesign the relevant system or its environment so that the problem is removed. This idealizes. It is better to solve than resolve, and better to dissolve than solve, because few problems stay solved for long. Dissolution requires more creativity than solution, and solution more than resolution. Unfortunately, creativity is a very scarce commodity. (p. 248)

In this organizational systems approach, we take the position that creative dissolution of the causal condition is the most desired problem-solving mission. The IRS can be fixed, as is, with basic components in place. Computer capability is enhanced, auditors become customer sensitive, and new business units are created. This would be a solution—the IRS at optimal effectiveness. Or, we could try radical dissolution such as a flat tax or the use of a sales tax, thereby dissolving some or all of the troubling conditions of the IRS.

Exactly what are problems in organization? Are they difficulties in reporting structure, management behavior, or personality and leadership style? When executives, managers, and consultants approach organizational problems, several characteristics of their styles are apparent:

- Problems are approached from a narrow one-dimensional perspective.
- Solutions are thought of as compromises between two or more opposing points of view.

These two assumptions and patterns of behavior dramatically limit the effectiveness of our problem solving in the complex organization.

We need a model of organization to begin our discussion of diagnosis and response.

Organizational and Sociotechnical Systems Concepts

Enhancing organizational effectiveness requires a conceptual picture of the whole organization (Fuqua, 1993; Ridley, 1993). Two points are keys to this perspective of problem solving and consulting:

- A view of the nature of organization enhances our ability to teach and practice organizational problem solving and consultation.
- Academics and professional managers must increase their use of organization theory and systems thinking in consultation, teaching, and practice.

The roots of the model used here are the sociotechnical concepts of Trist and colleagues beginning during the 1950s (Trist & Bamforth, 1951; Trist, Higgins, Murray, & Pollack, 1963). They recognized that the organization was a social system and that, along with the task and technology demands, designers must address the social psychology of the company (Katz & Kahn, 1978). This thinking has continued to contribute to our understanding of autonomous work group functioning (Susman, 1979) and the design of the organization (Pasmore, 1988; Trist & Murray, 1993). Current texts build this thinking into the perspectives on organization design, change, and development (Cummings & Worley, 2001; Daft, 1998).

Several commentators have given us a view of the scope of organization and management problems in field efforts to promote change and development. In their presentation of reengineering concepts, Hammer and Champy (1993) used a diamond to outline four problem areas: business processes, values and beliefs, management and measurement systems, and jobs and structures (p. 80). Cowan (1993) presented points of potential organizational problems in the views of executives as including external environment, strategy, production, operations, management information systems (MIS)/data processing, accounting, marketing, communications, customer management, and personnel (p. 122). Harrison (1994) listed eight elements as potential sources of problems: inputs, outputs, technology, environment, goals and strategies, behavior and processes, culture, and structure (p. 29). Hammer and Stanton

(1999) emphasized attention to organization processes as the means to improvement. All these authors were giving us conceptual maps to help us with diagnoses. Importantly, all were asking us to target the rich and "deep structure" of the organization (Old, 1995).

Organizations: Definition and Systems

The following comments on the history of organization theory will bring us to the durable organizational point of view presented by Kast and Rosenzweig (1970). Their model, expanded over the past 10 years with the work of other theorists and practitioners, will be used to guide our systems analysis of organization and management problems of many types.

We can view the history of organization theory through the emergence of various schools of thought that proposed, at their time, to present the correct theories of the architecture and functioning of the organization (Shafritz & Ott, 1996). Each new theory became the accepted perspective on the nature of organization as each school of thought replaced another's popularity and position of authority. Theorists competed for dominance or for recognition that they had found the truth. Peaceful coexistence with previous theorists was not possible, at least until more recently.

Each school of theory—named in an early Scott (1961) review as *classical/structural, neoclassical/human relations,* and *modern/systems*—attempted to develop a picture of the "reality" of corporate evolution and operation. Each group of organization theorists presents a description of complex reality and teaches its followers (e.g., students, researchers, practicing executives) to "see" reality in that way. Unfortunately, this tutoring has hindered the ability of new theorists to see other dimensions as parts of a more complex whole. Thus, the main schools that have evolved over the history of organization theory, adding more recent views of stakeholder networks and culture as the essence of organization, actually are emergent dimensions of the same reality. Through many arguments, there are no winners because proponents of "opposing" theories are fighting over and through different dimensions of organizational reality. Problem-solving failures can be attributed, at least in part, to this inadequate understanding.

For example, we could define the IRS problems in relation to the period of organization theory development. During the classical period, the IRS would be troubled by structural and technological deficiencies—the emphasis of organization theorists at that time. The answer would be to fix the table of organization and restructure.

During the human relations period, IRS problems would be defined as psychological. The causes would be individual attitudes, motivation, and satisfaction. The answer would be team building, sensitivity groups, and motivational seminars.

In our ongoing period of systems thinking, IRS problems are viewed as a complex set of interlocking deficiencies. The causes lie in the pattern of interrelationships, for example, an incentive system that distorts citizen relationships and leads to employee dissatisfaction and turnover. The answer lies in multiple interventions to change technology, structure, management style, and culture. The newer focus is on interlocking structures and especially on the processes of organization management (Garvin, 1998).

Systems theory proposes general principles as the formative guidelines for all organizations. These general principles are either characteristics (e.g., environment, purpose, structure, hierarchy, boundary) or actions (e.g., adaptation, differentiation, integration). The principles are viewed by systems-thinking organization theorists as primary elements for understanding the nature of organization for all organizations—from the IRS, to Microsoft, to the Hospital of the University of Pennsylvania. During the late 20th century, theorists viewed the organization as a whole guided by values and principles, by interacting subsystems, and by structures and processes of integration. A complex web of interlocking systems (both social and technical in nature), these systems include the task and core technology, the skills and abilities needed to complete the work, and the individual and group behaviors that comprise a social system.

We must know what an organization is if we are to solve organizational problems. Some years ago, Kast and Rosenzweig (1970) offered a model that is described and elaborated throughout this book. According to Kast and Rosenzweig (1985),

> We view the organization as an open, sociotechnical system composed of a number of subsystems. Under this view, an organization is not simply a technical or a social system. Rather, it is the structuring and integrating of human activities around various technologies. The technologies affect the types of inputs into the organization, the nature of the transformation processes, and the outputs from the system. However, the social system determines the effectiveness and efficiency of the utilization of the technology. (p. 113)[1]

This model—a sense of the organization as an interlocking set of five sociotechnical subsystems—is derived from the history of organization theory.

Kast and Rosenzweig's 31-year-old conception of the organization is consistent with current sociotechnical thinking accepted in the field. They viewed the organization as open to the environment and as composed of several subsystems under the following five titles:[1]

1. The product and technical subsystem
2. The structural subsystem
3. The psychosocial subsystem
4. The managerial subsystem
5. The culture, goals, and values subsystem

The subsystems and their relation to the organizational environment are represented in Figure 1.2. In this approach to problem solving and consulting, this mental model is the underpinning—the architectural target for design, development, and change (Nadler, Gerstein, Shaw, & Associates, 1992). It is necessary to briefly describe the nature of each of these subsystems because they will become the targets of our diagnostic and problem-solving work. The following descriptions of the subsystems are based on Kast and Rosenzweig's original work and adapted with the research and thinking of other theorists.

1. *The product and technical subsystem.* This refers to the knowledge required to design, develop, distribute, and support goods and services. The product and technical subsystem includes the "core work" of the public agency or private company—retail sales, manufacturing, teaching, providing medical care, collecting taxes, and so on. The product and technical subsystem develops as a result of the task requirements of the organization and varies depending on the particular activities of the organization as a whole and of its subunits (e.g., departments). The technology for manufacturing automobiles differs significantly from that used in an oil refinery or a software company. Similarly, the products and technology of a hospital emergency room are different from those in a university department. The product and technical subsystem is shaped by the production and delivery process, by the specialization of knowledge and skills required, by the types of machinery and equipment involved, and by the layout of facilities.

We can examine manufacturing processes. For example, at Lockheed, managers were concerned about growing workers' compensation claims. A se-

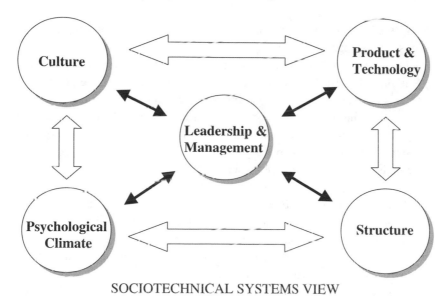

SOCIOTECHNICAL SYSTEMS VIEW

Figure 1.2. Organization and Management Problem Solving: The Diagnostic Targets

nior ergonomics engineering specialist led an internal team with representation from manufacturing, engineering, operations, production, materials processing, medical personnel, and safety engineering. The team was searching for a technical system flaw (Kelley, 1995).

In our case, the technologies used to assess, track, and collect taxes are the "technical system components" of the IRS. These include tax forms, tax tables, and audit processes. The product and technology help determine the organization's structure as well as its psychosocial climate, two more of the subsystems.

2. *The structural subsystem.* This involves the ways in which the tasks of the organization are divided (differentiation) and coordinated (integration) Organization charts, position and job descriptions, and rules and procedures define the structure in a "formal sense." Structure also is defined by patterns of authority, communication, and workflow. The organization's structure is the basis for establishing formal relationships between the production processes and worker psychology. Many examples of flawed performance are encouraged by wrong-headed reward systems that provide structural support for undesired behaviors

(Kerr, 1995). Interactions and relationships link those technical and psychosocial subsystems and can bypass the formal structure.

In our example, the IRS commissioner thinks that the unit structure at the IRS is flawed and is a prime cause of citizen dissatisfaction. Responding to problems of poor coordination and inefficiencies caused by the separation of specialists, he has proposed a business unit structure. IRS offices will be organized into four or more units: individual taxpayers, big business, nonprofits, and small business. With knowledge, skills, and resources better integrated in these units, citizens will receive higher quality service.

3. *The psychosocial subsystem.* Every organization has such a subsystem—the psychosocial dynamics of individuals and groups in interaction. Forces outside the organization, as well as internal characteristics such as technology and structure, help to establish the organization's psychological climate within which employees act out their roles performing their assigned duties. Subsystem elements include individual behavior and motivation, status and role relationships, and group dynamics as well as the values, attitudes, expectations, and aspirations of the people in the organization. As a result of this unique mix, psychological climates differ significantly from organization to organization. Certainly, the climate in which a computer analyst works is different from that of a nurse on a pediatric unit or a doctor in emergency surgery. Psychosocial aspects of the organization are both shaped and supported by management.

In our example of a federal agency, abusive, surly, and unfair treatment by IRS agents has come to the attention of congressional committees. Agents work in a climate where citizen abuse is tolerated, may be rewarded, and is thought to be helpful in management success. What will federal executives do to attack the problem that is here defined as psychosocial in nature—a combination of attitudes, motivation, and rewards? Behavioral strategies will be part of the solution (Berry, 1999).

4. *The managerial subsystem.* This is the integrator relating the organization to its environment; setting the goals; developing comprehensive, strategic, and operational plans; designing the structure; and establishing evaluation and control processes. Managerial activities traditionally have been described in terms of planning, organizing, developing, directing/leading, and controlling. More recently, the focus is on design, education, and stewardship as core duties (Senge, 1990). These duties are performed through a series of management roles—interpersonal, informational, and decisional (Mintzberg, 1975). Manage-

ment coordinates and integrates the production, structural, psychosocial, and cultural subsystems.

In our case of the IRS, the commissioner is responsible (*leadership*) for creating an organizationwide plan that will improve tax collection and audit processes (*product and technology*) with a new *structure* and a more "citizen-friendly" *psychological climate*. Deficiencies in IRS performance may be viewed as a *management* failure.

5. *Organizational culture.* This is the last of the five subsystems. To be successful and survive, the organization must meet social requirements—the goals and values of the external environment. Here we include the concept of corporate culture (Schein, 1990; Smircich, 1983) and the ability to understand culture as part of the problem-solving and consultation process (Lundberg, 1993). This subsystem links the goals and values of the members of the organization with those of the broader society. In our example, the IRS was created for social system purposes— -the assessment and collection of monies for the support of our collective government. The IRS must fairly fulfill its purpose—collecting taxes—or else it will lose citizen support. Failure to complete the task due to technological breakdowns or inequitable application would erode societal support.

These five subsystems are considered "internal" to this perspective of the organization. There is an "external suprasystem." The environment is considered to be all forces outside the "boundaries" of the organization (defined by the five systems). These forces can include a diversity of issues such as national and international trends as well as climatic and competitive situations (Figure 1.3). A sample of the rich mix of aspects includes the following:

- Economics
- Politics
- Technology
- Social factors and demographics
- Law
- Education
- Culture
- Natural resources
- Globalization

Environment

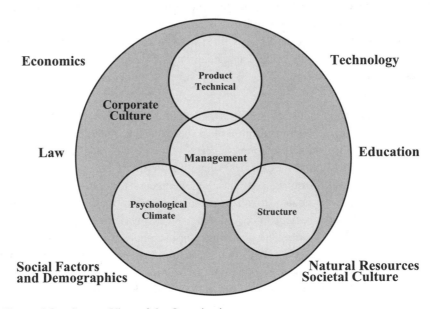

Figure 1.3.   System View of the Organization

We could add others that are related—communications, transportation, and so on. All can potentially affect problem solving from outside the organization.

With this perspective, every organization and management problem is potentially a five-system problem—plus the environment. This approach to problem solving both evolves from and reinforces our understanding of organizational thinking. Early views of organization failures and of problem-solving approaches emphasized the structural and technical subsystems. The human relationists and behavioral scientists advocated for the importance of the psychosocial subsystem, focusing their attention on motivation, group dynamics, and related people-oriented factors. The systems school (multiple subsystems) concentrated on methods of integration and linkage processes. Each approach to organization and management, or each school of theory, emphasized a particular subsystem with little recognition of the importance of the others. Figure 1.4 presents the full richness of subsystem variables in this view of the organization. Importantly, they all are potential points of trouble—targets for organization and management problem solvers.

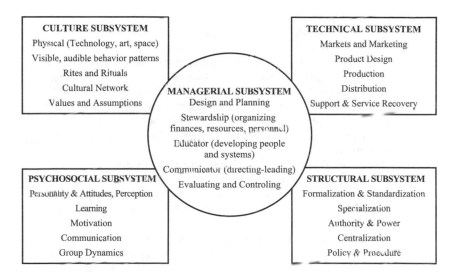

Figure 1.4. Organizational Analysis: Key Subsystem Variables

Quality of work life efforts, popular over the past two decades, increasingly took a whole organization perspective, changing climate, reward structure, and management style (Weisbord, 1987). For example, problem solvers at Continental Airlines address values, expectations, and teamwork as well as schedules and hub structures (Davidson, 1997).

This model of the organization is not without criticism. A summary of commentators' concerns, with some advice on the model's use, would include the following:

> There is incomplete knowledge of the five systems so that they are somewhat "black box like" (no one really knows what is in each). Subsequently there is little work on the validity of these contributors to the design and operation of companies. A problem solving team could use the model just as a discussion tool, keeping in mind that it is a somewhat artificial and not completely tested model of organization. If this is accepted, the group should proceed to use it but with the following additional limitations.
>
> *The model fosters system-by-system attention with limited focus on the interactive effects.* Because of the complexity in each of the topic areas—product, psychological climate . . .—consultants should remember that in reality all of the systems are working simultaneously and that their interactions are key. When the leaders commit to change beginning with statements of core values

and desired culture, they are also implying possible change in incentives, product design, production and delivery system, different attitudes, and even collaboration with the community.

The model is static in orientation, so the perspective can undercut our knowledge that companies are social systems and as such are constantly changing. While the IRS leader is launching task forces to look into technical issues of performance and a shortfall in service to citizens, staff may have already moved to make changes in policy and procedure. And when those changes are made, others are in the design stage, where ongoing efforts to continuously improve quality do not stop.

The intuitive clarity of the five systems of the model helps problem solvers to quickly see what must be done, but it simultaneously helps [to] undercut recognition of how complex organizations are. Here the culture material presented is brief and clear. In practice, executives and researchers devote whole careers to understanding what culture is and how to change it.

The separating of the systems is necessary for the presentation, but it is an artificial construction that can cause us to forget the nature of organizations—as integrated whole, product with structure with climate with leadership. At the IRS, we are trying to consider whether a culture change is necessary. But it is hard to separate out the potential effects of psychological climate, product quality, and leadership (determined commitment to serve the nation). Thus, as you pay attention to culture or product, you must constantly keep the other systems' effects in mind.

Each of the system's variables is not yet specific and quantifiable, i.e., the metrics are as yet not fully developed and cannot take us easily beyond the qualitative judgment. When a senator suggested we change the IRS culture, he was questioned by a second senator asking: "How citizen friendly is the IRS culture now?" This is a very good question—one very hard to answer with the level of science that the senators are accustomed to. We have made great strides in measurement, but each of the systems is a construction of reality that is open to much interpretation. (Ziegenfuss & Bentley, 2000)

Sociotechnical Systems Thinking

Although we use the label, we have not fully discussed what we mean by *sociotechnical systems* thinking and what the implications are for problem solving. Several classic articles offer detailed descriptions of the elements of sociotechnical theory (see, e.g., the earlier writings of Cherns, 1975; Cummings & Srivastva, 1977; Trist et al., 1963). The development of this theory and practice was summarized by Fox (1995) and Trist and Murray (1993). Here we review the main assumptions and concepts underlying the view that the organization is both *social* (culture, goals, values, psychology) and *technical* (production processes, structure, management, planning and control systems). We use the IRS case for illustration.

Sociotechnical systems theory is based on optimistic assumptions about human behavior in the workplace, as was noted some years ago:

- Many employees have the capacity and desire to make greater contributions through their jobs than ordinary organizational structures, processes, and workplace designs allow.
- To unleash employee motivation, organizations should allow employees to carry out activities relevant to their job tasks.
- Employees are not fixed as to their abilities but [rather] have the capacity to become either more or less than they currently are. (Chisholm & Ziegenfuss, 1986b, p. 318)

Experiences in the workplace also affect employees' needs and expectations. In short, one product of the organization is people. Because individual employees' skills and the motivation to employ these skills constitute key elements of, for example, the technology of health care delivery systems, the organization truly needs to view its employees as human resources.

Sociotechnical systems theory suggests that work roles and work units can be designed to respond flexibly to changing demands related to tasks performed and the environment. The capacity to perform in various ways and the ability to select appropriate responses are built into a sociotechnical systems work system. This approach contrasts sharply with traditional organization design principles of organizations that dictate the breaking of jobs into simple elements— so that the costs of training and replacing personnel may be eased—and otherwise follow closed-system principles derived from the concept of scientific management.

The term *sociotechnical systems* implies several types of internal and external congruence for work systems. The concept of congruence—or joint optimization—between technical and social systems is a design principle. The support systems of the organization, including those providing training, selection, payment, and so on, should be designed to foster and reinforce desired behaviors (Cherns, 1975). For example, wage incentives tied to individual performance actually inhibit efforts to develop work teams with group goals.

How does this perspective relate to our public agency's problems? In our IRS case, systems thinking implies several points about problem solving. First, we expect that IRS employees are responsible and interested in doing good work. They are not the villains painted in news reports. Rather, they are caught up in conflicting structures and system performance demands that compel them to "lean on" taxpayers. Because the IRS is divided into hierarchical structures, employees are unable to make discretionary judgments in a timely and flexible fashion. And because of incentive systems, they are put in a position of undercutting the service function that we, as taxpayers, think we are paying for. The problems are both social-psychological and technical in nature, calling for consultation that recognizes this duality (Cummings, 1993). In short, the IRS systems are not consistent; they are incongruent.

The concept of congruence (Nadler & Tushman, 1980) implies the need for a fit among the culture, reward, and control systems of an organization and the design of specific work processes, employee roles, and departments. Efforts to make changes in one area affect other areas of the organization. System congruence requires interrelated attempts delivered in a coordinated fashion to improve organizational functioning and impact such as production, productivity, and quality of work life. This approach is based on several assumptions.

- *Whole* organizations, not just individual *parts,* contribute to high- or low-quality problem solving. The wide array of IRS problems will not be solved with a new computer system.
- *Whole* means that both *social and technical* aspects of the organization are considered as appropriate targets of improvement action. Congressional hearings cited the lack of modern computer technology *and* surly behaviors by agents.
- Quality organization designs require *attention to structure* (components and policies) and *process* (decision making and group dynamics). IRS leaders are now considering redesign of their structure, a revision of the quota system for judging job performance, and streamlined decision making.
- *Relations between the parts* of an organization are crucial to the improvement of quality of the whole—to problem solving. Treatment of citizens may improve when the IRS quota structure is revised. But management also must revise its control and performance assessment methods when beginning to institute culture change.
- Quality is viewed as *synergistic,* meaning that the whole is more than the sum of the parts and that multiple initiatives (rather than single actions) are called for to solve problems (multisystem actions). IRS leaders now plan to restructure, to upgrade computer technology, and to address agent behaviors that are making the IRS seem "customer unfriendly."

- Both producer and user *inputs* are crucial for problem definition and understanding, meaning that information from key stakeholders is necessary to develop problem solutions. Congressional hearings were held to collect feedback about the IRS from citizens and to provide political leaders with an opportunity to review current agency operations.

- *Transformation processes* are the focus of attention because they lead to and explain problematic outcomes and are the means to improvement. How the audits are chosen, whether IRS teams are focused on similar markets (e.g., small business, nonprofits), and methods of electronic processing all are receiving attention.

- Avoiding *entropy* (organizational decay) is an underlying assumption because, in a dynamic environment, quality will decrease if aggressive actions are not taken to periodically assess and continue improvement). Congressional hearings were both reactive and proactive in that the IRS received a top-to-bottom review that some citizens and staffers viewed as a reaction to public problems, whereas others viewed it as an overdue periodic assessment.

- The approach recognizes the importance of *open systems thinking*, meaning that the external environment influences problem solving and that external opinions and measures (benchmarks) are important. The IRS "problems" surfaced when political leaders began to receive many complaints. Politicians and citizens from the "outside environment" (beyond the walls of the IRS) are forcing the changes.

- *Contingency* and *equifinality* thinking means that organizing for problem solving is dependent on the situation and that each organization must create its own unique improvement plan. Although IRS leaders can learn about successful development and redesign of other public and private companies, they must devise their own unique plan for improvement. And there are many ways of solving problems.

- This philosophy and practice imply that *systems are purposeful and planned,* meaning that problem solutions in structures, processes, and outcomes also are purposeful and planned. The IRS problems will not be solved by accident. Their resolution will occur only by a planned attack that recognizes the complex interrelated aspects of product/technology, structure, psychological climate, management, and culture.

Organizational Systems and Development Processes

Systems thinking is critical to addressing organization and management problems because a model of the organization is *implicit* or *explicit* at four points in the problem-solving process: diagnosis, planning, action, and evaluation.

First, managers and consultants must *diagnose* the organizational "locale" of their problems. To put it in quality management language, in what systems are the root causes? Diagnosis requires an understanding of the nature of organization, as Harrison (1994) argued so effectively. From the brief organization theory history, we know that in the not-too-distant past, diagnosis would focus on technology and structure as the key sets of variables. When a performance problem such as the one at the IRS surfaces, one mental set leads us directly to structure. A change in the table of organization—a reorganization—is the quick recommendation. This is not necessarily the cause of the problem, but it is the implicit mental model followed by the problem solvers. Problem solvers would "see" a structural problem as a cause of the organization's poor performance. We even have recent examples of this non-systems thinking. The writings and work of the reengineering advocates are a prime example of this limitation. In the very popular book *Reengineering the Corporation,* Hammer and Champy (1993) focused their attention on the product manufacturing and delivery processes of private companies. Although great gains were made in process efficiency, they did not "transform" the organization. In a follow-up book, *Reengineering Management,* Champy (1995) admitted that there was a missing piece—the managerial system. A broad perspective of the organization promoted by the systems model expands the diagnostic targets right from the start.

So, we have found that narrowly defined technological and structural views of the organization no longer are appropriate. The systems view has brought in the external environment, the psychological system, management behaviors, and corporate culture and has exposed the complexity of this "mess" of connected problems. Each approach to organization and management problem solving, like that of the reengineers, emphasized a particular subsystem with little recognition of the importance of the others and with little understanding that problem solving and consulting is multisystem in nature.

More recent approaches view the organization as an open sociotechnical system with subsystems and interactions that, in total, are *co-producers* of organization and management behavior (and of problems). Organization behaviors are explained as a result of the *converging influences* of goals and values, technology, structure, and psychosocial and managerial characteristics and actions.

How is organizational systems thinking used to teach and practice problem solving and consultation (Ziegenfuss, 1992)? The sociotechnical systems view is both a general perspective and a specific model that defines all public and private organizations. The five subsystems are the internal elements examined when tcaching and practicing problem solving through internal and external consulting. As a whole, these subsystems and their interrelationships *are* the organization to be analyzed, planned for, and acted on—the targets of interventions.

Teaching. To teach graduate management students about the consulting process, students are asked to analyze cases using the model to create a diagnosis, a plan for action, and impact measures of the changes (Ziegenfuss, 1996). The model drives group presentations of diagnosis, planning, action, and evaluation, and it helps students match problems with intervention tools and techniques.

Practice. In consulting practice, the model has been used regularly to guide board members' and senior managers' analyses of their organizations' strengths and weaknesses as a part of strategy formation. Between 800 and 1,000 senior managers and board members have used the model during the past 10 years as part of a strategic planning process. Along with internal "diagnosis" of the internal state of the organization, the model guides vision building (descriptions of the desired corporate future) by outlining a rich perspective of the organization future (Massie-Mara & Ziegenfuss, 2000; Ziegenfuss, 1989).

Research. The model also has been used in a series of research studies, for example, to attack medical malpractice (Ziegenfuss & Perlman, 1989), to identify barriers to quality improvement (Ziegenfuss, 1991), to create a conceptual plan for actions to improve quality (Ziegenfuss, 1992, 1993), as part of the scheme for a Delphi study of desired characteristics of departments of medicine (Jacques, Bauer, & Ziegenfuss, 1993), as a conceptual map for understanding the impact of organization change (Ziegenfuss, Munzenrider, & Lartin-Drake, 1998), and for organizing health care cost containment efforts (Ziegenfuss & Bentley, 2000).

The organizational systems model, as adapted here, has been used extensively as a part of a way of teaching consultation and engaging in consultative practice. It offers both elegance and simplicity, making it accessible to both students and managers. We can use the model to help us address the many problems of the IRS. And we can use it as a conceptual model for attacking problems of all types from diagnoses to action in many fields and industries.

Stakeholders

We now must consider who is involved in any given problem because we need their ideas, we need their advocacy, and we need to address their resistance to change (Golembiewski, 1993; Mitchell, Agle, & Wood, 1997). The IRS case is only one example. Each problem in any field involves a set of interested parties, labeled by some authors as *stakeholders*. To address the problem effectively, we must know who has a "stake" in a successful change (problem solving). For example, a team created to address the IRS problems would list the involved "parties to the problems." Who are they? Politicians, employees, tax attorneys, and citizens would be a good start.

Tschirhart (1996) defined stakeholders and the reasons why we attempt to manage them in problem-plagued organizations such as the IRS and in virtually all problem-solving and consulting engagements:

> Skilled management of the interactions of organizations with their stakeholders may help organizations achieve their missions by reducing the negative effects of dissatisfied stakeholders and encouraging support from key stakeholders. An organization's stakeholders include its employees, volunteers, board members, funders, suppliers, clients/consumers, regulators, contractors, competitors, collaborators, and any other actors who have a stake in the organization's performance and/or the power to affect organizational performance. A stakeholder's claims or interests in an organization may be economic, legal, or moral. (p. 1)

In the IRS case, business owners have an economic stake. Audited citizens have a legal one. And all citizens have a moral stake in the fairness of this key governmental agency. In each case, the stakeholders must be identified, and their positions must be understood.

In his book *Stakeholders of the Organizational Mind,* Mitroff (1983) identified seven categories of stakeholders that help us develop an "inclusionary net" of interested persons (Table 1.1). Starting engagements with a stakeholder analysis tells us who we will have to attend to during the problem-solving process. Stakeholders always are present. To attack organization and management problems, stakeholders must be identified, and their values and positions must be understood. Without systematic understanding of their views, problem solving proceeds as if their needs will be met by chance. The identification and involvement of stakeholders helps us expand the range and depth of problem solutions. And by including those with a stake in the problem, we can begin to address and minimize resistance to change.

Table 1.1 Stakeholders

1. The *imperative* approach identifies stakeholders who feel strongly enough about an organization's proposed policies or actions to act on their feelings.
2. The *positional* approach identifies those stakeholders who occupy formal positions in a policy-making structure, whether internal or external to the organization (e.g., government).
3. The *reputational* approach is a sociometric one. It entails asking various knowledgeable or important persons to nominate those who they believe have a stake in the system.
4. The *social participation* approach identifies individuals or organizations as stakeholders to the extent that they participate in activities related to a policy issue.
5. Because one of the reasons for identifying stakeholders is to assess their leverage and influence in a policy system, it sometimes is adequate to identify only those who tend to shape the opinions of other stakeholders. The *opinion-leadership* method does this.
6. The *demographic* approach identifies stakeholders by characteristics such as age, sex, race, occupation, religion, place of birth, and level of education.
7. The final method selects a *focal organization* in a policy system and seeks to identify the individuals and organizations that have important relationships with the focal organization. Typical relationships include those of (a) supplier, (b) employee, (c) customer or client, (d) ally, (e) competitor or adversary, (f) regulator or controller (e.g., government), and (g) regulatee or controlee (e.g., subdivisions of a parent organization, legally controlled entities).

SOURCE: Mitroff (1983).

How does this view of the organization as interrelated sociotechnical systems relate to problem-solving action by internal teams or outside consultants?

Action Research and Organizational Development

We now know what problems are, we have a definition of the organization, and we can identify and call on stakeholders for their help and involvement. What processes do we use to attack problems?

In this approach, organizational problem solving is considered to be both "action research" and "organizational development." A brief definition from a popular text introduced the philosophy and method:

> Action research is a data-based problem-solving process of organizational change that closely follows the steps involved in the scientific method. It represents a powerful approach to organizational change and consists of three essential steps:
>
> - Gathering information about problems, concerns, and needed changes from the members of an organization.

- Organizing this information in some meaningful way and sharing it with the employees involved in the change effort.
- Planning and carrying out specific actions to correct identified problems.

An organizational change program may go through repeated cycles of data gathering, information sharing, and action planning and implementation. The action research often concludes with a follow-up evaluation of the implemented actions. (Hellriegel, Slocum, & Woodman, 1998, p. 592)

Action research has received increasing attention from both researchers and practitioners during the past 10 years, and the strategy often is used to address problems (Greenwood & Levin, 1998; Reason & Bradbury, 2001; Stringer, 1999). Organization and management problem solving can be viewed as an *action research activity that is part of an overall strategy of organizational development*. This "system and whole organization" orientation to problem solving has meaning for how problems are engaged. When we confront situations such as the IRS case, we can too easily be led to the replacement of leaders and the notion that restructuring will "fix" the organization. But in cases where problems, as in Ackoff's language, are an interconnected "mess," we will need multiple actions in multiple systems along with follow-up data and reevaluation. The IRS problem really is one of long-term change and development that will require experimental action and a wide range of methods. It is not simply a problem of a flawed leader.

Organization development is an umbrella term for the philosophy and methods of continuous improvement of every aspect of the company (e.g., performance quality, productivity, efficiency, culture, leadership). Some leading organizational development activities and concepts currently in common use were presented by French and Bell (1990) some years ago and are listed in Table 1.2. In a problem-solving engagement, one, two, or several of these activities may be used and integrated into a "whole organization" strategy for improvement. Although some of these are not systems thinking in orientation, we can employ them as part of a rich strategy that is based in systems. We advocate the use of different methods in a pluralistic and complementary manner (Jackson, 1995).

Organization and management problem solving involves the use of one or several of these methods to dissolve the conditions that have given rise to problems, conditions that may be rooted in product/technology, structure, psychological climate, management, and culture systems.

Table 1.2 Organization Development Activities

1. Diagnostic activities
2. Team-building activities
3. Intergroup activities
4. Survey-feedback activities
5. Education and training activities
6. Structural activities
7. Process-consultation activities
8. Coaching and counseling activities
9. Life and career planning activities
10. Open-systems planning
11. Action research

SOURCE: French and Bell (1990).

For example, at the IRS, the new commissioner might select a number of activities to foster organization development including the following:

- A diagnostic inquiry to determine the breadth and depth of the troubles at the IRS
- Survey feedback activities to collect and consider information from citizens and employees about both the problem diagnosis and some remedial actions
- Training in conflict resolution and conflict avoidance as well as in customer service sensitivity
- Coaching and counseling to improve supervisory skills
- Restructuring of the quota and incentive systems for monitoring performance

This "package" of organizational development activities will produce improvement because of the multisystem targets and the recognition of interactive effects. Now how does the problem-solving work flow?

Problem Solving and Consultation Phases, Interventions, and Engagement Questions

Exactly what happens when a problem-solving or consulting team addresses a problem? Managerial problem solving and consulting often, but not always, follows a series of phases or steps. Regardless of whether the problem solvers and consultants have a role within the organization, are located outside the organization, or are some combination of "insiders" and "outsiders," there are certain basic patterns of interaction between the client and the consultant. These are the "steps" of the process of problem solving and consulting. Here they are presented as phases, building on Lippitt and Lippitt's (1975) work. These authors described the consultant-client working relationship throughout a problem-solving experience with the description of the workflow applying to both inside and outside teams. When a team is formed to address the problems at the IRS or at any other public agency or private company, five phases comprise the flow of the "engagement" or task:

1. Contact, entry, and relationship building
2. Contract formulation and diagnosis/engagement parameters
3. Planning the goals, steps, and actions of problem solving (change effort)
4. Action taking and continuity of effort
5. Evaluation and termination

Each of the phases can involve joint and individual work activities between client and consultant (or problem solver). Each of these phases is now described in more detail.

Phase 1: Contact, entry, and relationship building. In the first phase, problem solvers and consultants must make contact with the organization and the relevant executives. The contact can be seen as the start of the consultation (Quick & Kets de Vries, 2000; Schein, 1987). As insiders, the staff might already know about the problem. Outside consultants must somehow learn that a problem exists. Most engagements begin with a referral, with the first contact being critical (Bowers & Degler, 1999). In our ongoing case, word of the internal problems of the IRS must be passed on to outsiders so as to stimulate outside pressure for change and to present a "call for help." Of course, this is a public agency with congressional hearings and front-page coverage. Still, "would-be consultants" must make contact with key insiders. Consultants, or an inside problem-solving team, must explore the need and readiness for change, the potential for collaborative work, and whether the willingness and courage to proceed are present. Both internal and external consultants must strive to "understand" the client (Long, 1999). In a high-profile problem such as that at the IRS, courage is especially needed.

Phase 2: Contract development and diagnosis/engagement parameters. In the second phase, we more fully define the nature of the problem and come to an agreement about the task (Norris, 1994). We may launch into a formal diagnostic process, sometimes with an engagement letter (Zabrosky, 1999) or, if an inside team, a "committee charge." At this point, we find out whether the client has fully developed a diagnosis of the problem. Organizational diagnosis, fully addressed as systems thinking by Harrison (1994), can be described as "the process of using conceptual models and methods from the behavioral sciences to assess an organization's current state and find ways to solve specific problems or increase its [the organization's] effectiveness" (p. 1). Harrison's view of diagnosis drifts into implementation activity. Diagnosis, in a more limited sense, is used here to guide the development of proposals for organizational change and improvement by consultants and their clients. At this point, stakeholders are identified and recruited.

When the diagnosis is complete and has shared agreement by inside and outside problem solvers, the team selected is often composed of *expert, process,* and *package of service* consultants. When diagnosis is unclear, process consultants are engaged early in the project to help the client understand the breadth and depth of the problem and to create and manage the problem-solving process.

This phase includes parceling out the roles and responsibilities including task assignments and time frames. Specific outcomes (in some contracts called "deliverables") also are defined and agreed on.

In the IRS case, experts in computer systems would be engaged to provide a second opinion on the degree of technological adequacy including how to bring hardware and software up-to-date. In recognition of the nature of tax work and citizen customers, training consultants might be engaged to offer workshops on dealing with difficult customers and team building. Both groups would have start dates, training delivery dates, and total costs clearly specified.

Phase 3: Planning. In this phase, the diagnostic activity is completed, with relevant data collected, analyzed, and fed back to the client and executives. In these early phases, the feedback of data in regard to the diagnosis is crucial. In the first several phases, the problem solvers collect data to develop or to confirm/disconfirm what the contact client has deemed to be the problem. The way in which feedback is handled as both art and science (Kuhnert, 1993) is vital to the development and maintenance of the relationship between consultants and the client. *High-quality* feedback emphasizes the "here and now," individual acts, and being nonjudgmental; it facilitates change, provides psychological safety, and helps to build the problem-solving community (Golembiewski, 1993, p. 331). Harrison (1994) added that feedback is effective when it is relevant, comparative, timely, believable, sensitive, limited, and practical (p. 76). The success of the plan for intervention depends on high-quality feedback.

Plans for intervention are defined with responsibilities and time frames. In this phase, the diagnosis is used to lead us to multiple actions targeting multiple systems of the organization.

What does the IRS problem-solving plan include? To this point, we have discussed several types of interventions:

- Exploring the nature of the problem/shared agreement on diagnosis
- Expert technical advice regarding hardware and software requirements
- Training packages to build customer service and teamwork competencies
- Restructuring of the IRS into business units
- Analysis and redesign of the quota and reward systems

A full plan includes clear task assignments with responsible persons and completion dates identified.

Phase 4: Action. In this phase, actions are taken by individuals, by groups in one or more departments, or by leaders throughout the organization. Restructuring, training, hiring, firing, new compensation systems, and/or new work policies are used to address the issues raised in the diagnostic and planning phases. This implementation work is recognized as both critical and challenging (Bates & Dillard, 1993).

Phase 5: Evaluation and termination. In this final phase, the success of the interventions is tested. We ask whether the problem has been solved, that is, whether the correct actions were taken to address the problems raised at first contact and verified in the diagnostic stage. This is, in some models, a pilot-testing effort with a cycling back to diagnosis and new action if negative results are found. If successful, the engagement is terminated. The termination process is actually a complex mix of technical completion of consultant duties and the psychodynamics of assessing the degree of success (Gilmore, 1993). The problem-solving partners agree that the task has been successfully completed.

At each of the stages, there is a need to communicate and, if necessary, to reframe (Kesner & Fowler, 1997). The flow of the phases seems a bit linear and rational, sometimes not well representing the fluid nature of real problem solving. But if we think of it as a broad "directional path," with movement back to earlier stages when appropriate, then it works as a descriptor of the process.

Problem-Solving Actions:
Philosophy and Style of Interventions

We solve a problem by *intervening* in it. "Interventions," or actions and activities designed to help, can be classified in many different ways, with Blake and Mouton (1982) listing five types or categories of interventions. These categories represent an amalgamation of philosophy style and methods, some of which are not compatible with our other philosophies of organizational development and action research. But they are common styles. Think of the problem solvers or consultants as puzzling out a broad approach that will guide their selection of tools and techniques as well as their demeanor during the engagement. Table 1.3 presents the original descriptions.

What interventions would we use in the IRS case? By following the Blake and Mouton model, we could consider a mix of actions reflecting different philosophies and styles, thereby adapting to client needs for different approaches to the helping process.

1. We could conduct seminars that explain the theories and principles of customer service to IRS employees, believing that the education would lead to changed behavior (*theories and principles*).

2. We could prescribe a set of management, technical, and structural solutions in a report to Commissioner Rossotti (as outside experts, we are asked for answers) (*prescription*).

3. We could confront IRS senior managers and employees with data from surveys of citizens about the state of customer service and their unfortunate experiences as taxpayers (*confrontation*).

4. We could help an internal team conduct a fact-finding and data analysis process that would be the stimulus action leading to change (*catalytic*).

5. We could meet regularly with the commissioner and senior managers to provide psychological support and security as they begin to move through a series of major actions leading to change (while in a fishbowl of political attention) (*acceptant*).

In other words, as problem solvers, we categorize our style and methods of responding to problems, a set of philosophy/style options that is used selectively. We can *prescribe* answers or *confront* the client with unsettling data or customer feedback. We can *teach* and *stimulate* or just provide *support*. The approach can be a mix that, in its diversity, promotes change. When catalytic efforts are successful, they (a) are unpredictable, (b) distribute power, (c) have power, (d) are intolerant of nonsupporters, and (e) are ongoing (Collins, 1999).

Table 1.3 Intervention Types

1. *Theories and principles.* By making theories and principles that are pertinent to the client's situation evident, the consultant helps the client to internalize systematic and empirically tested ways of understanding and acting. When learned so well as to be personally useful, these principles permit the client to view his or her situation in a more analytic, cause-and-effect fashion than has hitherto been possible. Thus, the client becomes able to diagnose and deal with present and future situations in more valid ways. From the outset, he or she can correct an immediate problem or can plan for long-range improvements on the basis of proven effective approaches. Interventions that bring theories and principles into use involve joining education and consultation in a single action. . . .

2. *Prescription.* The consultant tells the client what to do to rectify a given situation or else does it for him or her. The consultant assumes responsibility for formulating the solution as a recommendation to be followed. . . .

3. *Confrontation.* This action challenges a client to examine how the present foundations of his or her thinking—usually value-laden assumptions—may be coloring and distorting the way [in which] situations are viewed. Possible alternatives that might lead to more effective solutions may then come clearly into view. . . .

4. *Catalytic.* A catalytic intervention assists the client in collecting data and information to evaluate and possibly reinterpret his or her perceptions as to how things are, based on better or more extensive knowledge of the situation. In this way, the client may arrive at a better awareness of underlying causes of a problem and how to address or resolve it. . . .

5. *Acceptant.* The intention is to aid the client to develop a basic sense of personal security so that he or she will feel free to express personal thoughts without fear of being judged or rejected. The client may be helped to sort out his or her emotions and, in this way, get a more objective view of the situation.

SOURCE: Blake and Mouton (1982).

During each engagement, problem solvers and consultants must decide which engagement approaches should be used for what reasons.

How do these interventions fit into this model of problem solving and consulting? Problem-solving consultants and managers can ask themselves questions about their cases (as can students in a management class). These self-reflective questions are used to define the philosophical, stylistic, and methodological approaches to problem solving in any given engagement. Although the following list does not describe all options, four key questions help us define *the* approach to the problem (building on Blake & Mouton's, 1982, model):

Who is leading the engagement?

- The consultant and problem solvers (outsiders and insiders)

To whom is the work directed? Who is the client?

- Individual
- Group
- Intergroup
- Organization
- Large social system

Why is the team working on the problem? Is it to address an issue in one or more of the following systems?

- Product/technology
- Structural
- Psychosocial
- Managerial
- Culture, goals, and values

What is the general approach? Is it some kind of intervention philosophy and strategy, such as the following?

- Theory and principles
- Prescriptive
- Confrontational
- Catalytic
- Acceptant

The "why" in the model is very much driven by the diagnostic work based on this five-system conceptual view of the organization. The "what," in a broader sense, includes getting second opinions or technical assistance on topics such as computer technology and training systems (given the intervention approach). As we add more understanding to our knowledge of problem-solving and consulting practices, the options will expand.

The first question—"Who is leading the engagement?"—can be answered in several ways.

Problem Solvers:
Consultant Types and Roles

What type of problem solvers do we need at the IRS? What roles will they play? In a basic way, we can think of problem solvers as experts, as skilled pairs of hands, or as facilitators (Long, 1999). Within the overall approach of a systems-oriented problem-solving model, different types of consultants and consulting products (packages) can be used effectively if they are delivered within the total system context. Several writers have described types of consultants. Schein (1993a) referred to content experts, doctors, and process consultants (p. 653). No definitions of consultant types have yet gained full consensus, but they are described here with the labels *packaged service* consultant, *expert advice* consultant, and *process* consultant. Keep in mind that managers and their problem-solving teams can act as consultants as they solve problems, so these options apply to internal agents as well.

The *packaged service* consultant is an individual who provides a specific "prefabricated" program, usually an "off-the-shelf" item. Training, new hardware installation, and turnkey operations of all sorts are examples. Here we can think about the positive and negative images of "pre-fab." Characteristics such as speed of construction, standardization, quality, and volume come to mind. As we consider projects developed to high-quality specifications, we can come to see consulting packages as effective because they are well tested, are delivered repeatedly in different environments, and conform to expectations of high quality.

For example, employees in every field have received fliers and brochures that invite participation in a professional education program of one kind or another. It may focus on team building, conflict management, time management, or any one of a number of management concerns. A current list might include searching the Web, managing stress, giving effective presentations, improving computing skills, and using quality analysis tools. Such programs frequently are available through executive development centers at colleges and universities and often are designed and conducted by selected staff of the institutions. They are developed as "standard models" (products) designed to be offered in similar fashion to many organizations. Other programs also are offered by private groups or practitioners. During the 1990s, total quality management training and reengineering programs were popular examples.

According to Schein (1987), four assumptions underlie the use of the packaged service consultant:

1. The client has correctly diagnosed the problem.
2. The client has correctly identified the consultant's capabilities to provide the expertise.
3. The client has correctly communicated the problem and the nature of the expertise or information that is to be purchased.
4. The client has thought through and accepted the potential consequences of obtaining the information or the service. (p. 23)[2]

Think about these important assumptions. One must get the diagnosis right—on one's own. The programs are helpful when the registrants are certain that the contents of the programs are directly related to their professional or organizational needs. Most of the time, the fliers include descriptions of the programs being offered, the names and backgrounds of the people who will conduct the programs, and other information regarding fees, locations, and registration. The major advantage to packaged service activities are relatively low cost, opportunities to meet people with similar needs from other organizations, and concentration of effort (most seminars are designed to be 2- or 3-day intensive learning programs). In our example, the IRS team might use packages of consultation for training, for new technology implementation, for individual staff development, and for a new performance incentive structure.

A major disadvantage to such programs is that they cannot, by virtue of their target audience, be company specific. They rarely are designed to deal with each participant's particular or unique problems; they can lead to "cookie-cutter" thinking (Pringle, 1998). Another disadvantage is that the learning is not easily transferable to employees' company environments. By definition, there is limited follow-up, there is no ongoing education, and only rarely is there any evaluation of results. Finally, predesigned programs succeed because of their standardization (bringing efficiency and low cost) and fail due to lack of flexibility. The contents and teaching methods for the programs usually are "locked in." Only rarely can participants redesign the programs if they do not meet their expectations.

This packaged service consultant mode, then, assumes that clients can use a set of "predeveloped products" that can be applied in generic fashion across industries. For example, whole product packages are delivered repeatedly in almost identical fashion to the IRS and to companies in transportation, health care, and banking. Although there are some consulting services that can be offered in this way, not all such services can be. Expert advice on a problem specific to only one organization might be needed on an individual basis.

The second type of problem solver is the *expert advice* consultant. Four assumptions underlie the use of the expert consultant, sometimes referred to as the doctor-patient model of consultation. According to Schein (1987), this model is effective when the following conditions apply:

1. The diagnostic process itself will be seen as helpful.
2. The client has correctly interpreted the organization's symptoms and has located the sick area.
3. The person or group defined as "sick" will reveal the pertinent information necessary to make a valid diagnosis; that is, [the person or group] will neither hide data nor exaggerate symptoms.

4. The client will understand and correctly interpret the diagnosis provided by the consultant and will implement whatever prescription is offered.
5. The client can remain healthy after the consultant leaves. (p. 25)[2]

These expert consultants are asked to visit the organization to diagnose its "state of health or illness" or to examine a particular technical activity. This usually is done through observations of staff meetings and employee activities and through interviews with specialists and managers. Sometimes, extensive data are collected about an aspect of technology or of the production and delivery process. After gathering the necessary data, a comprehensive report is prepared, typically containing a description of the corporation and situation, an analysis of the problems, listings of key findings and recommendations, and a cost of implementation analysis. Here the consultants offer procedures and strategies for accomplishing recommended changes.

Expert consultants are brought in because, in theory, they are objective and minimize internal biases. But the consultants selected often result from clients' biases about the nature of the problems and solutions. Problem solving using outsiders is "given over" to acknowledged experts in specialty fields of organization (e.g., marketing, production, finance, human resources) and specific technology (e.g., information systems, engineering). Deep training and much experience and ability are added. The studies can be very expensive and often include the analyses and recommendations that would have come from the companies' own employees. Follow-up and implementation can fail because of the "light" commitment to the outsiders' analysis and recommendations. The diagnosis–planning–action–evaluation cycle is not so much a partnership with the client as it is a partnership with organization development approaches.

These two types of consulting approaches—packaged and expert—are used frequently, but there are reservations about their use. We often reject packaged programs because organizations have *specific* and *unique* problems, not *general* ones. The transferability of standard solutions is questioned. Expert consultation uses outsiders to solve company problems. Unless the organization happens to learn the problem-solving process—typically not a part of the assignment—it will have to call in the experts each time the problem comes up.

The third consultant type, the *process* consultant, is a professional group or individual focusing attention on how work is accomplished. This model is advocated by organization development specialists. According to Schein (1987), six conditions underlie the process consultation model:

1. The client is hurting somehow but does not know the source of the pain or what to do about it.
2. The client does not know what kind of help may be available and which consultant can provide the kind of help that may be needed.
3. The nature of the problem is such that the client not only needs help in figuring out what is wrong but also would benefit from participation in the process of making a diagnosis.
4. The client has "constructive intent," is motivated by goals and values that the consultant can accept, and has some capacity to enter into a helping relationship.
5. The client is ultimately the only one who knows what form of intervention will work in the situation.
6. The client is capable of learning how to diagnose and solve his [sic] own organizational problems. (p. 32)[2]

The process consultant analyzes and redesigns the way in which organization problems are defined and addressed. This problem-solving capability is the target of the help, which is focused on the needs of the client, much like a clinical inquiry in personal therapy (Schein, 1995). In this model, a diagnosis is made, the results of the diagnosis are shared with employees and management, and the needs of the organization are identified and clarified as a part of the consulting process. In collaboration with company staff, problems are prioritized, including the need for education and training. Problem-solving process helpers can be internal, such as a process improvement director in a medical center (Shimkus, 2000), or can be brought in from the outside. Consultants and the client jointly develop a program designed to meet the organization's needs. It is not generic or prepackaged; instead, it is client specific (Jacobsen, 1990). Education efforts are planned, conducted, and evaluated in a continuing cycle until organizationwide competence exists. Process consultation requires a long-term relationship between consultants and the client, in the process developing a shared interest in the success of the outcome. Although not completely analogous, "corporate coach" is another label (Miller & Brown, 1995).

For example, a process consultant could be hired to lead a search for an IRS future (Cahoon, 1993). The process consultant would not prescribe what that future would be (as a package or an expert might). Instead, the process consultant would establish a means by which the participants could analyze their environment and stakeholder needs, self-reflectively assess the conditions of the IRS as it is, and jointly begin to craft a vision of the IRS's future. Participation, commitment, and creativity are fostered by the design of the process. No expert directives are issued, and no "standard package" of public agency futures is likely to exist. Instead, the client is taught and coached, building continuing capability to problem solve (Washburn, 1995).

Although this is not an exhaustive comparison of the models, the presentation has highlighted significant differences in the approaches to the problem-solving and consulting functions. Many organization development and systems practitioners do not believe that package and expert engagements are helpful unless they are conceived as part of "whole organization interventions." As a conclusion to this review (and as a statement of my bias), the Organizational Development Institute (1981) further commented on the differences and strengths of the process approach:

> In the *purchase-of-service model,* it is the participants who must determine the value of what was learned. If they are satisfied, they wait for some sort of "follow-up program" to provide the next level of learning; and such follow-ups are relatively rare.
>
> In the *expert advice model,* the client system must determine the value of the information and recommendations provided. They [client system] must also take responsibility for putting these recommendations to work. The problem here is that many client systems often lack the skills necessary to do that and, consequently, these "best-laid plans" never materialize.
>
> In the *process consultant model,* the implementation of action plans is typically a mutual effort between the consultant and the client system. The client system wants the plans to work because it developed them. The consultant wants the plan to work because consultant success is very closely tied to the success of the client system. The major disadvantages of the process consultant model are that client systems may have to share with the consultant in the investment of time and energy during all phases of the project. Organization development (OD) projects are long-term efforts, usually taking 2 years or more, and OD requires a learning commitment on the part of the organization as well as a financial investment.

Now we increasingly recognize the change management aspects of successful organization development.

How would these three types of consultants appear in our IRS case? First, we could engage a firm to provide a package of customer service training seminars to all our employees. We would have determined that surly behavior toward taxpaying citizens was caused, in part, by the lack of training—"not knowing" how to behave with clients.

Or, we could hire an information systems expert to help us determine how to move the IRS data system into the 21st century. This outside expert would prescribe a set of technical solutions regarding the acquisition of new hardware and software.

Or, we could hire a process consultant to work with an internal team of IRS employees to diagnose the problems in organization and technology and to develop a shared plan for corrective action. The process consultant would not prescribe answers; instead, the consultant would teach and support problem solving by the internal team.

In fact, we probably would need to employ all three types of consultants to address the wide range of IRS problems.

All the consultants must draw on power to make change. Each type of consultant—expert, package, and process—uses some or all of the following five sources of influence (French & Raven, 1968) plus an amalgamation that I think of as "personal" power, meaning charisma plus:

- Legitimate
- Coercive
- Reward
- Expert
- Referent
- Personal

Expert consultants draw on their legitimacy and expertise and on their referent linkage to senior managers (with their coercive and reward power). Process consultants often have strong interpersonal skills—a contributor to their personal power.

As we consider the three types of consultants and problem solvers, we should remember that they can be internal or external to the organization or a team with a combined locus. In large organizations, there are experts of all types, including very well-developed education and training groups and quality improvement and reengineering teams.

For internal consultants, the advantages to being based inside the organization include the following:

- Knowledge of the culture
- Knowledge of power sources and levels
- Track record of success and credibility

- On-site availability
- "Sunk" and somewhat hidden costs
- Pressure for follow-up
- Awareness of the whole problem environment

For external consultants, the advantages to being based outside the organization include the following:

- Free of bias and political linkages
- Power of the "external expert"
- Freedom to offer unpopular recommendations
- New skills and knowledge and "extra hands"
- Direct costs (often high)
- Natural termination points

In each engagement, there is a combination of advantages and disadvantages in the makeup of the team that will influence the decision to use insiders or outsiders. An inside-outside collaboration often is used, but there can be problems of clashing perspectives and methods (Lacey & Samuels, 2000).

When problem solving, managers or consultants can deliver predeveloped packages, offer advice, or use process skills to help clients and employees problem solve. The stated advantages/disadvantages inform us about each model's applicability. The preceding arguments seem to favor process work. But *all three types* are in constant use by consultants and managers in all kinds of profit and nonprofit organizations. This situation will continue. The task is to *match* the type of consultant with the appropriate problem situation and the organization's needs. The matching process is helped by considering the roles that the consultants are expected to play in solving the organization's problems.

Consultant Activities and Roles

We need to further describe the activities that consultants and internal problem-solving teams undertake for their clients. Some years ago, Turner (1982) listed eight activities central to the consulting and problem-solving process:

1. Providing information to a client
2. Solving a client's problems
3. Making a diagnosis, which may necessitate redefinition of the problem

4. Making recommendations based on the diagnosis
5. Assisting with implementation of recommended solutions
6. Building a consensus and commitment around corrective action
7. Facilitating client learning, that is, teaching clients how to resolve similar problems in the future
8. Permanently improving organizational effectiveness

Each of the three types of consultants—packaged service, expert, and process—contributes some but usually not all of these activities, which are engaged in through the performance of roles.

When consultants work in organizations, they do so with a variety of purposes and functions. Lippitt (1975) defined eight roles that consultants can act in as they problem solve. This role set has been used to describe the roles of the ombudsman and the quality management specialist (Ziegenfuss, 1987a, 1988b). Both specialists are internal consultants. Others have defined the problem solver's roles as initiator, expert, and facilitator (Geberlein, 1989). Think of how the IRS team of inside staff and outside consultants will need to act in each of the following roles. Note that the roles fit managers engaged in participative problem-solving teams as well as outside consultants.

The roles are separated into *process* and *content,* language that distinguishes the *way* we work from the *substance* of the problems. In process roles, consultants and problem-solving teams contribute their efforts to developing and improving the way in which problems are attacked and resolved. In content roles, consultants are relied on for expertise and skills relevant to the specific nature of the problems. Acting in a process role, consultants can facilitate a meeting between two "warring" department directors. Acting in a content/ expert role, consultants may give an opinion about the safety of a bridge design or the options for new IRS software. Some consultants stay with one role, whereas others operate in a repertoire of ways (Lundberg, 1994).

The process roles of the consultant include the following four roles, with some examples of representative actions:

1. *Facilitator/Human dynamics specialist.* The consultant addresses the work process itself as a way of enhancing client competence. Here the consultant attempts to help the client to be more responsive to organization problems and more effective in solving them. In this role, the consultant helps to plan and facilitate meetings, engages in "shuttle diplomacy" to negotiate conflicts, and reports observations about meeting style and effectiveness to the client. At the IRS, managing the human dynamics of taxpayer and congressional relations

might require help to control emotions, constrain politics, and maintain a focus on solutions.

2. *Advocate role.* Some consultants are hired to be advocates for change and continuous improvement. As an advocate, the consultant works to influence the client to change in some way such as becoming informed about and use total quality management. For example, a consultant may be engaged to assist in strategic planning process design while simultaneously acting as an advocate for adaptation to a changing environment. Consultants could become advocates for new hardware and software or for improved customer service at the IRS.

3. *Collaborator in problem solving.* In this process role, the consultant partners with the client, announcing a desire to share the challenge of the task and the responsibility for success. The helping role complements the client work on the problem but does not displace it with a unilateral outside prescription. Consultants could work with the IRS commissioner to begin to change the culture and to develop a new structure of the agency.

4. *Reflector.* This role is defined by supportive active listening. As a reflector, the consultant assists in client decision making by asking questions that offer empathy and help to clarify, modify, or change a situation. The consultant is a "sounding board" to enable the client to verbalize and test possible diagnoses and solution alternatives—a "safe haven" for thinking out loud. Beset by angry citizens and congressional watchdogs, the IRS commissioner needs a secure and safe sounding board.

As a whole, these four roles are directed toward enhancing the client's understanding of the dynamics of problems and solutions. Content roles include the following: technical expert, fact finder, teacher, and alternative identifier.

5. *Technical expert.* One role of an internal or external consultant is providing specialist expertise in a field or function. The technical specialist, through his or her special knowledge, skill, and professional experience, is engaged to complement or supplement the skills and knowledge in the client organization. Consistent with the assumptions of the doctor-patient model, the client is responsible for problem diagnosis, for establishing the objectives of the consultation, and sometimes for implementation. Technical experts provide opinions and answers, for example, offering a recommended set of technical specifications for new computer hardware and software at the IRS.

6. *Fact finder.* All consulting involves some sort of investigative work. Fact-finding is an integral part of solving both technical and social-psychological problems. With an action research approach, the fact-finding can become applied research with methodological rigor. The depth, breadth, and length of the engagement define the thoroughness of the fact-finding process and related analysis (applied science). In this role, the consultant employs a wide range of qualitative and quantitative methods, from personal interviewing to statistical analysis. The IRS commissioner, confronted by public complaints and press reports, might ask consultants to survey citizens to determine the depth and breadth of their dissatisfaction with the agency.

7. *Teacher.* Consultants act as educators and trainers both directly and indirectly during engagements (Palmer, 1998). Some consultants provide training and education as a primary service, whereas others see the teaching as, for example, an "add-on" to survey work. Training programs (packaged consultation) offered to client organizations call for the teaching role almost exclusively. For example, in supporting strategic planning at the IRS, consultants hired to assist with the design of the planning process might be required to "teach" IRS staff and executives about strategy-making processes including methods for analyzing environmental changes.

8. *Identifier of options and recommendations.* Some consultants are employed specifically to offer options and recommendations. Other consultants help identify options in collaboration with the client. This role is particularly strong in the expert consultation model and is less apparent or absent in the process consultant approach. When the IRS commissioner began to see that the organization's structure was flawed, consultants hired by the agency could provide three alternative ways of organizing the agency with advantages, disadvantages (including especially costs), and feasibility.

In many engagements of significant size and duration, problem-solving managers and consultants act in a variety of the roles just noted, acting as both expert fact finders and process specialists at different points in the projects.

Consultant Skills and Competencies

Who will perform effectively as consultants or as members of insider-dominated problem-solving teams? McLean and Sullivan (1993) identified key competencies, and some years ago, Greiner and Metzger (1983) defined the essential personal characteristics required for success in this work. Now being developed is a uniform body of knowledge (International Council of Management Consulting Institutes, 1994), including codes of conduct, standards, and continuing education (Lightbown, 1993).

Many years ago, Sherlock Holmes demonstrated a number of key consulting skills in his famous cases—data gathering, determining vital facts, attending to detail, validating data, and analyzing alternatives (Webb, 1995). Some commentators with a bias toward the expert role have viewed the necessary skills as primarily technical and technological (Cooper, 1992). Others have indicated that the skill set is both social-psychological and technical, requiring the ability to develop trust and to sensitively provide feedback and support (Tagiuri, 1992). Moline (1990) identified categories of capability including orientation, consulting skills, project management skills, and industry or market skills. And once these skills have developed, practitioners and staff of both inside and outside teams must be retained. Otherwise, both expertise and client relationships are adversely affected (Morrell & Simonetto, 1999).

Skills and competencies can be tied to a single person, or they can reside in a team—the team collectively presenting the attributes required for a successful engagement. Large consulting firms and academic consulting teams (Kolenko, 1994) both bring this multifaceted perspective. When the IRS leadership looks for help, what are the selection criteria? Building on Greiner and Metzger (1983), the following competencies and skills are a good start.

Seven attributes comprise the leading professional skills and competencies required of members of inside problem-solving teams and outside consultants:

1. *Industry and/or functional expertise and experience.* This refers to background in an industry such as health care, retail, or manufacturing or in a specialty such as finance, marketing, or personnel. Background experience in public administration and tax law would fit the IRS engagement.

2. *Analytical and diagnostic.* This refers to the ability to integrate diverse streams of data to arrive at an understanding of the problem. Experience with collaborative diagnosis and problem solving is required if the approach is client centered. At the IRS, joint diagnosis would bring the client into the process, which would be very politicized from the outset.

3. *Methodological.* This refers to the ability to frame an approach to data collection, analysis, and feedback and to identify and employ change methods. In

a large engagement such as the IRS project, team members must have applied social science skills to enable them to define, collect, and analyze data.

4. *Teamwork.* This refers to the ability to appreciate and work with diverse internal and external team members (Drozodow, 1997). In the IRS project, members might represent management and information science, tax law, politics, and public policy, among other fields.

5. *Teaching.* This refers to the ability to interact with the client in an "educational mode," functioning as a teacher of technical and human relations skills (Senge, 1990). One view of surly IRS agents is that they were hired with that behavioral set. Another view is that they need to be taught new options and strategies for working with citizens.

6. *Writing and oral presentation.* This refers to the ability to develop and present project proposals (Minto, 1998) and final reports in high-quality writing and stimulating oral presentation. In some engagements, strategic storytelling works (Brown, 1998; McConkie & Boss, 1994). IRS consulting teams might need to present to both the agency management and congressional oversight committees. For the committees in particular, presentation and response skills will be key.

7. *Project management.* This refers to the ability to integrate multiple contributions, coordinate sometimes competing demands, and meet client deadlines. In high-profile projects such as the IRS case, delivery on time is critical.

All members of the consulting team must have base levels of the following personal attributes, including a strong bias and capability for self-inquiry (Badaracco, 1998). All members must know themselves and their contributions to the team.

1. *Tolerance for ambiguity.* This refers to the ability to work with uncertainty in diagnoses, work processes, and outcomes. The IRS case is a mix of organization design, politics, public policy, and law with no clear and easy answers.

2. *Openness to quantitative and qualitative data.* This refers to the ability to work with and integrate both objective numbers-oriented data and "softer" material from interviews and focus groups. IRS attention to quantitative measures of performance only is part of the problem.

3. *Relationship skills.* This refers to the ability to develop and maintain relationships with clients (Schaffer, 1997) and team members (Pick, 1992) including alliances (Sabath, 1992). IRS leaders will need both staff and congressional allies.

4. *Energy and stamina.* This refers to personal reserves that allow long days under pressure over long periods of time. For example, few congressional committees allow project teams to stop and rest.

5. *Ethics.* This refers to a desire to help within the boundaries of professional conduct (Prager, 1992). What can be done fairly in a sometimes hostile political environment? In a highly charged public engagement, consultants at the IRS will find that the truth has been "adapted" to fit positions and news headlines.

In building an internal change group or an outside consulting team, we search for candidates with these qualifications, recognizing that strengths and weaknesses can be balanced with other team members.

Problem-Solving Outcomes

How is the very real IRS case going? As reported in *USA Today*, the IRS commissioner gave an update on audits—one part of the progress:

> Rossotti says the reasons for the decline in audits include: a decade-long staff slide, antiquated computers, and IRS legislation—passed in 1998 amid a furor over alleged IRS abuses—that gave taxpayers new rights and IRS agents new customer service responsibilities that have taken them from enforcement. Even as its workload increased under the new law, the IRS's employment fell by 18,800 from the height of more than 116,000 in 1992. Many of those who remain have been reassigned from enforcement to training and customer service, the IRS says.[3]

Why do we often struggle to successfully implement solutions? Coates (1997) identified a number of reasons why organizational problem-solving efforts fail. Some of the leading reasons include inconsistencies between management's words and actions, unclear or overreaching expectations without a good measurement system to evaluate change, failure to realize that successful organizational change takes persistent effort that may last for years, absence of any long-term perspective dealing with systemic issues, capabilities of the consultant not being known or understood by management, and consultants tending to be proponents of one approach exclusively to help manage change. Sometimes, the failure is dramatic and costly. AT&T complained that it spent $500 million in a failed development and change effort (Puri, 1997). The failures are driven by a lack of understanding of the task and by poor execution. Let us think more about the task.

What do we expect to occur as a result of our consulting and problem-solving engagement? Shared understanding of the problem and commitment to resolution actions are two outcomes (Covin & Fisher, 1991). Do we want two department directors to end their conflict and work together as a team? Do we want our political critics to appreciate the turnaround at the IRS? We can consider a range of expected outcomes, from those that optimize the current conditions, to those that produce compromise from both sides, to a significant and dramatic redesign.

Ackoff (1987) helped us toward this perspective of problem dissolution:

> A problem is said to be solved when the decision maker selects those values of the controlled variables which maximize the value of the outcome, that is, when he [sic] has optimized. If he selects values of the controlled variables that do not maximize the value of the outcome but produce an outcome that is good enough, he has resolved the problem by satisficing. There is a third possibility: He may dissolve the problem. This is accomplished by changing his values so that the choices available are no longer meaningful. For example, the problem of selecting a new car may be dissolved by deciding that the use of public transportation is better than driving oneself. It may also be dissolved by moving to within walking distance from work so that driving is no longer required. We use "solving" loosely to cover all three alternatives. (p. 221)

How does this sense of outcome possibilities apply to the case of the IRS? There are three outcomes:

- *Satisficing* could be accomplished with incremental improvements in current IRS policies and procedures, some small changes in audit practices, and improved access to agents through expanded hours of operation and technologies such as 800 numbers and Web-based information.
- *Optimizing* could be accomplished by radically transforming the whole public agency. Computer hardware and software is acquired, the agency is restructured into business units, and agencywide training is employed to improve service, which is now measured by indicators and compared to other industry benchmarks. From the subject of jokes, the IRS is transformed into a model of a high-performance public agency.

- *Dissolving* of the problems could occur by creating a national flat tax or a sales tax, significantly reducing or eliminating many of the functions and structures of the IRS.

The approach to problem solving in this book, including the cases, requires us to consider both how we *solve problems* and how we *dissolve the conditions* that produce the problems in complex social organizations. Sometimes we are successful, and sometimes we are not.

What are some of the common and practical points of failure experienced by inside teams and outside consultants? Seven often encountered flaws in outsider engagements are when consultants offer fads; consultants rubber-stamp management decisions; teams answer questions when the answers already are known; senior consultants negotiate contracts but juniors are sent in to do the work; project length and scope are expanded; recommendations are not understood, thereby undercutting action; and consultants recommend what they do, thereby locking in the client (Shapiro, Eccles, & Soske, 1993). Not all consultants work in this manner, but the problems have a familiar feel.

When projects "work," what happens? In some cases, it is believed that the results come from incremental gains (Fishman & Moses, 1999). In other cases, problem solving represents a stretch or strategic leap forward (Hamel & Prahalad, 1993). One view of "high-impact" consulting specifies the key elements of problem solving success as a focus on results, willingness to change, speed, ongoing cycles (e.g., diagnosis, solutions, evaluations), and teamwork ("High Impact Consulting," 1997). Another suggests that successful outcomes result from top management support and a sponsor, consultant competence, and the consultant mode (Jang, 1998). Still other authors insist that it is results—not activity—that should drive problem solving (Schaffer & Thomson, 1992). In all cases, we are looking for specific tangible results expressed in the client's terms (Schaffer, 1995).

Analyzing Engagements: The Case Report

The preceding description of the consulting and problem-solving engagement can be combined to describe the full experience of moving through a problem, from *diagnosis* to *approach* to *impact*. The questions that drive the problem solving are represented on the checklist in Table 1.4 and are used to guide case discussion both in class and in professional assignments.

Table 1.4 Case Analysis Guidelines/Instructions

Step 1: Diagnosis

 a. *Problem identification.* What are the critical diagnostic issues/problems and the reasons for seeking help?

 b. *Sociotechnical systems analysis.* Develop the diagnosis and identify expected primary and secondary subsystem involvement—product-technology, structural, psychosocial, managerial subsystems, and culture.

 c. *Stakeholders.* Who are the critical stakeholders in the case? Describe them as types imperative, positional, reputational, social participation, opinion leadership, demographic, and organizational.

Step 2: Approach and plan

 a. *Plan for action.* Identify the consulting approach, process, and methods to be used:
- *Consultants:* expert–process–package
- *Why:* information, facilitation, second opinion, objectivity, etc.
- *Needed activities:* diagnostic, team building, survey, education and training, restructure, process, coaching, counseling, strategic planning, action research, etc.
- *Methods:* theory, prescriptive, confrontational, catalytic, acceptant, etc.
- *Roles:* content/fact finder, technology expert, educator, alternative identifier, process reflector, advocate, process specialist, etc.
- *Power:* expert, reward, coercive, legitimate, referent, personal, etc.
- *Who:* individual, group/team, intergroup, organization, larger social system, etc.

 b. *Personnel needs.* Define who is to be used in the consultation and why.

 c. *Time and responsibility.* Who does what and when?

 d. *Costs.*

Step 3: Evaluate problem and organization impact

 a. *Sociotechnical organization changes.* Define any long-term macro and micro system changes expected (system by system, if appropriate).

 b. *Problem.* resolved–solved–dissolved

 c. *Additional data needs.* What additional data would you like and why?

Summary

 This first chapter presented a description of a systems and consulting approach to organization and management problem solving. We can summarize the elements of the model by again using the IRS example. First, we consider the IRS problem to be sociotechnical in nature. It is more than creating an up-to-date information system; it also includes the culture and psychology of the agency. We can take this beginning diagnostic view further by analyzing whether the problems at the IRS are primarily technical, structural, psychosocial, managerial, or cultural in attempting to identify the leading problematic systems so as to initiate the first corrective action. As we begin our diagnosis, we consider that there are many stakeholders with a critical investment in the problems and the proposed solutions—employees, senior managers, citizens, politicians, tax lawyers, and others. Each stakeholder's position must be considered for the solution to be successful, and many stakeholders will have contributions to the problem's resolution.

Once the diagnosis is complete, we can select an internal or external consulting team. In many engagements, this selection is decided prior to diagnostic work. The IRS team's recommended actions will be prescriptive, catalytic, and educational, and they will rely on a range of methodologies dependent on the type of problems defined. For example, the IRS problem of computer inadequacy may require outside experts who will offer a prescriptive set of hardware and software suggestions. A process consultant may be brought in to help the agency plan for the future and to conduct some team-building sessions with the demoralized staff (under political attack in Washington, D.C.).

Consultants will be expected to offer second opinions as outside experts, or they will be counted on as a process team engaged in internal organization development. Frequently, the approach chosen is an action research one. Not all solutions to the IRS problems can be defined in a "master solution plan." Instead, they will emerge from some action/evaluation/redesign strategies, converting problem solving into organizational learning. Finally, the problems will be solved with a transformed IRS, or we will have successfully dissolved the conditions that produced it in the first place (e.g., with a flat tax).

The balance of the book offers further information on the locale of the problems—five organizational systems—and cases illustrating problem-solving interventions in those systems. The variety and depth of the cases are purposeful, reflecting what real teams and managers face. As you read the cases, consider how you and your own team would address the problems.

Notes

1. From F. E. Kast, *Organization and Management: A systematic contingency approach.* Copyright © 1985 by The McGraw-Hill Companies. Reprinted with permission.

2. From E. H. Schein, *Process consultation* (Vol. 2). Copyright © 1987 by Pearson Education, Inc., Upper Saddle River, NJ. Reprinted with permission.

3. From USA TODAY, Copyright 2001. Reprinted with permission.

2

Solving Product and
Technical Problems

The imperatives of technology and organization, not the images of ideology,
are what determine the shape of economic society.
—John K. Galbraith, *The New Industrial State*

With this chapter as a start, each of the organization subsystems defined in
the model is further described. Several cases illustrating problem solving and
consultation regarding that one aspect of the organization are presented. The
product/technical subsystem is the subject of this chapter.

The Nature of the Product/Technical System

Managers, executives, and consultants confront a broad range of problems
driven by the product and technological production requirements of their respective organizations. Machines, production systems, and the knowledge to

make goods and services are not smoothly integrated without problems. The cases in this chapter are *product/technical* problems that differ by industry and company. Kast and Rosenzweig (1985) defined the organization's technical component as follows:

> The organization is not simply a technical or a social system; it requires structuring and integrating human activities around various technologies. The technical system is determined by the task requirements of the organization and is shaped by the specialization of knowledge and skills required, the types of machinery and equipment involved, the information-processing requirements, and the layout of facilities. (p. 207)

To understand the technical requirements, imagine that products must be a response to a market; must be designed, produced, and delivered; and must be supported. The core technical work of an organization includes, for example, engineering in a car company, teaching in a university, and clinical care in a hospital. In the case of the Internal Revenue Service, the product/technology component includes the tax rules, the various forms for citizens to complete, and software for processing and audit procedures. Too often, we associate *product* and *technical* with equipment and machinery, but this subsystem is broader than that, as Kast and Rosenzweig originally noted:

> Some of the misunderstanding is due to the lack of a precise agreement on the meaning of technology. The terms technology and technological change have many meanings, ranging from specific to broad connotations. In the narrowest view, these terms are associated with machine technology, the mechanization of the means of production of goods and services, [and] the replacement of human effort. This mechanistic view emphasizes such visible manifestations of technology as the supersonic airplane, assembly lines, electronic computers, transportation systems, and the vast complex of facilities and equipment necessary for developing a space shuttle system. This emphasis on physical artifacts is understandable because the machine is the most obvious manifestation of technology. From the anthropological approach, the history of technology is often associated with the first use of primitive weapons and tools. The ability to use these instruments was a major distinguishing characteristic of humans from lower animals. However, it is an oversimplification to associate the advancement of technology with the history of tools and machines. Machines are merely the physical artifacts of technology. . . .
>
> In the most general sense, technology refers to the application of knowledge for the most effective performance of certain tasks or activities. Technology converts spontaneous and unreflected behavior into behavior that is deliber-

ate and rationalized. Jacques Ellul gives a broad connotation to technology or, as he calls it, technique. "In our technological society, technique is the totality of methods rationally arrived at and having absolute efficiency (for a given stage of development) in every field of human activity." He suggests that technology has come to dominate every field and is geared to the achievement of efficiency and rationality in all human endeavors. The definition we are using in this chapter is:

> Technology is the organization and application of knowledge for the achievement of practical purposes. It includes physical manifestations such as tools and machines but also intellectual techniques and processes used in solving problems and obtaining desired outcomes. (p. 208)

Technology in all its forms contributes to the design, production, distribution, and support of core products and services in both the private and public sectors. The following are cases discussed in this chapter:

- Hospital physicians and executives study the feasibility of a new courier service for laboratory tests.
- Private and public sector leaders search for ways of assisting unemployed and displaced workers.
- University librarians ask why their faculty and student customers are not using more of the library's products, from search to reference.
- Teachers confront the challenge of expanding computer use in the school curriculum.
- Hospital directors face community questions about access to and quality of care.
- Ford and Firestone executives search intently for the causes of tire defects and rollover risks of sport utility vehicles.

All these cases address problems of product and technology.

Managers and consultants faced with product and technology problems focus their "diagnosis–planning–action–evaluation" cycles on this subsystem. In an information service company, we might focus initially on hardware and software equipment. But the knowledge base and the methods of interacting with users are important as well. Product and technology problems vary by industry, field, and organization type. Consider these examples:

- Schools' product/technical subsystems involve teaching, research, and community service.
- Manufacturers' product/technical systems involve the design and production of computers, toasters, and refrigerators.

- Hospitals' product/technical systems involve treatment of acute illness as well as prevention and education to promote wellness.
- Law firms' product/technical systems involve research, trial presentation, negotiations, and client counseling.

The possible illustrations are endless. The point is that all organizations have a design and production process that integrates knowledge and equipment to create and deliver goods and services. Each of these technical processes experiences problems from time to time and requires continuous improvement, radical reengineering, or even new innovative products. Consultants are called in to help executives and managers address these technical problems and others. Or, executives develop internal problem-solving teams to tackle their companies' technical problems.

Importantly, each problem-solving team must focus on the interactive effects. The underlying assumption is that most of the problems are based in one system (technology-product), but the causes and solutions involve other subsystems as well (e.g., structural incentives, employee psychology, management behavior).

Our first case concerns a hospital laboratory.

Case 2.1   The Hospital Laboratory Feasibility Case

Center Community Hospital (hereafter Center Hospital) is an in-house laboratory faced with competition from a freestanding commercial laboratory. Executives wanted a feasibility study conducted for a laboratory tests courier service (pickup and delivery) for physicians in private practice. Hospital executives were worried that the local freestanding commercial laboratory service was cutting into the hospital's business. The chief executive officer engaged consultants to analyze the product-related technical and financial questions involved in establishing a courier service.

At the start of the study, the consultants approached it as a simple and straightforward feasibility question: Could the hospital technically deliver and prosper financially by developing this courier program? However, as the study began to unfold, it was revealed to the consultants that the courier feasibility study actually was embedded in a series of strategic questions for the hospital. For example, did the hospital want to remain the primary provider of laboratory services in that community? Would the hospital do whatever was necessary to maintain its competitive position in laboratory services—including upgrading technical equipment and shifting personnel? Did Center Hospital want to address some personnel questions that were becoming barriers to growth in the hospital laboratory? An outside team was chosen to address the problem.

The case questions are in three sets:

I. Diagnosis
   What is the presenting problem?
   What systems are involved?
   Who are the stakeholders?

II. Approach
   What is your plan for action?
   What personnel are needed?
   How much time is required, and who has responsibility for the solution?

III. Impact
   What systems are expected to change?
   What happens to the problem?
   What additional data are needed?

Some general case facts about the hospital were available to the consultants. They are provided in Table 2.1.

Case Context and Purpose

This study was developed to address several current needs of Center Hospital, specifically the following:

- A need to extend the hospital's linkage to physicians with only loose ties to the hospital, that is, increase the strength of the linkage with doctors
- A need to determine whether a laboratory test pickup and delivery service is feasible, both technically and financially

The study was proposed as a tool for assisting management in evaluating the merits of the courier service as a new product proposal.

The primary tasks were described in the contract as follows:

Table 2.1 Case Facts: Center Community Hospital Laboratory

1. Business: Provision of health/medical care
2. History: More than 100 years of service to the community
3. Location: Mid-Atlantic
4. Products/Services: Health care; 411-bed facility providing general medical and surgical services
5. Territory: Small city and surrounding areas, one of five hospitals in the city
6. Customers/Clients: People seeking medical care, primarily small urban-area patients
7. Employees: 1,908 personnel
8. Ownership: Not-for-profit, nongovernmental
9. Revenues: Unknown
10. Reason for consultation: Increase linkage with physicians

- To identify and evaluate courier service technical requirements including equipment, facility, personnel, and financial resource requirements that would be needed
- To evaluate physician acceptance of the new mechanism
- To create recommendations for management regarding project authorization, design, and implementation
- To determine whether the pickup and delivery service would be financially feasible

In short, the purpose of the study was to determine whether the development of the courier service would be technically and financially feasible as well as helpful to the hospital in achieving its objectives of further linking with and serving physicians in the area.

Procedure

The procedure involved a review of critical factors necessary to the development of the pickup and delivery mechanism using the following means to collect data: personal interviews of hospital management and physicians, analysis of official laboratory price lists, assessment of laboratory equipment and procedures, and location mapping of expected customers. The interviews and official record analyses were directed at developing information on the following topics: the need for the service; physician attitudes and willingness to support the service; program design; resource requirements; equipment, personnel, and finances; start-up requirements; and mechanisms for evaluating progress.

Lack of time and resources available, and the limited willingness of physicians to be interviewed, created natural constraints on the study. A sample of physicians was selected for personal interviews, and a follow-up questionnaire was mailed to all other physicians not interviewed. The final physician sample included those who were interviewed personally and those who returned questionnaires.

The following physician specialties were represented by individual interviews or by the returned questionnaires: family practice, neurology, obstetrics/gynecology, internal medicine, pediatrics, radiology, emergency medicine, radiology, and ophthalmology. The physician group participating in personal structured interviews or in the mail survey represented about 40% of the physicians using the hospital laboratory. In addition, laboratory, management, and other organizations' representatives (10 persons) were interviewed.

It was quickly learned that a private competing commercial laboratory was operating that offered pickup service, lower prices, additional services (e.g., staff supplement during vacation periods, regular customer service visits, extensive free supplies). The strategic question for hospital executives and senior laboratory staff was as follows: Does the hospital compete, buy out the commercial laboratory, or leave well enough alone? The summary from the problem-solving report is presented next.

The Report: Hospital Laboratory Test Courier Feasibility (Executive Summary)

There is little dispute among those in the health industry that their organizational environment is turbulent. Changes in hospital directions and operations are coming fast now. One area of concern is the current technical and financial status, as well as the future viability, of individual clinical departments.

Departments are being inspected one by one to identify their strengths and weaknesses and to assess where their future opportunities lie. Increasingly, more health care executives are taking a strategic systems-oriented approach. They are considering many alternatives in light of their fundamental missions and their survival, believing that they can help shape their own futures. In conducting the feasibility study, the consulting team recognized and addressed this need to think strategically.

FINDINGS

The findings and suggested recommendations of the study are as follows:

1. The competition between a commercial laboratory and Center Hospital is, and will continue to be, very strong, centered on both costs and the range and depth of services.

2. Physicians would, in general, consider switching to the Center Hospital laboratory provided that costs and services were at least equivalent.

3. There were no concerns expressed by the physicians regarding the technical quality of service of the Center Hospital laboratory. In fact, all physicians surveyed noted that the quality was good.

4. Although the report did not exclusively target laboratory product and technical concerns, several physicians noted that Center Hospital test profiles were not as extensive as those offered by competitors. For example, the commercial laboratory's comprehensive screen yields 25 results, whereas Center Hospital would require seven screens to yield the same 25 results.

5. If the Center Hospital laboratory were to decide to expand its services, then a pickup and delivery service would be only one of the services needed to compete effectively.

6. Price of the laboratory services appears to be the primary criterion leading physicians to use the commercial laboratory.

7. The potential gain from the additional revenue generated *solely* by the pickup and delivery service is not considered to be significant and could be zero.

8. The costs of startup and operations are relatively high compared to the small potential gain from adding only a laboratory courier service as the activity for generating increased laboratory work.

9. The courier service question actually is embedded in a *set* of strategic planning considerations that must be addressed by the Center Hospital laboratory.

10. The analysis of the courier service for pickup and delivery identifies larger issues relating to the future of the hospital laboratory (a strategic planning need).

The resulting general recommendation was that the hospital should delay development of the courier service until it can determined whether this will be one new activity in a whole set of strategies designed to increase laboratory business.

Instead of a simple answer to the new product and financial feasibility question, laboratory personnel were confronted with a series of long-term questions including the following. First, does the hospital laboratory want to compete with commercial laboratories with a full range of products and services? Second, what total *set* of business development strategies are possible? Third, are the laboratory personnel prepared for a change to a competition-oriented culture? Fourth, are these alternative structures for laboratory services located solely within the hospital (e.g., contract management)? The feasibility study was transformed into a strategic planning problem for the laboratory's future.

The answer to the question of courier product feasibility as a sole change in the laboratory is clearly based on the physician responses. It would not produce a "flood" of increased business for the laboratory, and it might not result in any new business. From that point of view, the pickup and delivery service is not financially feasible. But the courier problem is embedded in several broader concerns that involve the future initiatives that the laboratory might take and its current and future competition.

To be competitive now and in the future, Center Hospital *must initiate* courier service and make other product and service changes. But the courier service is only part of the change required for the Center Hospital laboratory to be fully competitive with private profit-making laboratory services. As a sole initiative, courier service is *not* presently financially feasible. The team recommended that the laboratory delay a final courier service decision while the laboratory conducts its own "future study" in conjunction with the management of the hospital.

The laboratories currently competing with the hospital are vigorous in their entrepreneurial spirit and in their capability to provide a wide range of services at low cost. Competing with them directly will be an exceedingly difficult task given the current laboratory orientation (which is toward quality clinical service, not business/sales development). To make the changes, the Center Hospital laboratory service would need to undergo cultural, structural, and product changes that would produce multiple business development strategies. It appears that unless multiple initiatives are undertaken, even a modest increase in business created by a courier service would not generate sufficient income to justify the expenditures.

Therefore, the team recommended that the laboratory initiate a strategic planning process with staff, physicians, and directors in collaboration with the hospital's senior management team. This strategic future study would consider new equipment and products, business development strategies, competition, a wide range of alternatives (e.g., contracts with outside laboratories), and the full range of alternative designs and business development activities available to the laboratory (only a few of which have been mentioned here). This would enable the laboratory service to consider the pickup and delivery mechanisms as part of a much broader and deeper strategy for its future.

This recommendation rests on the view that a courier service alone would not be sufficient to entice the physicians not currently using the Center Hospital laboratory to switch. Physicians cited costs as their primary reason for using another laboratory, but they also included a number of other services such as staff support, free supplies, and a greater range of tests available. A number of physicians said, "I have to have a reason to switch; just making the service equivalent will not do it." The courier service is *necessary but not sufficient* given that the competition already provides that service *and* is providing extra services for its customers.

RECOMMENDATIONS

The following recommendations are offered as a result of the laboratory courier service study:

1. The hospital should delay development of the service and consider alternative strategies. For example, the courier service is absolutely needed and should be initiated given a *longer term* strategy to become fully competitive with outside laboratory business. Alternatively, other arrangements (e.g., a reference laboratory) might eliminate the need for the hospital to create its own courier service.

2. The hospital should consider initiating courier service if the start-up costs are exceedingly low. For example, if a vehicle and staff already are available from the hospital, then a low-cost, low-risk pilot project could be created. To the extent that vehicles and staff must be acquired prior to start-up, the start-up should be investigated carefully.

3. The hospital also must consider the intangible payoffs from the courier service. These intangibles would include increased hospital linkage to new physicians, some increased referrals, and market protection. To the extent that the initiation of courier service is very low cost, the intangible payoffs could be sufficient to make it an extremely viable investment.

4. The laboratory and hospital management should explore outside laboratory services management. The key word here is *explore.*

5. The hospital should consider a buy-out of the in-town laboratory competitors. It is possible that the competitor could be merged with the hospital laboratory, thereby creating a new laboratory service.

This case has described a product feasibility study that began as a very "simple" and limited problem but ended by surfacing a wide range of strategic management decisions. As such, it is a case example of the presence of significant strategic issues in seemingly "ordinary" product development decision making.

This feasibility study was conducted to address three current needs of Center Hospital: (a) a need to extend the hospital's linkage to physicians with only loose ties to Center Hospital, (b) a need to explore any new revenue-generating ideas that are consistent with planning committee policy and management objectives, and (c) a need to determine whether the laboratory pickup and delivery service is a feasible one. Specific tasks included the following: identify and evaluate technical requirements such as equipment, facility, personnel, and financial resources; evaluate physician acceptance of the new mechanism; create recommendations for management regarding project authorization, design, and implementation; and determine whether the pickup and delivery service would be financially feasible. The study procedure involved the collection of data through personal interviews and a mailed questionnaire to physicians, official laboratory records, and a comparison of pricing lists and contracts with other hospitals.

This case involved the so-called "simple" decision of whether to add a courier service. The expense was not very great, but the executive team wanted a financial feasibility review. Although the project size was small, the ultimate potential impact on the laboratory's culture, technical work, and personnel was not. The study surfaced a fundamental concern for the future of the laboratory.

Case 2.2   Displaced Workers

We all live in communities where downsizing and reengineering are a corporate way of life. What happens to workers displaced from their jobs? How do plant closings, company failures, and manufacturing relocations affect a community as a whole? One community decided that workers were a valuable resource that needed to be protected even in the face of economic change. This community initiated a problem-solving approach at the local level to preserve and protect a critical technical resource—employees.

The case questions are in three sets:

   I. Diagnosis
       What is the presenting problem?
       What systems are involved?
       Who are the stakeholders?

II. Approach
What is the plan for action?
What personnel are needed?
How much time is required for the project, and who has respon-
sibility for the solution?

III. Impact
What systems are expected to change?
What happens to the problem?
What additional data are needed?

Some general case facts about the community were available to the consultants.
They are provided in Table 2.2.

In this case, an outside team working in collaboration with community representatives was used to address the question of displaced workers. This is their
report.

A Study of Displaced Workers in Mapletree: Needs, Services, and Developmental Requirements

EXECUTIVE SUMMARY

A study of the needs and services for unemployed and displaced workers in
Mapletree was conducted to address three questions:

1. What are the needs and experiences of displaced and unemployed workers in
   Mapletree?
2. What are the perceived strengths and needs of the social service system now
   supporting displaced and unemployed workers in Mapletree?
3. What changes or new developments are required to create a strengthened social service system for unemployed and displaced workers in Mapletree?

Working in collaboration with the sponsors—the Mapletree Area Labor Management Council (MALMC) and the Unemployment HELP program of Allied
Churches—researchers and consultants from University College collected new
information and examined existing data and surveys.

The process of the study required information from the Mapletree community including the numbers of unemployed and displaced workers, employers,
and social service agency directors. Data were examined in three ways. First, a

Table 2.2   Case Facts: Mapletree, Pennsylvania

1. Business: Manufacturing
2. History: Incorporated as a city in 1910
3. Location: South-central Mid-Atlantic
4. Products/Services: Diversified but mostly manufacturing
5. Territory: City/County population of 96,000
6. Customers/Clients: City/County residents
7. Employees: 3,611 county employees
8. Ownership: Public
9. Revenues: Unknown
10. Reason for consultation: Address the needs of workers for jobs and management for workers

systematic mapping of the service agencies was conducted including data on services provided, financial support, times of operation, and eligibility. Second, focus groups were conducted separately with groups of unemployed and displaced workers from minority and gender populations to identify their perceptions of problems in finding jobs. Focus groups with corporate representatives also were conducted to obtain employers' perspectives on the strengths and needs of the social service system. Third, a mail survey of a random sample of unemployed workers was conducted to collect needs data.

Major study findings included the following:

1. Unemployed and displaced workers believe that available and useful services exist but sometimes find it difficult to obtain information about available services, especially about job openings, job training, and retraining programs.
2. The network of social service agencies is fragmented and overlapping in responsibilities and without any clear delineation of service specialization.
3. Corporate representatives believe that the social service system is extensive but complex and decentralized.
4. An integrated plan and a communitywide effort are needed to develop a coordinated social service system.

As a result of the study, the researchers recommended the following:

- The creation of three task forces to address these problems: one on agency coordination, a second on corporate involvement, and a third concerned with education/training needs

- The design and development of a coordinated social service system with communitywide public and private support

PROBLEM

The MALMC identified a need to obtain information on the status of unemployed and displaced workers in Mapletree County. *Displaced workers* are defined here as those persons who have lost their jobs because of layoffs or plant closings and whose job skills are not in demand in the Mapletree labor market. Officially, Mapletree County has a 13% unemployment rate, which translates to approximately 8,000 persons. Of this total, only about 1,500 are receiving unemployment compensation.

The MALMC is concerned that there is little available data about the extent of the difficulties faced by unemployed and displaced workers in Mapletree County. Many receive little or no warning about layoffs or plant closings. Most receive little or no assistance from their former employers to help them enter job training or retraining programs or to help them find other jobs. Consequently, some displaced workers have had problems finding replacement jobs that use their job skills. In addition, some of these displaced workers have not been eligible to take part in available job training and job placement services. Some have been out of work for so long that they have exhausted their unemployment benefits and no longer are listed on the unemployment rolls. The MALMC proposed to survey displaced workers and employers in Mapletree County to gather information about this problem including the following:

- Assessment of the needs of unemployed and displaced workers
- Identification of services available to unemployed and displaced workers
- Creation of responses to the trends and needs

The MALMC will use findings of the study to develop planning and programming for human resources in Mapletree County, thereby contributing to improving the economic climate.

The MALMC asked the Center for the Quality of Working Life at University College to conduct a study of displaced and unemployed workers in Mapletree County. Through its Unemployment HELP program, Allied Churches' long involvement with these problems in Mapletree County led that group to join with the MALMC to identify the following questions as critical to addressing the unemployed and displaced worker problem in Mapletree County:

1. What is the experience of workers in Mapletree County who have been displaced due to long-term layoffs or plant closings?
2. Are present job training and retraining programs adequate for the needs of displaced workers?
3. What is the experience of workers relative to job training and retraining programs?
4. Who is at risk now? Can some job classes or skill areas be identified that could be considered to be at "high risk" for displacement because of changing market or technological factors?
5. Is a Job Search program needed by unemployed workers and by Mapletree employers? (Job Search is a cooperative labor-management program to help prepare employees facing long-term or permanent layoffs to find new jobs.)

This study addressed these issues identified by the MALMC, Allied Churches, and members of the Mapletree community. Four activities were the focus of the researchers and consultants:

- Reviewed available data regarding long-term unemployment in Mapletree County
- Interviewed and surveyed samples of unemployed and displaced workers to determine their perceptions of available job training and placement programs and their needs for these services
- Interviewed sample of employers to determine employer perceptions of available job training and placement programs and to determine their perceptions of needs for training and job placement services
- Initiated recommendations for a comprehensive program to address future needs of displaced workers in Mapletree County.

STUDY PLAN AND METHOD

The study plan used a three-part design that involved service agencies, displaced workers, and corporate representatives and that was directed toward developing a model for assisting displaced workers.

Part 1: Service mapping. The first part of the study involved mapping the already existing services for displaced workers in Mapletree County. Service agencies were identified and classified by Allied Churches staff on the basis of mission, core activities, clients served, costs, and funding sources. Allied Churches staff developed the database by contacting social service agencies in the Mapletree area.

Part 2: Focus groups and survey. Samples of displaced and unemployed workers were identified. Three focus groups were organized from sample members for specialized focus group interviews. Issues explored in the focus groups included layoff or termination experiences, training and placement needs, knowledge of available services, and extent of available corporate and "referred agency" services. Allied Churches staff identified participants and coordinated these sessions. The sessions were conducted by the University College team.

Two focus groups were held with corporate representatives to explore their perceptions of the same issues. The leading questions were "Have corporations been able to build linkages with the community agencies?" and "What has been their overall experience?" MALMC and Allied Churches staff identified participants and coordinated these sessions. These sessions were conducted by the University College team at neutral community sites.

A survey of unemployed workers was conducted. The survey was necessary because the focus groups identified issues that the sponsors and consultants jointly determined required additional information to clarify. The director of the Mapletree office of the State Office of Employment assisted in developing a sample for the survey and in distributing survey forms to clients in the sample.

Part 3: Program development. Based on the data gathered, a set of program recommendations designed to meet the needs of both unemployed and displaced workers and employers was developed. The recommendations include both short-term and long-term actions for the MALMC and related agencies and corporations to consider.

Study process. A step-by-step process to carry out this study plan was followed. The process included participation by MALMC and Allied Churches staff to ensure that a full range of both labor and management needs was identified. Staff views were solicited throughout the process.

The Center for the Quality of Working Life at University College worked with the MALMC and the Unemployment HELP program of Allied Churches to produce this report. University College provided study design guidance, conducted the focus groups, analyzed the data collected, and prepared the draft and final reports. MALMC and Allied Churches staff assisted with meeting coordination, data collection, and study design and final report preparation.

The steps in the study process are reproduced in Table 2.3.

STUDY SAMPLES AND PROCEDURE

Representative samples of social service agencies, unemployed and displaced workers, and corporate managers were selected from current files available in Mapletree County, from MALMC files, and from other local sources. Sample sizes for the service mapping, the focus groups, and the survey were determined to fit the nature and complexity of the design and the degree of accuracy desired. The samples are described as follows.

Service mapping sample. All service agencies that represented themselves as serving the unemployed were surveyed. All 16 nonprofit agencies completed the survey form and are listed here. In addition, 2 private agencies—Psychological Practice Group and Regional Service Clinic—participated in the survey.

Delta Socialization Services
Minority Outreach Employment Center
Employment Generating Services, Mapletree County
Office of Employment and Training
Growth for Single Parents and Homemakers
Office of Vocational Rehabilitation
American Farmworkers Opportunity
Cumberland Employment Service
State Office of Employment
County Office of Employment
Rehabilitation and Industrial Training Center
Senior Community Service Employment Program
Skills Training Center, Community Council
YWCA
Mapletree County Area Agency on Aging
Mapletree Spanish American Center

Focus groups. A total of five focus groups were held, three with unemployed and displaced workers and two with employers. Focus groups were held with unemployed and displaced Hispanic workers at the Spanish Center and with unem-

Table 2.3 Steps in Study Process

Step 1: Linking up (October/November)

    A. Meet with Mapletree Area Labor Management Council representative and Allied Churches staff

    B. Establish committee and initiate study design process

    C. Draft proposal for study

Step 2: Study development (December/January)

    A. Assemble materials

    B. Meet with committee

    C. Refine design and proposal

    D. Review with committee

    E. Finalize study design and proposal

Step 3: Develop samples (January/February)

    A. Identify subgroups of interest

    B. Develop sample frames for service mapping and focus groups

    C. Review with committee

    D. Draw samples

    E. Prepare focus group schedules

Step 4: Conduct focus group sessions (March)

    A. Meet with worker and corporate groups

Step 5: Tabulate and analyze focus group data (March/April)

    A. Conduct data coding and entry

    B. Conduct data analysis

Step 6: Consider need for additional survey (April/May)

    A. Develop survey form

    B. Develop sample in cooperation with the Mapletree Office of Employment

    C. Conduct survey and analyze survey data

Step 7: Begin drafting program recommendations (April/May)

Step 8: Draft report and review (May/June)

    A. Review with committee

    B. Review with select readers

Step 9: Prepare final report (May/June)

Step 10: Strategize to implement findings (June)

---

ployed and displaced black workers at the Minority Outreach Employment Center. The focus groups for unemployed and displaced women workers and for corporate representatives were conducted at the community library. Focus group attendees were selected in cooperation with service agency administrators. Group sizes ranged from 4 to 10 participants. The groups were designed to stimulate interactive discussion of the issues and problems from the perspectives of the subject groups. The central questions were "What do displaced and unemployed workers feel are the general problems they face with regard to finding jobs in Mapletree County?" and "Are there any specialized problems experienced by certain subgroups?"

For unemployed and displaced workers, the questions were designed to lead group members through the process they experienced from notification, to the actual unemployment experience, to their thinking about their future job prospects. The questions appear in Table 2.4. For corporate representatives, the questions were directed at securing knowledge of their understanding of the service system, their views on support for displaced workers, and their suggestions for future program development. The questions appear in Table 2.5.

Survey sample and procedure. A survey of displaced workers was conducted to secure further information directly from workers. The sample was drawn from the files of the Office of Employment (OE). A total of 200 workers were randomly selected based on the criterion that they had been unemployed long enough to qualify for mail-in service rather than personal visits to the OE office. OE staff developed the sample from their records. Each worker was mailed a questionnaire and a stamped self-addressed envelope for return directly to the team at University College.

STUDY RESULTS

The results of the study are presented in Appendix 2.1 at the end of this case. The survey response rate (25%) was modest. Unfortunately, "stressed" groups such as unemployed persons are reluctant to participate in survey research; hence, survey response rates tend to be less than optimal. Despite this, the combined methodologies used in this project—focus groups, service mapping, and a mail survey—provide a useful "snapshot" of conditions in the Mapletree area. Similarities in the findings gathered by way of the different methods make us confident that the data gathered are useful. By using these multiple methodologies, we have been able to develop an "understanding" of the community and the displaced and unemployed workers and to offer recommendations for addressing the needs.

Table 2.4 Displaced Workers Focus Group Questions

A flow model of the displaced worker experience guided the questioning through three steps:
1. Notification of layoff/termination
2. Layoff/unemployment experience
3. Perceived employment prospects

A. Notification/Support:
1. How much warning of the coming layoff did you receive from officials—company and union—and how much did you receive through the "grapevine" (rumors)?
2. What was the extent of *company* information and support regarding placement, training/retraining, and benefits regarding unemployment?
3. What was the extent of *union* information and support regarding placement, training/retraining, and benefits regarding unemployment?
4. Did you receive information and assistance from other sources such as media—newspapers, television, radio, brochures/handouts—and community groups?

B. Describe your layoff experience regarding the following:
1. How was your job search from the OE office, company, union, and community agencies?
2. Did you receive retraining or information from any source—union, company, OE, and so on? (type of program: union sponsored, company sponsored, or community agency program; financial arrangements: self-financed, union, company, or public sources)

C. Describe your prospects for the future including the following:
1. Jobs: How long have you been looking? What is available? Do available jobs underutilize your skills or not pay enough? Are you qualified for available jobs? Are you looking?
2. How helpful have available services been—from the union, company, OE, community agencies, and training programs—regarding referrals and sensitivity to your needs?

D. Do you have any other comments to make?

FINDINGS AND DISCUSSION

The findings of the study are organized in three parts: focus group findings, service mapping findings, and survey findings. A summary of each is presented in what follows, with the subsequent discussion addressing implications and program development.

Focus group findings. Three of the focus groups involved displaced workers in discussions of their needs and the services received. Their comments are summarized as follows.

Table 2.5 Corporate Representatives Focus Group Questions

The topic was introduced by describing the purpose of the study, offering a brief definition of displaced workers that was generic in orientation (e.g., all levels, all types of workers). The questions were as follows:

1. Describe/Characterize the climate in Mapltree County for displaced workers.
2. Are services currently available for displaced workers? If so, then name two.
3. What services do you think displaced employees would need the most?
4. What are the benefits to a company in assisting displaced workers?
5. What are the benefits to the economic development effort in Mapletree deriving from assisting displaced workers?
6. Who should operate services for displaced workers (public or private groups)?
7. How should services for displaced workers be funded?
8. What occupational and skill groups are at risk for becoming displaced workers during the next 5 to 10 years?
9. How would you rate the community's adequacy of training for providing displaced workers with new knowledge and skills (both before and after they are displaced)?
10. What is your opinion about the idea of creating a joint effort to address the problems of displaced workers (e.g., a public-private partnership)?
11. What should be the key services and characteristics of a model displaced worker?
12. What else should we know about the displaced worker issue in Mapletree County?
13. Would you be willing to join a task force to create a model program?

1. *Reasons for displacement:* The unemployed cited the primary reasons for unemployment as layoffs, plant closings, and skill changes.

2. *Service rating:* Unemployed persons rated the services they have received as in the middle or somewhat positive.

3. *Best and worst services:* Unemployed persons indicated that the best services they received were job skills training programs, whereas the worst services they received were those related to their contacts with OE staff and with making actual contacts regarding job openings. Much of their frustrations with the OE stemmed from two sources: (a) the paperwork required to establishing their eligibilities for unemployment benefits and (b) the inability of OE staff to help them find good jobs.

4. *Corporate assistance:* Unemployed persons generally reported that they received little or no support from their previous employers, although help was extended by some organizations. There was organizational uniqueness; some helped, whereas others did not.

5. *Training:* Unemployed persons indicated that referral to and linkages with appropriate training generally were weak or nonexistent.

6. *Problems blocking unemployment:* Unemployed persons indicated that the problems blocking their unemployment included the following:

- Lack of information about available jobs
- Low pay and few/no benefits in available jobs
- Age
- Education
- Training
- Transportation
- Child care

7. *Job finding:* Unemployed persons only infrequently received actual job-finding assistance.

8. *Service needs:* Unemployed persons indicated that they needed help most in (a) getting job referrals and (b) job search skills (e.g., resumé writing, interviewing, filling out applications).

9. *Pay levels:* Unemployed persons frequently indicated that pay levels for available jobs were too low to justify their job searches. That is, in connection with day care and travel expenses, it did not "pay" to work.

10. *Job potential:* Unemployed persons indicated that their job potential was not adequately recognized and that they were stymied by the lack of current experience for available jobs.

Corporation representatives also were interviewed in focus groups. Their comments are summarized as follows.

1. *Climate:* Corporate representatives indicated that there is a reasonable support system for displaced workers in Mapletree County (with qualifiers such as complexity and ease of access, as noted later).

2. *Service availability:* Corporate representatives indicated that some services are available for displaced workers, but they were uncertain as to the accessibility and location. They know and speak highly of the Job Placement Service at the OE and cited it most often as the source they used when seeking workers.

3. *Service needs:* Corporate representatives generally were unclear about what the critical needs of displaced workers are.

4. *Corporate benefits:* Corporate representatives clearly recognized the benefits of supporting displaced workers through the transition to new jobs (e.g., corporate image, ability to recruit in the future), and they particularly regarded the development and maintenance of a communitywide labor pool as a key economic development need.

5. *General benefits:* Corporate representatives indicated that the community needs to ensure the retention of the workforce and that some collaborative corporate initiatives for displaced workers could help to support the economic development effort (e.g., labor pool).

6. *Service system control:* Corporate representatives indicated that a public agency should control the service system but that it should be a joint public-private initiative ensuring that the system is responsive to private needs.

7. *Funding:* Corporate representatives indicated that services for displaced workers should be publicly funded, but they recognize the need for private contributions to the system as well.

8. *At-risk occupational and skill groups:* Corporate representatives did not report that any particular occupational or skill group is any more at risk than another, but they cited a general risk for all occupations and skill groups if area economic development efforts are not successfully undertaken, particularly in the fields of training and education.

9. *Training adequacy:* Corporate representatives indicated that the training opportunities generally are present but are sporadic and beneath the level required to meet the needs of employers and the community, especially in areas such as computer training and computer-related manufacturing technologies.

10. *Educational preparation:* Corporate representatives indicated that the educational preparation of job applicants from the Mapletree area is deficient in significant ways in both literacy and math preparation. One employer said that if his company had to upgrade its manufacturing technologies to more sophisticated levels, then it probably would have to relocate elsewhere to find an adequate workforce.

11. *Joint initiatives:* Corporate representatives indicated that they would be willing to engage in joint initiatives to create an expanded and developed service system for displaced workers.

12. *Social service characteristics:* Corporate representatives indicated that the key characteristic in a model program for helping unemployed and displaced workers would be a centralized referral source—one-stop shopping for ease of both individual and corporate access.

13. *Importance:* Corporate representatives generally indicated that the labor pool development and retention problem is significant and should be addressed by public and private leaders. They further stated that they would be willing to assist by contributing time on task forces and through the organizations in which they already are involved such as the Chamber of Commerce, the Manufacturers Association, and the MALMC.

The preceding comments from corporate representatives are consistent with identified needs and the views of the other groups.

Service mapping findings. As a result of the surveys collected from the service agencies, we were able to generate some observations about the network of agencies currently providing services to unemployed and displaced workers. The comments and findings are as follows.

1. *Complexity:* There are many agencies offering social services in the Mapletree area. Taken together, they create a complex web that often is too dense for corporations and unemployed persons to penetrate and that may contain both duplicate (e.g., counseling) and missing services (e.g., job search and skills training, actual referrals).

2. *Entry:* There is no easy access for either individual or corporate referrals except for the identification of job placement assistance at the OE.

3. *Funding sources:* The funding sources are primarily governmental (either state or federal).

4. *Client service load:* There are many clients receiving services, but the extent of services received by individuals and the effectiveness are unknown.

5. *Race:* Both blacks and Hispanics indicated that there are some unique problems (e.g., prejudice, language problems) for them to overcome in attempting to use the service system.

6. *Referral sources:* The referral sources are diverse and scattered among service types, with the potential for agencies to *refer to each other* without clients making successful connections with services or employers.

7. *Training:* Training services generally are available, but they are received by relatively few persons and might not be applicable to the open jobs.

8. *Fragmentation:* The service system is divided and/or fragmented beyond the ability of individuals and corporations to address and understand.

9. *Service differentiation:* It is very difficult to understand the actual services that would be defined as the agency's products in an individual way. That is, how can one agency be distinguished from another?

10. *Service times:* There is only one agency that lists evening hours and only one agency that lists Saturday hours, two times during which unemployed or displaced workers may be likely to attempt to obtain services.

11. *Regional thinking:* There does not seem to be an interest in establishing a regional network of services that could be used to support specialized training (e.g., in combination with other local communities) and that would fill in some of the gaps in the Mapletree social service system.

Survey findings. The findings from the survey of unemployed workers conducted with the help of the OE listing are summarized as follows.

1. *Unemployment rationale:* Large numbers of the displaced workers (54%) identified their reasons for unemployment as layoffs.

2. *Service rating:* The majority of unemployed respondents to the survey rated available employment services positively (excellent, good, and fair ratings totaled 70%).

3. *Best services received:* Among respondents who identified a best service (only 34%), the most frequent services mentioned were some form of job search and skill training received at one of the service agencies.

4. *Worst services received:* Unemployed respondents, for the most part, had no comment. But of the few who did identify worst services, the most fre-

quent response concerned their experiences at the OE. The team learned that most unemployed persons were seeking more help in finding jobs than the OE was able to provide and that this was a source of frustration to clients.

5. *Ex-employer assistance:* Most unemployed persons (78%) stated that they received no help from their ex-employers.

6. *Job training suggested:* Unemployed persons in large numbers (96%) reported that no one—ex-employers, unions, the OE, and so on—suggested training or retraining to them.

7. *Job training referral:* Again, 96% of the unemployed persons did not have locations to which they were referred for job training.

8. *Good jobs:* More than half of unemployed persons (52%) indicated that there are good jobs available in Mapletree County.

9. *Problems with or barriers to employment:* Unemployed persons most frequently listed the following as factors: pay too low, no information about job openings, age, education, and lack of training.

10. *Attendance at job search training:* Fully 84% of the unemployed persons had not attended job search training.

11. *Attendance at job skills training:* Again, 84% of the unemployed persons had not attended job skills training.

12. *Help required:* Unemployed persons suggested that there are three leading types of assistance most required: job referrals, job openings, and resumé writing.

RECOMMENDATIONS

Based on the data gathered in the focus groups, in the service mapping process, and from the survey, the team made eight recommendations that we believe would assist displaced workers in Mapletree County.

1. Coordinate the existing service system. One problem appears to be the lack of an integrating mechanism across all the existing service agencies. Problems of service duplications and service gaps exist. Any attempts to address these problems must be communitywide and should be undertaken as a partnership of public and private efforts.

2. Develop an easily recognized information source for system access for the unemployed and for corporate referrals. Both unemployed persons and corporate representatives reported feeling intimidated by the web of agencies. A single entry point and telephone number would help.

3. Heighten employee/employer and community recognition of training/retraining needs. Employees, employers, and the community all must recognize that promoting job training and retraining is in everyone's best interest.

4. Expand training in new and modern technologies of all types in Mapletree County. The community apparently has not extended training efforts as far or as deeply into new technologies as is needed, particularly regarding computer-related technologies (e.g., computer-assisted design and production technologies, scheduling and operations methodologies).

5. Invigorate the means for linking educational/training groups (schools) with employees and expected employment training needs. Although linkages may exist now, they do not appear to be as strong or as effective as they need to be. Employers must make their assessments of educational preparation inadequacies in Mapletree County known to educators.

6. Develop a consortium to coordinate job training programs to assist Recommendations 3 and 4. This would be a group with a specific task of defining and addressing educational and training needs on a cross-organizational basis. No additional organization would be needed if some existing group could assume responsibility for the organizing of a training and educational consortium.

7. There are three job-level support services needed for displaced workers: (a) expanded transportation services, particularly between city-based unemployed persons and outlying plants; (b) expanded language training (Spanish-English and English-Spanish); and (c) expanded child care development services. These services may be available now, but they need to be coordinated.

8. Create a corporate labor/sharing jobs pool. This pool would extend the use of existing labor resources by sharing information among employers about job classes and skills available because of layoffs and plant closings.

To address these recommendations, we suggest the creation of three task forces: one targeted at agency coordination, a second for corporate responses, and a third to address education/training needs. A suggested process to initiate task force activity is presented in Figure 2.1. The task forces should involve key

Figure 2.1.   Unemployment Task Force Group Structure and Process

actors from all sectors of the community. These task forces should focus on further defining systems needs, refining these recommendations, and developing action plans to implement them.

Steps toward implementation are as follows:

1. Identify a relevant organization to coordinate creation of task forces.
2. Each task force should follow the following four-step process:
   a. Assess community needs in the subject area (e.g., services coordination, corporate responses, education/training).
   b. Create a "vision of the future" in the subject area (e.g., coordination of services to unemployed/displaced workers in a consolidated organization).
   c. Compare the assessment of the present (Step 1 output) to the desired future (Step 2 output) so as to identify gaps.
   d. Create a plan of action/steps to move from the present to the future.

Appendix

Tabulation of Findings of Unemployment Survey

Question 1: How long have you been unemployed?

Category	Frequency	Percentage
Less than 6 months	41	82
6 to 12 months	4	8

Category	Frequency	Percentage
1 to 2 years	4	8
More than 2 years	1	2

Question 2: How did your unemployment come about?

Layoff	27	54
Closing	5	10
Skill changes	1	2
Other	17	34

Other descriptions:

Change of ownership/Termination/Sold to new owner
Change of ownership
Drop in sales
Ethnicity
Fired/Terminated because of absenteeism
Fired/Termination
Fired for disagreeing with boss
Fired
Health/Pinched nerve
Job misrepresentation
Quit
Redefinition of position
Seasonal/Lack of work
Seasonal/Lack of work
Seasonal/Subcontractor
Seasonal work
Seasonal/Lack of work

Question 3: How do you rate services for unemployed persons in Mapletree County?

Category	Frequency	Percentage
Excellent	2	4
Good	17	34
Fair	16	32
Poor	7	14
Don't know	7	14
No response	1	2

Question 4: What are the *best* employment services you have received?

Church charities/Showed different avenues and gave encouragement
Compensation
Consolidated school of business/Excellent job search program
Employment agencies/Good job opportunities
Employment Fast/They had the most variety
Job services
I'm learning an interesting and skilled vocation
Updating of job-hunting skills

Local bureau/ They appear to try to help you
Mail service/Don't have to meet any crabby people
New options/Classes on job-finding skills
Newspaper
Return to school/Furthering skills
Office and newspaper want ads
Mapletree Tech Institute/Help with interviewing, resumé writing, and associated skills

Question 5: What is the *worst* employment service you have received?

Agency/They want to give me minimum wage
Bracks Group/Big buildup, no further contacts
Employee attitude
Employment office/No interest from employees of the office
Temp services/I was always overworked and underpaid
Unemployment office/Lack of opportunities at livable wage
Unemployment office/Attitude/Want me to support family on minimum wage
Unemployment office/Smart attitude, waste of time, not interested

Question 6: When you lost your job, did your ex-employer offer to help you?

Category	Frequency	Percentage
No	39	78
Yes	11	22

How helped:
   Arranged for new options
   Gave me unemployment checks to draw on
   Good references
   Hired an outplacement service
   I was told I'd be called back
   Nine weeks' severance pay
   Offered to help but never did anything
   Promised approximate return date
   Said I'd be called back
   Seminars on finding jobs at unemployment agency
   Severance pay
   Will call back in fall

Question 7: When you lost your job, did anyone (e.g., ex-employer, union, unemployment office) suggest a job training program?

Category	Frequency	Percentage
No	48	96
Yes	2	4

Question 8: If anyone (e.g., ex-employer, union, unemployment office) did suggest that you go into a job training program, where were you sent?

Category	Frequency	Percentage
No response	49	98
Made response	1	2
Response: Their plant		

Question 9: Do you think that there are good jobs available in the Mapletree area?

Category	Frequency	Percentage
Yes	26	52
No	9	18
Not sure	15	30

Question 10: If you are having problems in finding a good job, what do you think are the main reasons? (Check all that you think are important.)

Category	Frequency	Percentage
Pay too low	28	56
No information about job openings	21	42
Age	19	38
Education	12	24
Lack of training	11	22
Lack of jobs in Mapletree area	10	20
Lack of jobs you can do	7	14
Race	4	8
Sex	2	4
Child care	1	2
Transportation	1	2
Other	11	22

Other categories:
    Fact that I was fired
    Lack of good jobs in my field
    Lack of work in my line of work
    Need more job counseling for job placement
    Not enough experience
    Too many other people applying for good jobs
    Not hiring people with my type of management skills
    Overqualified
    Overqualified
    Very specialized skills
    You have to know someone in the business

Question 11: Since becoming unemployed, have you attended any programs that teach you *how to find another job?*

Category	Frequency	Percentage
No	42	84
Yes	8	16

What job search program have you attended?
    "Get That Job" tape
    Consolidated School of Business
    Growth Program
    New Options
    Personalized outplacement service
    Unemployment bureau
    Unemployment program at unemployment office
    Mapletree Tech Institute electronics program

Question 12: Since becoming unemployed, have you attended any training programs to *learn new job skills*?

Category	Frequency	Percentage
No	42	84
Yes	8	16

What skill training program have you attended?
   Consolidated School of Business
   Secretary
   Real estate
   School bus driving/Lethal weapons training course
   Student teaching
   Thompson Institute/Computer programming
   Mapletree Tech Institute/Electronics program

Question 13: What kind of assistance do you think would help you find a good job?

Category	Frequency	Percentage
Job referrals	24	48
Job openings	18	36
Resume writing	12	24
Interviewing	8	16
New/Updated job skills	7	14
Dress	2	4
Applications	6	12
Anything else	11	55

Anything else descriptions:
   Available transportation
   Business agent
   Career that will be in demand for a few decades
   I'll be called back after Labor Day
   Job counseling
   Juggling home, child, part-time job, school, and unwilling husband
   Knowing who is hiring instead of hit and miss
   More listings in local newspaper
   Most jobs aren't advertised
   Typing/Computer training
   Where to get specific training

Question 14: How old are you?

Category	Frequency	Percentage
20s	10	20
30s	12	24
40s	17	34
50s	8	16
60s	3	6

Question 15: What is your sex?

Category	Frequency	Percentage
Male	27	54
Female	23	46

Question 16: What is your racial/ethnic background?

Category	Frequency	Percentage
White	48	96
Black	2	4

Question 17: How far did you go in school?

Category	Frequency	Percentage
Attended high school	8	16
High school GED	1	2
High school graduate	14	28
Attended college	8	16
College graduate	5	10
Attended vocational tech	14	28

Vocational tech training:
  Adult education/Typing
  Courses/Business school
  Floriculture
  Television servicing
  Two-year vocational drafting program
  Mapletree County vocational tech
  Auto body
  Electronics tech/Associates degree
  Trade school
  Two years of electricity
  Typing II/Word processing

Question 18: What was your last job title?

Blue collar (16)
  Assembly worker
  Candy packer
  Floor lady/Garment industry
  Group leader and setup
  Machine assembling operator
  Machine operator
  Mechanic/Carpenter
  Power plant insulator
  Candy maker and sales
  Driver/Forklift and truck

Freight handler
Laborer/General
Machine adjuster setup
Machine operator
Packer
Sewer/Upholstery

White collar (15)
Buyer
Clerk
Clerk/Dyehouse
Clerk/Purchasing
Clerk/Greenhouse attendant
Information specialist
Secretary
Split ticket distributor
Clerical associate
Clerk/Customer service
Clerk/Office
Clerk
Computer operator
Receptionist/Law office
Secretary/Receptionist

Technical (4)
Artist/Paste-up
Electrical maintenance
Technician/Health physics and radiation monitor
Welder/Layout

Supervisory (4)
Master mechanic supervisor
Supervisor/Plating
Master scheduler
Supervisor/Computer operator
Managerial (6)
Manager/Sales and purchasing
Manager/Food store
Manager/Telecomm
Manager/Sales
Manager/Grocery
Manager/Sales

Professional (5)
Engineer/Design
Mechanical designer
Recruiter/Trainer/Real estate
Engineer/Electrical
Teacher

Case 2.3   Library Use

Introduction

Hambrick and McMillan (1989) presented a brief overview of focus groups, their uses from a managerial and research perspective, and a sample of applications. One major use of focus groups is for problem definition in support of management decision making. This section describes how focus groups not only helped to define a managerial problem better but also expanded the boundary of the problem.[1]

The Problem: Its First Definition

Based on various usage statistics, the director and staff of a university library realized that there was notable underuse of library resources and services. They asked another university's applied research center to propose a study that would help them better understand the problem.[2]

Discussions between the researchers and library staff established the following three working assumptions:

1. The undergraduate students at the university, like many college students, will do as much or as little library research as their professors demand. Thus, the faculty play a key role in students' use of the library.
2. The faculty themselves might be unfamiliar with some library resources available to them and their students.
3. There are important differences among the library needs of various disciplines. For example, a chemistry professor and student might have library needs that are different from those in the social sciences.

A self-study of the Michigan State University library system supported Assumptions 1 and 3. That study revealed that the three most common reasons given by undergraduates for using the library are to study (35%), obtain research information on a specific subject (17%), and find a specific book or periodical article (11%). These activities are commonly associated with assignments. The same study suggested that frequency of use may be tied more to curriculum than to any other factor.

With these assumptions as the starting point, the parties agreed that the first investigation of underuse of the academic library should focus on the faculty.

Library Use

Studies on the use of library resources often employ measures such as the number of users, frequency of use, expressed needs, peak times, recurring difficulties, specialties of users and staff and their handling and deployment, stock requirements and regulations, service quantity, frustration of requests, lead times in delivery of documents, user and nonuser penetration, and costs of supply (Hannabus, 1987; Shapiro & Marcus, 1987). Although these statistics provide useful information, they do not help identify issues that may underlie library use. In this particular instance, the researchers conducted a brainstorming session with the library staff to develop questions that would guide the research effort. The actual questions were as follows:

1. What are faculty information and instructional needs?
2. How should students learn about libraries?
3. Do faculty perceive that the library is underused by students and/or faculty?
4. If so, why is there an underuse?
5. How can the library staff best aid the faculty in student research?
6. What programs, if any, would the faculty like to see made available to them in terms of library staff working with the students?
7. What are the base and optimal expectations of the faculty?
8. Are the faculty aware of new technologies available to them and their students?
9. How can the library assist its users or potential users—both faculty and students—to handle the almost unlimited access to information now available through the library?
10. What kinds of new technology or information would the faculty like the library to provide?

Neither the library staff nor the researchers were convinced that these questions exhausted the issues that should be discussed. In fact, they both thought that identifying other issues would be as important as answering the questions that already had been identified.

Focus Groups: What and Why?

One approach to answering such questions involves a population or sample survey, making use of either a questionnaire to be completed by the respondents or an interview schedule to be completed by trained interviewers in dialogue with respondents. This approach also typically gathers demographic or quasi-demographic data on respondents and, therefore, allows a researcher to compare faculty in naturally formed groups. For example, one might compare the responses of liberal arts faculty to those of engineering faculty, or one might compare responses of "technologically informed" faculty to those of faculty who are not so informed. This way of thinking leads to a quasi-experimental design and approach (Cook & Campbell, 1979). Although this approach may lead to differences that can be clearly stated, it often does not help identify underlying issues.

Van Maanen (1982) noted the disadvantages associated with quantitative quasi-experimental designs in studying organizations:

> the relatively trivial amounts of explained variance, the lack of comparability across studies, the failure to achieve much predictive validity, the high level of technical and notational sophistication rendering many research publications incomprehensible . . ., and the causal complexity of multivariate analysis, which . . . make change-oriented actions difficult to contemplate.

Furthermore, Goodall (1984) suggested, "Research done in the great scientific traditions tend[s] to encourage simplistic reductionist assumptions and explanations . . ., usually at the expense of more complex interpretive possibilities." Radin (1988) emphasized the role of qualitative methods in practitioner-oriented research, reminding us that *qualitative* is not to be equated with *nonempirical*.

Both Greenbaum (1987) and Krueger (1988) provided useful introductions to focus groups as a tool for applied research. Krueger described a focus group as

> a carefully planned discussion designed to obtain perceptions on a defined area of interest in a permissive, non-threatening environment. It is conducted with approximately seven to ten people by a skilled interviewer. The discussion is relaxed, comfortable, and often enjoyable for participants as they share their ideas and perceptions. Group members influence each other by responding to ideas and comments in the discussion.

The director and staff of the library desired to gain feedback from faculty users about their own and students' use of the library. They recognized, as did

Katz, Gutek, Kahn, and Barton (1975), that where there was no direct check on their products or services, the need for systematic feedback from the people being served was all the more necessary. (Ideally, this study would include information gathering from students and librarians as well as from faculty; however, the research client and sponsor wanted the study limited to faculty.)

The open-ended approach of focus groups allows participants to comment, to explain, and to suggest notions quite different from any they would offer in answers to highly structured questions. This opportunity, in fact, characterizes the difference between focus groups and structured surveys or other kinds of quantitative research. More than a half century ago, Rice (1931) noted that the interview as a fact-finding vehicle is flawed in that the questioner takes the lead and the interviewee is more or less passive. The most important information or perceptions might not be disclosed because the questioner provides a direction that leads away from them. In short, Rice suggested that the interview might yield data in areas more likely to represent the interviewer's ideas than those of the interviewee.

In summary, the focus group method was chosen because of the library's determination to come to a better understanding of library use and related issues rather than merely to gain a statistically supportable conclusion.

Although there is no way of determining the exact ideal group size, Krueger (1988) noted that the typical focus group is composed of 7 to 10 people, whereas Greenbaum (1987) claimed that the most desirable size is 8 to 10 people. The group participants usually have something in common and have some characteristic that identifies them as useful for the research at hand. The current research effort made use of two focus groups of 10 faculty members each.

As faculty, the group members' knowledge and expectations of the library, their teaching methods, and their types of assignments all influenced the students' use of the library. The group participants represented the broad spectrum of academic disciplines. As is generally true in choosing participants for focus groups, there was no intent to choose a statistically representative sample of individuals. The first group represented the following disciplines: engineering, foreign languages, geography, political science, psychology, sociology, and religion. The second group was drawn from biology, chemistry, education, English, foreign languages, management, mathematics, music, and political science.

Focus Group Discussions

The author served as the moderator of the focus groups. The discussions developed in such a way that the groups addressed all 10 of the initial questions as well as other issues without the moderator having to pose all 10 questions to either group.

There was no analysis of the librarians' questions prior to the conduct of the focus groups. Consequently, the moderator did not see their views of the issue as technical, psychosocial, or anything else in particular. Conducting any such analysis before the focus group sessions could prompt a moderator to guide the discussion in a biased manner. The first question posed by the moderator served as an icebreaker and a stage setter: "How long ago did students in your class last use the library, and what did they use it for?" Whenever necessary throughout the discussion, the moderator posed prompting questions such as "Does anyone see it differently?" and "Would you explain that further?" Depending on the flow of the discussion, the moderator posed one of the substantive questions, all of which appear in Table 2.6. Comments from the faculty, rather than additional questions from the moderator, brought other issues to the surface.

The following themes emerged from the focus groups:

1. Students use the library almost exclusively to complete assignments that require specific library resources.
2. Faculty express a strong desire to have a greater variety of print material available in the library for students to read as needed and to browse through.
3. Faculty expect the library to be the supplier of academic resource material. They want the library to catalog and otherwise support non-print material (e.g., tapes, satellite programs). The library should be a place in which to find books as well as a path to other sources.
4. Students should learn about the library as a tool through progressive need-to-know assignments in their regular courses. Developing these assignments is a joint faculty-library responsibility, with the faculty having the greater share of the responsibility. Faculty pointed to "Writing Across the Curriculum" as a model that might be applied to library use.
5. When requested, the librarians do an outstanding job of explaining library resources to students. The librarians and the faculty might work together to identify what students should learn at different stages of their educations. Developing library literacy and library skills among the students is a joint faculty-librarian responsibility. There currently is a strong sense of faculty-librarian cooperation. In the faculty's view, the librarians are a real asset and

Table 2.6 Research Questions Related to Internal Subsystems

Librarians' Questions	Goals and Values	Technical	Psychosocial	Structural	Managerial	Environment
1. What are faculty information and instructional needs?			X			
2. How should students learn about libraries?		X				
3. Do faculty perceive that the library is underused by students and/or faculty?		X	X			
4. If so, then why is there an underuse?		X	X			
5. How can the library staff best aid the faculty in student research?		X				
6. What programs, if any, would the faculty like to see made available to them in terms of library staff working with the students?		X				
7. What are the base and optimal expectations of the faculty?			X			
8. Are the faculty aware of new technologies available to them and their students?		X				
9. How can the library assist its users or potential users—both faculty and students—in handling the almost unlimited access to information now available through the library?		X				
10. What kinds of new technology or information would the faculty like the library to provide?		X				

are very willing to work with the faculty and the students; the librarians are willing to go out of their way to be helpful.

6. There is a strong, but not unanimous, feeling among the faculty that the library director does not foster or encourage the kind of library interaction that they feel is valuable—a view that they believe the librarians also hold.

7. Many believe that the library is underused. Many question the way in which library use is measured, whereas others claim that improved design of texts and readers, easy access to copies, and student and faculty subscriptions reduce the need for traditional library support. In addition, students may be intimidated by all that is available in the library.

8. Some faculty are keenly aware of new technologies. They desire out-of-library access to databases and card catalogs. Other faculty are notably less aware of what is available. Orientation sessions are very helpful for those who choose to attend them.

Having almost unlimited access to bibliographies, abstracts, and other lists of sources generates frustration if the library is likely to have just a small proportion of listed items. More journals, including online journals, are wanted. There is a strong desire that access be made available through home and office personal computers. The catalog should include non-print material.

The library is at a rather advanced stage of technological support, probably more than students—and at least some faculty—are able to use. There is strong, if not widespread, feeling that some of the money spent on more advanced technology might be better spent on printed matter.

9. The faculty recommended that a focus group session be conducted with the librarians to get their views on some of the same issues.

The thrust of this research lies in the relationship between "what we got" and "where we started." In this case, the results of the focus group discussions matched the librarians' questions. Rather than just developing a somewhat one-dimensional linkage, that relationship was explored within the context of an open systems model.

Analysis in an Open Systems Context

There is no one best way of viewing reality, and there is no one best theory of organization. Each theory of organization—classical/structural, neoclassical/human relations, modern/systems/culture—attempts to describe how it views the organization and how its theory explains the organization. The viewpoints, explanations, and theories do not change the reality. In this particular instance, as in others, the open systems model "works"; that is, it contributes to an organizational analysis through self-understanding.

The model of Kast and Rosenzweig (1985), and its adaptation by Ziegenfuss (1985, 1989), provides the structure for the present analysis. In that model, the library is viewed as being composed of interwoven subsystems, namely managerial, structural, psychosocial, technical, and goals and values. The library exists, in turn, within the larger environmental suprasystem, which is the university and its environment.

Paisley (1968) noted that in studying information users one must consider a series of systems with the user at the center rather than treat the user in isolation. Mick (1980) included situational and environmental variables in his study of library users. Hiscock (1986) concluded that libraries need accurate studies of the needs and behavior of their users if they are to be guided by user needs rather than by technology.

Analysis in qualitative research involves "judgment calls . . . [or] decisions (some big, some small, but all necessary and consequential) that must be made without the benefit of 'objective' rules that one can apply with precision" (McGrath, 1982). Ott (1989) pointed out that this problem, unfortunate as it may be, is not unique to research on organizational culture or to the use of qualitative methods. It might just be more obvious that we are incorporating judgment calls when we use qualitative research methods.

LIBRARIANS' QUESTIONS AND OPEN SYSTEMS

We can now review the initial set of 10 questions posed by the library staff and attempt to identify which internal subsystem is, or which subsystems are, most relevant to each question. Where there is more than one subsystem strongly related to a particular question, we consider that question as related to both subsystems. Where we note that a question is related to one subsystem, we do not suggest that the question is unrelated to all others. To gain a better understanding of the library staff's views and the faculty's views on the issue of library underuse, we develop associations between the librarians' questions and subsystems and then between faculty issues and subsystems.

As noted in Table 2.6, Librarian Questions 1 and 7 concern the needs and expectations in the realm of the psychosocial subsystem. Librarian Questions 3 and 4 concern the use of materials and technology by individuals as well as whether and why they are underused. These fall in the realm of the technical and psychosocial subsystems.

We categorize all the remaining questions as related mainly to the technical subsystem (Table 2.6). Librarian Questions 2 and 8 relate directly to knowledge of the library and the technology it makes available. Librarian Questions 5, 6, and 9 relate to processes that the library staff can undertake to improve (increase) the students' use of the library. Librarian Question 10 refers specifically to equipment and support services that a library may provide.

Based on Table 2.6 and the related reasons, we conclude that the library staff view library underuse mainly as technical and secondarily as psychosocial. The research question, then, becomes one of how the faculty view library underuse.

FOCUS GROUP RESULTS AND OPEN SYSTEMS

We associate Faculty Issues 1 and 5 (Table 2.7) primarily with the psychosocial and structural subsystems. Both of these concern student behavior patterns and what the faculty and librarians can jointly do to influence those patterns or work habits. We see Faculty Issues 2 and 3 as primarily psychosocial, related strongly to the work habits and instructional needs of faculty.

Faculty Issues 4 and 8 relate directly to knowledge and, therefore, to the technical subsystem and to the needs of students and faculty—the psychosocial subsystem (Table 2.7). The faculty see developing need-to-know assignments as a joint faculty-library responsibility. That view results from the value (goals and values subsystem) that they place on students' library literacy and from their understanding of the roles of faculty and librarians within the university (structure).

Faculty see the library director's activities (managerial subsystem) as creating an atmosphere in which the librarian is inclined or disinclined to interact fully with faculty. Faculty Issue 6 relates essentially to the managerial subsystem. Faculty Issue 7 clearly points to the relationship between the environment and the library (Table 2.7). Access that students have to materials outside the library, either from other libraries or through the well-developed books of readings and cases, illustrates the faculty view that changes in the environment may alter the students' need for traditional library services.

As noted earlier, this kind of research effort ideally would involve focus groups not only with the faculty but also with students and the librarians themselves. The faculty also identified the need for conducting focus groups with the

Table 2.7 Faculty Issues Related to Open Systems Model

Faculty Issues	Goals and Values	Technical	Psychosocial	Structural	Managerial	Environment
1. Students use library mostly for assignments			X	X		
2. Faculty want print material			X			
3. Faculty want non-print material catalogued			X			
4. Students learn about library through need-to-know assignments/A joint faculty-library responsibility	X	X	X	X		
5. Developing a library curriculum/Already strong faculty-librarian cooperation		X		X		
6. Library director does not encourage librarian-faculty interaction as completely as needed					X	
7. Whether library is underused is questionable/Other materials have changed students' need for library						X
8. Faculty are variably aware of new technologies/Many desire out-of-library access/Already much technology available		X	X			

librarians to explore the latter's view of their own role, perhaps their evolving role.

It appears from an analysis of Table 2.7 that faculty view the issue of library underuse as a systemwide issue, perhaps involving the psychosocial system more than any other but, nevertheless, reflecting the influence of all subsystems. Importantly, the faculty certainly do not see the problem of library underuse as primarily a technical one.

Conclusion

What started as a series of questions seeking primarily technical answers evolved into a broader organizational analysis. Presenting both the original librarians' questions and the issues that emerged from the faculty focus groups in the context of an open systems model provided a method of analysis that broadened the scope of the original problem. Clearly, developing a technical fix, based on a summary of answers to the librarians' questions, would not take into account the broader issues and would have little chance of solving those problems that are not essentially technical.

Notes

1. This case was formally presented as an article published in the *Journal of Management Science and Policy Analysis* (McKenna, 1990) and is presented here as an edited version with permission.

2. To maintain confidentiality, the university that is the subject of this case will remain anonymous. The author (McKenna) appreciates the contributions of Michael Young and Mark Kiesling of the Institute for State and Regional Affairs, Pennsylvania State University at Harrisburg.

Case 2.4 Computers in High School: Oakton School District

High schools across the country have been struggling with how to acquire and implement computer technology. Faculty and students have expressed interest in the potential of computer technology and the Internet to enrich the curriculum. The superintendent of schools appointed a faculty committee to address the school district's needs and to create a plan and process for implementation.

Faculty were interested in how they could secure resources for equipment and how they would be able to measure the effects of increased computer use. The committee contacted a local university and a consulting firm for ideas on how to proceed. Faculty decided that they wanted to study the use of computers and the difficulties encountered in expanding the new technology. They produced the following work statement for consideration by the university and the consulting firm.

MEMORANDUM

TO: Interested Universities and Consulting Firms

FROM: Faculty Committee on Computer Technology

   The purpose of this project is generally to increase the use of computers by faculty in their high school courses through a *computer implementation self-design process*. There has been little research on the social and technical effects of simultaneous computerization of high school departments. There is, however, little doubt that nearly all departments will continue to go through this process during the next decade.
   The key results expected from the project are as follows:

- Increased faculty use of microcomputers in their course work, research, and consulting
- Increased knowledge of the social and technical alterations caused by computers on the school district's organizational culture
- Increased understanding of design features that link users and computers more effectively
- Increased knowledge of the implementation process by which computers are successfully integrated into a school system

The project is to be specifically addressed to high schools, but these concerns cross grade levels.

Problem

   School district leaders and faculty are confronted with the problem of computer acquisition, use, and overall acceptance. Oakton School District has both cost-of-acquisition problems and acceptance problems. There is relatively little written material in the academic literature on the social and technical aspects of computerizing a whole school system simultaneously.
   The problem, then, is one of designing the technical and social systems necessary to fully integrate computers into departmental management, teach-

ing, and professional development. For example, with regard to departmental management, the problem involves computer use in at least four areas: Internet use, word processing, budgeting (spreadsheet), and database management (e.g., student records, scheduling, bibliographies).

The extent of each faculty member's use of computers in teaching involves, to some degree, exposure and pure ease of "access." The problem's solution requires work on both administrative and teaching aspects—two areas in which there is a nationwide need, with many school districts facing the same problem.

Intensive analysis of how school systems' "organizational cultures" respond to these problems is critically needed to speed the acceptance of computerization *and* to increase "implementation approach" knowledge and success. The proposed work extends the interest of the administration and faculty in bringing computer equipment to faculty and students. And it extends this committee's interest in evaluating organizational systems change and in increasing productivity and the "quality of teaching life." The research will lead to designs and processes for more effectively integrating computers into the social and work structures of secondary school systems. The school, in this case, is using itself as the study subject.

Procedure

The procedure for the study will be as follows. Each faculty member will receive one personal computer, depending on the nature of the equipment supplied. Students will be invited to use the computer through the course work process (as *newly redesigned* by the faculty member to include the computer). The "student use time" will be a part of the research findings.

The project will be run participatively using both the faculty committee and a faculty computer systems steering committee. The research committee will be responsible for formulating and guiding the design and implementation of the research aspects of the proposal. The systems steering committee will be responsible for ensuring that the computer system (e.g., hardware, software selection, training documentation, manuals) satisfactorily addresses faculty and student requirements.

In general, the research will focus on a broad range of organizational impacts. An organizational systems model will be used to identify changes in goals/values, teaching and curriculum, technical improvement, structural and psychosocial adjustments, and managerial needs. For example, how will the computer affect the goals and values of the department? Will computers be a core value of the teaching and academic curriculum? As another example, how will computers affect and be affected by the psychological climate? Will the increasing knowledge and use of computers create competition among faculty users? The committees will further specify the design as they begin work in collaboration with university and consulting teams.

Case 2.5   Westside Hospital:
Services Distribution

Westside Hospital is a 450-bed community hospital located in a small urban city with a population of about 100,000. The hospital has been in operation for some 75 years at the same location. During this time, the hospital has grown from 85 beds to a modern facility complete with all of the latest technology and a staff trained at some of the best schools in the country. It is located in a wealthy section of the city, but one in which deterioration is beginning to appear.

The management team has been essentially intact for the past 10 years. Team members appear to operate smoothly with consensus as to direction, policy, and operations. The management team was aware that some community members were beginning to express some dissatisfaction with the hospital, but the team was not concerned given that the issues were not apparent or loudly expressed. Management was taken by surprise when a community group publicly presented a report blasting the hospital for inadequate services to the poor, citing in particular a significant difference in infant mortality rates. "Access and quality are in question," the group said. The group called for a reinstatement of taxable status for the hospital, suggesting that the additional tax revenue could be used to serve poor patients. Because the report was front-page news, the hospital management team met immediately to begin an analysis and create a response.

Several issues quickly surfaced at the first meeting of the team. The staff confirmed that there were differences in infant mortality rates, although they did not know why. Second, staff recently had completed a patient origin study including a review of patients from the major specialties (obstetrics/gynecology, psychiatric, medicine, surgery, pediatrics, and newborn services). The data indicated that most patients came from high-socioeconomic districts. Third, the team recognized that the staff refer most "poorer" patients across town to the city hospital. Fourth, the team admitted that the staff composition, although in compliance with governmental guidelines, was not very diverse in ethnic and minority mix.

As a result, the chief executive officer decided to complete an organizational systems analysis of the problem. The analysis would have two components: (a) diagnosis of the hospital subsystems elements so as to identify the problem causes and (b) a policy change plan that would address the needs identified, whether they be quality of care, management insensitivities, or misperceptions.

Each member of the management team was asked to (a) identify the technical and other problems in the organizational systems and (b) suggest policy changes to address them.

Case 2.6   The Ford/Firestone Problem

Few consumers have not heard about the national controversy over the Ford sport utility vehicles and the seemingly defective Firestone tires. Both companies quickly appointed internal problem-solving teams, and both companies employed outside expert consultants to help them understand the problem.

Here it seems that the focus of attention should be on the product and technology of both companies. Is there a defect in the Firestone tire that leads to loss of tread and subsequent accidents? If so, then is this a defect of design or of misuse? The problem-solving team naturally would focus on product and technology.

At Ford, the team would quickly get to this product/technology topic as well. Its attention would be on the design of the company's sport utility vehicles, the vehicles' propensity to roll over, and the impact of tire separation. Design, production, and crash-testing engineers would dominate the team. Technical quality control would be the highest priority subject.

If there is one case that seems to be a product/technology exclusive, then this is it. Unfortunately, it is not so simple, and not just because the technical questions are very complex. It seems that some of the data about risk and technical inadequacy were available inside the companies *prior to* the national publicity. Why were these data not used by *management?* If the data were not distributed, then what does that tell us about the *culture* of both organizations and about the *psychological climate* that supports open communication and knowledge sharing?

Using the two companies' Web sites (Ford: www.ford.com; Firestone: www.firestone.com), develop a team and an analysis of the multiple dimensions of this problem.

Note

1. From F. E. Kast, J. E. Rasenzweig, *Organization and Management: A Systems and Contingency Approach.* Copyright © 1985 by The McGraw-Hill Companies. Reprinted with permission.

3

Solving Structural Problems

*There is nothing more difficult to take in hand,
more perilous to conduct, or more uncertain in its success
than to take the lead in the introduction of a new order of things.*
—Niccolò Machiavelli, *The Prince*

Some organization and management problems have to do with the way in which a department or a whole company is structured. The problems are not product related or technical; that is, they do not concern production processes or the application of technological knowledge. Nor are they issues of vision and values that might call for a review of culture and strategy. In this chapter, we consider "restructuring" as a problem-solving response.

The Nature of Organizational Structure

In the opening case concerning problems at the Internal Revenue Service (IRS), Commissioner Charles Rossotti remarked that restructuring to address the problems will be completed quickly. What is structure, and how can we think about structure as a problem area in organization and management systems?[1]

> Structure involves the ways in which the tasks of the organization are divided (differentiation) and coordinated (integration). In the formal sense, structure is set forth by organization charts, by position and job descriptions, and by rules and procedures. It is also concerned with patterns of authority, communication, and work flow. (Kast & Rosenzweig, 1985, p. 115)[1]

In the classical view of organization theory, structure involves division of labor, unity of command, authority and responsibility, span of control, and departmentalization. In practice, structure can be defined formally by "what is on paper" in job descriptions and organization charts. But it goes beyond paper. Kast and Rosenzweig (1985) noted,

> Very simply, structure may be considered as the established pattern of relationships among the components or parts of the organization. However, the structure of a social system is not visible in the same way as a biological or mechanical system. It cannot be seen but is inferred from the actual operations and behavior of the organization.
>
> The distinction between structure and process in systems helps in understanding this concept. In the biological system, the structure of the organism may be studied separately from its processes. For example, the study of anatomy is basically the study of the structure of the organism. In contrast, physiology is concerned with the study of the functions of living organisms. In the study of a social system such as an organization, it is difficult to make this clear-cut distinction.
>
> We agree that the structure of the organization cannot be looked at as completely separate from its functions; however, these are two separate phenomena. Taken together, the concepts of structure and process can be viewed as the static and dynamic features of the organization. In some systems, the static aspects (the structure) are the most important.
>
> In the complex organization, structure is set forth initially by the design of the major components or subsystems. It is the internal differentiation and patterning of relationships with some degree of permanency that is referred to as structure. The formal structure is frequently defined in terms of the following:
>
> 1. The pattern of formal relationships and duties the organization chart plus job descriptions or position guides.
> 2. The way in which the various activities or tasks are assigned to different departments and/or people in the organization (differentiation).
> 3. The way in which these separate activities or tasks are coordinated (integration).

4. The power, status, and hierarchical relationships within the organization (authority system).

5. The planned and formalized policies, procedures, and controls that guide the activities and relationships of people in the organization (administrative system). (p. 234)[1]

William Daft, an organizational theory researcher, has defined eight characteristics of structure common to all types of organizations, whether they are corporations, hospitals, units, or departments. Some or all of these—formality, specialization, standardization, hierarchy of authority, centralization, complexity, professionalism, and personnel set—are the subjects of problem-solving attention from internal or external teams of problem solvers and consultants.

For example, the IRS case raised the question of whether citizens were treated in a standardized way as intended by law and regulation. Or, do some citizens receive either better or worse treatment? Part of the answer to this question is found in examining how well IRS staff are distributed across the country in divisions and departments that support equitable organizational performance. Rossotti believes that the IRS could be restructured into four business units: individual taxpayers, big business, tax-exempt entities, and small business. Should authority and power for performance review and case discretion be more centralized or less so? These are questions that closely involve structural design.

We can think of structure as a set of elements—part of the architecture. Structure consists of the following:

- The overall policies, procedures, and controls (administrative system)
- Formal linkage and duties (described in a table of organization and job descriptions)
- How tasks are distributed in units and departments and/or employee responsibility assignments (differentiation)
- Coordination of tasks and duties (integration)
- Complexity
- Power and hierarchy (authority system)
- Personnel configuration and mix

Any or all of these can contribute to organization and management problems in both private and public sector organizations, undercutting effectiveness. Structure is not the whole organization; it is only one of five subsystems in the model we are using. When structural problems are defined as the primary problem, they must be addressed with a structural solution.

One hospital quality management project used structural actions such as changes in job responsibilities and reporting relationships. Leaders began with the question: Who should be in charge of quality? If that person is to be a vice president, then should his or her duties be expanded to include facilitation of and education for total quality improvement? Should that person report directly to the chief executive officer? Each question has, in part, a structural answer.

Multisystem change is the problem-solving path to organizational effectiveness. Structural actions for problem solving rearrange the parts of the organization, for example, to increase productivity and quality of working life by removing structural blockages. Structural problem solving uses job descriptions; task assignments; task coordination; reporting hierarchy; and policies, procedures, and controls as tools of improvement.

Here we review cases in which the *primary* system in need of attention is the structural one. In this chapter, five cases are presented addressing or reporting on compensation structure, a university reorganization, a structuring of community services agency, a proposed high school merger, and the expansion of an airline.

Case 3.1   Sanitation Service: Sanicorp Compensation Case

A public sanitation service faced both recruiting and long-term development questions. The board was unsure about whether compensation levels were appropriate for the current level of operation and whether they were adequate for the significant growth anticipated. Board members planned to initiate an internal study but decided against it. Instead, they used outside consulting assistance. The case questions are as follows:

    I. Diagnosis
        What is the presenting problem?
        What systems are involved?
        Who are the stakeholders?

   II. Approach
        What is your plan for action?
        What personnel are needed?

How much time is required, and who has responsibility for the solution?

III. Impact
    What system changes are expected?
    What happens to the problem?
    What additional data are needed?

Along with the case analysis questions, consider the following:

1. Does this review answer the board's questions about compensation?
2. Will compensation changes address the organizational problems?
3. Are only financial issues the concern here?

Some general case facts are provided in Table 3.1.

In this case, the problem identified by the client was thought to be a weak compensation structure. The consulting team presented a report following 3 months of study. The report is summarized here.

Executive Summary

Problem. The purpose of this study is to examine the compensation levels of management at Sanicorp. The board and the staff believe that it is necessary to determine whether compensation levels are equitable relative to other organizations and whether they provide for appropriate future growth at Sanicorp.

Method. The levels of compensation were compared to those of similar management jobs in city, state, and federal organizations in the area. The comparison was conducted to determine whether the levels of compensation are within the range offered by other employers. Other factors affecting compensation levels also were examined.

Findings and discussion. The compensation levels are not fully competitive with similar positions in the local area. Results of this lack of competitiveness can mean job turnover, thereby costing Sanicorp knowledgeable employees and creating difficulty in recruiting qualified personnel. In addition, the compensation levels might not be appropriate for Sanicorp's future growth and development. In

Table 3.1 Case Facts: Sanitation Company—Sanicorp

---

  1. Business: Trash and refuse disposal
  2. History: Company established in 1949
  3. Location: Small urban community
  4. Products/Services: Removal of refuse from city residents
  5. Territory: Diverse community in city only
  6. Customers/Clients: City residents
  7. Employees: Exact number unknown, estimated at 38
  8. Ownership: City owned
  9. Revenues: Unknown
  10. Reason for consultation: Recruitment and retention problems

---

view of plans for its future, the compensation levels must be brought in line with the increased responsibilities that managers will be asked to assume.

Recommendations. There are three central recommendations:

1. Create a study group composed of the board and staff to address compensation needs that will correlate with Sanicorp's future growth and development.
2. Increase salary levels to parallel those of local competitors.
3. Develop a salary scale that delineates steps and career rates for management positions.

A study process for a board and staff task force is included.

THE ISSUES AND PROBLEMS OF SANICORP

Sanicorp's salary problem can be defined in terms of four components.

1. Currently, there is an increase in *competition* for well-qualified personnel in management and support positions in both the public and private sectors. Each agency and business presents its compensation package and then proceeds to look for the best possible candidate in terms of education, personality, and job goals. The more attractive the compensation package is, the better the qualifications of the prospective employees are likely to be. Better qualified workers, in turn, will improve the performance, growth, and success of the agency.

The first question is, does compensation enable Sanicorp to be competitive in creating a pool of talented applicants from which to draw?

2. Compensation and job conditions are two major factors in *job turnover.* Job turnover is costly. Time is lost in searching for replacements and in training the replacements. Along with training, new employees require a period of time in which to match the efficiency and knowledge of the former employees.

For these reasons, it is important to minimize the amount of turnover in any organization. Salary levels provide the initial incentive for employees, but it is the total compensation package that reduces turnover. Other relevant aspects of the compensation package are incentives, non-cash benefits, performance appraisal, and workforce development.

Along with basic salary, there is a long list of attractive factors in a compensation package including the following:

- Unemployment compensation
- Incentive payment
- Life insurance
- Hospitalization and surgical insurance
- Incentive plans
- Overtime pay
- Shift differential pay
- Pension programs/retirement
- Agency vehicle
- Clothing/equipment allowance
- Workers' compensation
- Medical and dental services
- Credit unions
- Paid leave or time off for the following:
  Vacations
  Holidays
  Sick leave
  Death in family

The second question is, do the basic salary and additional compensation benefits enable Sanicorp to minimize job turnover?

3. *Equity* in compensation levels that match job skills is a major factor in *employee satisfaction.* For example, a computer programmer must be paid a

salary comparable to other computer programmers in other organizations. A secretary who takes dictation and is asked to make minor administrative decisions should not be at the same salary level or pay scale as a file clerk. Unfortunately, salary increases of people rising within the organization often are based on their previous positions rather than on their new responsibilities. It is important to have career path development for each position defined and equitable salary levels established for each step. If a file clerk aspires to a secretarial position, then he or she should be able to determine exactly what skills need to be acquired and what compensation will be received for acquiring them. Equity within the organization is easier to achieve than equity with other employers. The following is a list of some of the factors that make external equity so difficult:

- Problems of job content
- Established internal wage relationships
- Differences in stability of employment
- Corporate policies
- Working conditions
- Variations in fringe benefits
- Financial conditions of the organization

The third question is, do current salary levels have reasonable internal and external equity?

4. Examining and defining key skills for each job is not just an exercise in *job description*. The purpose is to match personnel with positions and appropriate salaries. In most organizations, job descriptions outline the major responsibilities for each position. A closer look at skills required to carry out responsibilities will help ensure appropriateness in the comparison of compensation levels. In addition to specific skills such as computer programming, other job factors affect compensation. Job factors include the following:

- Level of responsibility
- Amount of supervision
- Number of employees supervised
- Decision-making responsibility
- Risk level of those decisions for the organization

Thus, the final question is, are the salaries appropriate for the nature of the jobs as defined by the job descriptions?

Method. The approach to the problem outlined previously involved analysis of existing data, official forms and records of Sanicorp, and collection of additional information regarding local salary levels. There were four basic steps:

1. Review materials related to the purpose and functions of the company including policy book, job descriptions, and salary scales.
2. Review data secured by staff from similar companies.
3. Collect additional salary information about comparable positions in state and federal government and in nonprofit organizations.
4. Integrate these data sets to provide a basis for board-staff analysis and decision making.

The results of the data collection are presented next. The findings (not presented in detail here) suggest that compensation was inadequate and that Sanicorp should further address the problem with an internal study group.

The consulting team suggested a five-phase process to assist implementation of the compensation structure redesign. The following steps are offered as a starting point, with "adaptation" to the study process expected.

Phase 1: Start-up. The first phase requires about 1 month and involves organizing the salary structure redesign process.

1. Identify the general task for all participants—the development of a revised salary structure.
2. Select a study group of 6 to 8 board members.
3. As a group, initiate discussion to identify specific problems associated with implementation of salary changes (e.g., changes in positions, services, equity, location, and/or facilities).
4. Develop consensus on the objectives such as the following:
   - To define the existing salary situation (using this report)
   - To identify problems and changes likely to occur in the areas during and after salary change
   - To develop a model of a desired salary system
   - To compare the existing elements of the salary structure to the agency's design
   - To create a plan for managing the salary structure change

5. Develop a work plan with procedures and schedule with executive director and staff support.

Phase 2: Current organization compensation. In Phase 2, comprehensive analysis of the current salary system is undertaken to lay the groundwork for change needs (using this report as a base).

6. Identify the areas of the organization and the jobs that will be the focus of the study and change.
7. Review the information that is needed to analyze these areas (this study plus other data).
8. Identify what information is available and review methods for collecting additional required data such as union and city requirements and responses.
9. Using the data, develop a current consensus on the salary situation.

Phase 3: Other organization analysis and comparison. Phase 3 is designed to identify other organizations that have created models of a desired salary system.

10. Identify other public and private organizations similar in character, and secure data on these organizations' salary systems (again using this report as a base).
11. Identify and analyze problems that might emerge from effects of salary change.
12. Compare the current organizational situation to that of other situations to estimate possible and desirable changes resulting from salary change implementation.

Phase 4: Plan development. In Phase 4, a plan for the full development and implementation of the new salary system is created using the study group's work as a base.

13. Identify needs for salary change and the order in which changes should occur.
14. Create a comprehensive plan for salary system implementation including assistance required and strategies for dealing with noninvolvement and resistance such as the following:
    *   Action steps to be taken
    *   The rationale for activities and positions
    *   Person(s) or group(s) responsible

- Dates by which activities are to happen
- Establishment of an action schedule and method for proceeding

Phase 5: Study summary and continuation considerations. Phase 5 concludes the study and evaluates progress of salary change implementation.

15. Review the process and results of the implementation planning to determine (a) whether the objectives were met and (b) if so, whether they were met in the manner intended.

Case 3.2   University Reorganization

One university provost recognized the changing environment including competition for students, rising costs, regulations, and the need to consider structural changes during the coming decade. An internal task force of faculty was used for consulting and problem-solving advice. This report was developed by the faculty chairman and his committee colleagues.

Consider the following case questions:

I. Diagnosis
   What is the presenting problem?
   What systems are involved?
   Who are the stakeholders?

II. Approach
   What is your plan for action?
   What personnel are needed?
   How much time is required, and who has responsibility for the solution?

III. Impact
   What system changes are expected?
   What happens to the problem?
   What additional data are needed?

Some general case facts are provided in Table 3.2.

Table 3.2   Western State University

---

1. Business: Postsecondary education
2. History: Founded in 1960, 4-year campus center
3. Location: Warren, Kansas; 8 miles from the state capital
4. Products/Services: Opportunity to earn a baccalaureate degree in 1 of 20 academic majors; also offers 14 master's degree programs and 4 doctoral degree programs
5. Territory: Majority of students in-state, other students from other western states
6. Customers/Clients: Enrollment 6,500 students (undergraduates and graduates)
7. Employees): 205 faculty members
8. Ownership: State
9. Revenues: Tuition and fees more than $8,500 per year
10. Reason for consultation: Consider needs for structural change in new decade

---

Report of the Ad Hoc Committee on Reorganization

A team of "internal problem solvers" (7 faculty) produced the following report on options for restructuring this campus of a large state university. This report is an edited version of the one developed by the 7-member faculty group.

HISTORY AND STUDY PURPOSES

Historically, the Western State University academic model has been that of a comprehensive university. The university strives for excellence in both professional studies and liberal arts, albeit with a more selective set of disciplines. The mission of Western is fourfold: to be innovative, to be interdisciplinary, to be high quality, and to meet the needs of the region. The college is in a position, as a major urban campus, to meet the academic and service requirements of the local community while seeking national recognition for the quality of its faculty.

Since its founding, the Western campus has emphasized both professional and humanistic programs and has used a variety of administrative organizations to do so. Initially, options and programs provided structure. By the mid-1970s, divisions were employed. By February 1979, the campus had grown into 11 programs, an organization generally felt to be cumbersome and inefficient. Later in 1979, Western consolidated into its present configuration of 5 instructional divisions plus a library division. Enrollment in Fall of 1980 was 3,500 undergraduates and 1,700 graduate students. In 1990, college enrollment was about 5,000. Current enrollment is more than 8,500 and growing.

Western was designed from its inception to be "a programmatic response to a fluid situation" and has mirrored the university-at-large in its organizational development and changes. For example, the liberal arts program emerged in 1970 as part of a plan to form core colleges to consolidate administratively dispersed departments. The consolidation was intended to better provide the desired level of education and research plus the resources required. This new organization reflected the university's commitment to support the increasingly popular arts and sciences.

Strategic planning over the past 5 years has led to significant administrative and academic reorganization. The majority of these initiatives to date have focused on technology, the sciences, and professional areas. The university is now directing attention to liberal arts and sciences, and to recruiting a new dean of education, as it prepares to reassess the need for resources in these areas. For strategic planning purposes, the university also should conduct an academic administrative review of the humanities, behavioral science, and education programs to follow up on major initiatives accomplished in the business and public affairs divisions.

Enrollments are strong in the programs to be reviewed; indeed, admissions activity in psychology, teaching, and multimedia disciplines reflects a growth in national interest. For example, elementary education enrollees increased from about 110 to 250 in the span of a few years, and total humanities enrollment grew 37.7% in 1 year. Acute shortages during the 1990s for teachers at all levels underscore the need to review and evaluate education programs and their connections to liberal arts and behavioral science. Western must be positioned to take advantage both of current concerns that teacher preparation includes more discipline-based courses and of the national resurgence of interest in elementary and secondary education. Finally, unless a university achieves excellence in its core disciplines, it cannot achieve greatness in its professional programs—or in any program—given that all students require strong general studies foundation steeped in intellectual rigor and creative vitality.

In approaching its task, the review committee at Western is charged to consider the following overarching question: What is the optimal administrative configuration for liberal arts, education, and related professional programs given the mission of Western and the projected needs of its constituencies during the period from 1995 to 2005?

Areas of consideration include the following:

- The best climate and structure to encourage interdisciplinary courses and activity as well as to promote diversity and internationalization within the curriculum
- The advantages/disadvantages of an administrative consolidation of liberal arts, behavioral science, and education programs in developing graduate curricula, with particular attention to thesis supervision
- Pros and cons of administratively functioning as departments rather than divisions, with particular attention to promotion- and tenure-related issues
- The administrative configuration most supportive of research productivity including collaborative efforts
- Issues related to building a coherent viable summer school educational program
- The impact of strengthened administrative interrelationships on future program development

INTRODUCTION

Western administrators offered a proposal for reorganization of several academic units in Spring 1995. Recognizing significant external changes in local and national environments—costs, competition, regulatory mandates, and so on—the administration believed that it was necessary to review the organization of the university to ensure a continuing best fit with future environmental demands, particularly with regard to liberal arts and education.

National interest in the liberal arts, and in addressing the performance of the nation's secondary education system, has become a leading concern. Western needed to investigate the implications of these national concerns and how they could affect the structure of the college.

A joint faculty-administration committee was formed to collect relevant information on these issues and to present recommendations for reorganizing, if appropriate.

The committee was charged to address the following: What is the optimal administrative configuration for liberal arts, education, and related professional programs given the mission of Western and the projected needs of its constituencies during the period from 1995 to 2005? The charge also suggested that the committee address the relationship between administrative structure and (a) climate for interdisciplinary work, diversity, and international activities; (b) advantages of consolidation; (c) departmental structures relative to tenure and promotion; (d) research productivity, particularly collaboration; (e) summer school; and (f) future program development.

PROCESS

The committee decided to take a longer term, planning-oriented approach to proposed reorganization in response to this task. An open process, soliciting much input from faculty and administrators, was thought to be an appropriate procedure. The committee met with all chairs, with the provost/dean, and with the primary faculty groups originally involved—behavioral science, education, and humanities—and held two open forums to enable all faculty to comment. In addition, faculty were invited to submit written comments and questions.

The following meetings were held during Spring and Fall 1995:

- Individual meetings with each director
- Individual meetings with the provost and associate provost
- Group meetings with faculty and chairs from education, humanities, behavioral science, and public policy
- An open meeting to generate input from faculty
- A second open meeting to review findings and opinions

The questions presented to individual administrators and faculty were as follows:

1. What external threats (outside of the university) are relevant to the reorganization question?
2. What external opportunities (outside of the university) are relevant to the reorganization question?
3. What internal strengths are relevant to the question?
4. What internal weaknesses are relevant to the question?
5. How does the possibility of reorganization fit with the university's mission and vision of the future?

The critical issues identified by faculty and administrators are discussed next.

Vision/Mission issues. Faculty and administrators identified vision and mission issues related to the structure of the campus:

- Lack of vision for the campus as a whole
- Degree of fit of campus vision with the university's vision of achieving "top 10" public research university status

- Applied/Professional versus liberal/general education
- Nontraditional structure

Any recommendations for structural change were expected to address these vision-mission issues.

External and internal threats, opportunities, and needs. Reorganization usually is undertaken in response to compelling external and/or internal pressures and needs. The committee asked faculty and administrators to identify the critical *external* threats and opportunities and the *internal* strengths and needs that create a compelling case for reorganization.

The responses from faculty and administrators and committee discussions are presented in what follows. The comments are pooled as a result of committee discussion and do not necessarily represent the views of specific faculty or administrators.

The key external issues, which reorganization options would need to address, include the following:

- Competition (both with other institutions and with other companies)
- Image and visibility
- Resource availability
- Accreditation (both state and national)

Reorganization also is driven by the needs of the internal organization. From the individual and group meetings, faculty and administrators focused on the following internal issues:

- Tenure/Promotion (both control and manageability)
- Loss of courses, teaching load, program development, and course areas
- Unit loyalty
- Collegiality
- Autonomy
- Interdisciplinary nontraditional programs

The committee used these perceived external threats and opportunities and internal needs both as criteria to evaluate the necessity of restructuring and as criteria by which to judge the effectiveness of the current and proposed configurations.

FINDINGS

From the meetings and subsequent committee discussion, the committee developed the following key findings.

1. Regarding vision and mission, there was almost uniform agreement about the lack of a clear vision codeveloped and shared by the faculty and academic units, and there was much vagueness on the vision and mission of the campus.

2. Regarding image and visibility, groups consolidated for nonacademic reasons present a vague and misleading image to anyone not intimately involved in the structure. Programs such as education, mathematical science, and behavioral science need more visibility and identity than they have at present.

3. There appears to be too much focus on short-term budget issues and not enough attention paid to long-term planning.

4. There is ongoing addition of new programs, course offerings, and responsibilities without selective elimination of existing ones, resulting in a progressive fragmentation of faculty time and lack of depth in some areas.

5. Insufficient funding and inadequate resources prevail in virtually all areas—for faculty, equipment, staff support, routine supplies, and so on. Restructuring will not improve the situation unless it provides a unique opportunity to address these problems.

6. Regarding external resource availability, support is not thought to be significantly affected by most structural alternatives. Regarding internal resource availability, potential allocation change raises much concern among smaller groups that expect to be dominated by larger groups. Strong leadership was seen as a critical need.

7. Program development is now hampered in smaller units when they are part of larger groups with different goals.

8. Concerns about tenure and promotion were greatest among faculty who expected to be joined in academic units with which they have little in common. It was considered that the situation would require significant effort to make it workable/acceptable and would add perhaps yet another administrative layer in the process.

9. Organizational change is likely to be successful only if faculty need and support the new structure. They do not support further consolidation at this time.

CONFIGURATION OPTIONS

As a result of the data presented in the findings, the committee created the structural configuration options presented in Table 3.3. The committee analyzed each of the configurations. The following summarizes the discussion of each option.

OPTION ANALYSIS

In summary, the options described in what follows are similar in nature. The differences tend to focus on whether units are independent or linked to other units and the choice of unit names. Many of the arguments apply to each of the configurations.

I.   Five units—existing structure

Option I, the existing structure, was thought to need change for several reasons:

1. Competitive pressures are pushing public affairs and engineering toward becoming schools.
2. Existing programs in larger divisions dilute image and hamper visibility.
3. Budgetary and programmatic conflicts exist.
4. Long-term development is hampered.
5. Some felt a need for a balanced structure with a new direction.

The strongest rationale for retention of the existing structure was that the university did not yet have clarification on mission and vision. Because structure is the mechanism through which an organization carries out its mission, lack of a clear mission/vision precludes the choice of a structure to carry it out.

II.   Seven units (two schools)

Option II proposes seven freestanding academic units: schools of business administration and engineering technology; divisions of humanities and public affairs; and math, computer science, and science.

Table 3.3 Configuration Options Identified

Nonparallel structures

Option I: Five units (existing organization)
    School
        Business administration
    Divisions
        Behavioral science and education
        Science and engineering technology (with math, computer science, and science)
        Humanities
        Public affairs

Option II: Seven units
    Schools
        Business administration
        Engineering
    Divisions/Departments
        Education
        Behavioral science
        Math, computer science, and science
        Humanities
        Public affairs

Option III: Seven units
    Schools
        Business administration
        Engineering
        Education
    Divisions/Departments
        Behavioral science
        Math, computer science, and science
        Humanities
        Public affairs

Option IV: Seven units
    Schools
        Business administration
        Engineering
        Public affairs
    Divisions/Departments
        Behavioral science and economics
        Math, computer science, and science
        Humanities
        Education

(Continued)

Table 3.3 Continued

Parallel structures

Option V: Three units
  Business administration
  Engineering
  Liberal and professional studies
    Behavioral science
    Economics
    Education
    Math, computer science, and science
    Public Affairs

Option VI: Five units
  Business administration
  Education
  Engineering
  Liberal and professional studies
    Behavioral science
    Economics
    Humanities
  Math, computer science, and science
    Public affairs

Option VII: Four units
  Business administration
  Engineering
  Liberal and professional studies
    Behavioral science
    Economics
    Humanities
    Math, computer science, and science
  Public affairs

Option VIII: Four units
  Business administration
  Education
  Engineering
  Liberal arts
    Behavioral science
    Economics
    Humanities
    Math, computer science, and science
    Public affairs

NOTE: The ad hoc committee on reorganization developed this preliminary set of options through discussions with faculty and administrators.

Included among the review comments was that organizational effectiveness usually is defined by management theorists as the extent to which an organization makes the best use of scarce resources in achieving its goals by means that are acceptable to its members and the extent to which achieving these goals provides some socially useful function in larger society. It is not clear that Option II is substantially different from the existing structure and, therefore, would make better use of resources. It might even require additional administrators, or a different role for chairpersons, to make it work.

Perhaps most important, the faculty involved in the programs that would be appended elsewhere on the organization chart have not suggested that this structure would be more satisfying to them than the existing one.

Option II's major advantages appear to be increased visibility and autonomy for the programs involved. But it is not so much better than the existing structure that it should be adopted in the absence of strong faculty sentiment in favor of becoming a school, division, or department.

III. Seven units (three schools)

Option III was configured using three schools (business administration, engineering technology, and education) and four divisions/departments (social and behavioral sciences; math, computer, and natural sciences; humanities; and public affairs).

Included among the review comments was that, with regard to *external factors* (e.g., competition, image/visibility, resource/funding, accreditation), the committee believed that, given its proximity to state government and pressures from other campuses, the public affairs division should be moving quickly toward school status. In Option III, public affairs would be prohibited from taking full advantage of many significant opportunities by not being designated a school.

The committee also believed that, in terms of external factors, giving education the status of school should be a desirable medium-term goal. Because education has not been given the personnel and resources necessary to capitalize on the outstanding climate for growth, a move to a school would be premature at this time. But education was seen as being sufficiently different from all other units in nature and, therefore, in need of its own identity. With proper funding, vision, and leadership, education could very well achieve school status. This move would, in turn, enhance image and visibility, allow the unit to compete more effectively with other teaching/training institutions, increase outside funding potential, and strengthen accreditation prospects.

With regard to internal factors (e.g., tenure/promotion, course offerings, unit loyalty, collegiality, autonomy, interdisciplinary programs), the committee acknowledged advantages of Option III for more specialized homogeneous review of dossiers by departments, greater autonomy, and some increase in unit loyalty. This diversification into seven units, however, also was perceived as militating against greater collegiality as well as the creation and maintenance of interdisciplinary nontraditional programs.

Finally, in terms of vision and mission, the committee reiterated that public affairs needs to move swiftly toward school status and that education should be a separate unit provided with sufficient personnel and financial resources to encourage significant growth. Option III's proposal to move engineering technology in the direction of school status also was viewed as highly desirable and appropriate, especially with the advent of competition from a nearby facility.

IV. Seven units (three schools)

Option IV calls for a structure with three schools (business, engineering, and public affairs) and four divisions/departments (behavioral science, science, humanities, and education).

Included among the review comments was that the schools concept would strengthen competitive position, image, fund-raising, and accreditation for each of those units, although the accreditation effect would be weak. Department titles would not affect the other units.

The schools would create *stronger* internal management potential with greater autonomy and loyalty. There would not be a loss of courses, but there might be barriers to interdisciplinary program development (with more formality and autonomy in schools).

This structure, like the others, cannot be fitted to a vision that is unclear. Development through schools is consistent with the university's direction. There still remains a set of disconnected units.

V.   Three units

Option V calls for three units in the structure: business, engineering, and liberal and professional studies. The problems with Option V center on the third unit (liberal and professional studies); the committee seemed to have no difficulty with the first two, which in fact already exist as separate entities.

"Liberal and professional studies" as a designation for an academic unit seems to raise more questions than it might resolve. It could potentially include virtually any fields—even business administration and engineering technology—so the label provides no clear understanding of what the unit might contain to anyone outside of, and to few within, the institution. Because the programs are now (and likely will continue to be) selective rather than comprehensive, it seems desirable not to foster misunderstandings about the offerings.

The inclusion of public affairs in this unit is particularly problematic in that, of all the present divisions, this one is most clearly related to the university's location near the state capital. It also is the first to offer an autonomous doctoral program, and it seems destined for further growth. Inclusion in a larger unit, such as is suggested by Option V, could inhibit public affairs faculty in their attainment of wider public and academic visibility.

Economics faculty seem to belong (at least in this college) in the business administration school, where their courses are required in several curricula, rather than in a larger unit, where they would offer only electives. There might be accreditation issues inherent in this model.

VI. Four Units

The academic structure set forth in Option VI consists of four units. In addition to separate administrative units in business administration minus economics and in engineering and math science, other units would be established for education and for liberal and professional studies.

Analysis of this option resulted in its rejection. First, it was acknowledged that there was an inherent vagueness in the label "liberal and professional studies." Most of the academic programs at Western—including education, engineering, and business—could be categorized as professional studies. Furthermore, it was suggested that public affairs, which is included in the liberal and professional studies unit, would lose its strong identity and would adversely affect its vitality in competing with similar academic programs that are locating in the region.

VII. Four units

Option VII would link humanities with some other elements traditionally found in a liberal arts school including the social sciences, economics, math, and science.

The reviewers believed that, with benevolent leadership, such an option could work. But there are two significant concerns. The first is the degree to which this reorganization would improve programs with respect to such concerns as raised in the original charge; this is questionable. The second is that the education program currently appears to be weakened by its association with behavioral science. There is little evidence to suggest that it would fare any better under this particular reorganization.

In short, there is little that is compelling about this model, although it presents few significant problems so long as there is effective leadership at the program level (e.g., education, behavioral science) as well as at the overarching (school) level.

VIII. Five units

The primary reasons for rejecting Option VIII are the same as those for rejecting the other parallel options. These basically relate to the difficulties that arise when various disciplines are united for nonacademic reasons such as aiming for a parallel organizational structure.

The problems associated with this type of structuring have the greatest impact on smaller units that are joined with larger units with which they have little in common. These issues include the following:

- Visibility and image (this type of unit presents a vague and misleading image to anyone not intimately involved in the structure; the structure distorts the image of the subunits involved and, in some cases, completely obscures their existence)
- Tenure and promotion (whether faculty are being judged, even at the division level, by true peers)
- Program development (very difficult when the goals of the smaller unit are different from, or even in conflict with, the goals of the larger unit)
- Resource availability (although resources are short overall, their distribution is not seen to be equitable)

RECOMMENDATIONS

The committee agreed on two major recommendations:

1. Create an interactive process that will enable a shared vision and mission for Western to emerge. This vision and mission should provide the basis for future structure.

2. As an interim action, create the following separate programs to increase development opportunities: behavioral science, education, and math and computer science.

In response to the main question in the charge to the committee—restructuring for liberal arts—the committee rejected the concept of an easy reorganization into a liberal arts unit. There are no easy linkages, but more important, combining existing units would not take the university very close to a full liberal arts school. The university would be short by many faculties in fields ranging from science to languages to arts, and it would be short by millions of dollars. A massive infusion of new funds was seen as unlikely. In fact, the committee was continually informed about resource shortages. So, why should the university invest limited resources in filling out liberal arts in light of more clearly articulated needs in programs such as education and engineering technology?

A fully developed liberal arts program would require both economics and political science. Because these programs are intimate elements of existing divisions, pulling them out would be damaging given the development status of business and public affairs. Without economics and political science, the "liberal arts concept" falls substantially short.

In addition, and perhaps most important, the committee believed that reorganization into a major liberal arts thrust is a significant strategic issue. This must be discussed widely in terms of the vision and mission for Western. The concept of liberal arts was not rejected but was deferred to a future point in vision and mission planning.

Lack of clarity on vision and mission was a key finding. A major reorganization can be successful only within the context of an academic/intellectual vision of the future. Because structure is the mechanism through which vision/mission is implemented, structure decisions must follow rather than lead.

The committee suggested an interim structure that makes limited changes in the short run. The structure would include one school (business administration), three potential schools (engineering, public affairs, and education), and four divisions/departments (behavior science, humanities, math and computer science, and library). The two units moving toward schools—engineering and public affairs—would need to follow the extensive planning and development path followed by business administration. Following this path would be possible over the next several years and would help address competitive pressure quickly.

The divisions/departments would be able to generate greater autonomy and development. For example, education also could progress toward school status. The sciences and humanities could pursue both independent and linked development, as those faculties deem appropriate. Movement toward a liberal arts structure could occur if faculties believe that this is the best route for the future.

The committee believed that these changes could be made very quickly. The changes appeared to be acceptable to faculty, based on individual and open meeting comments, and this interim structure would not interfere with further developments when vision and mission questions are settled. In short, there were some immediate gains, with flexibility for future change.

Why did the committee suggest an interim structure while the university clarifies vision/mission questions? The committee was able to define several reasons:

1. The proposed separation deals with units that already are functionally separate.
2. The units' current combination impeded functioning (e.g., goal conflicts, planning uncertainties).
3. Program development will be hampered.
4. Tenure and promotion for some programs are not currently handled by peers.
5. Visibility and image of the affected programs will be enhanced.
6. Competitive position will be enhanced (e.g., education).
7. Budgetary clarity and a more equitable distribution of resources within the programs will be possible.
8. Interdisciplinary studies will not be affected and may be enhanced with further separation.
9. Research productivity may be enhanced by organizational clarification.
10. Summer school programs will not be affected.

These were persuasive points for the committee. Committee members were able to agree on the two main recommendations and believed them to be consistent with both faculty and program needs developed during the fact-gathering process.

Case 3.3   Matrix Design:
Church and Community Services

Faced with increasing change in its service system and with new opportunities for growth, one community service director requested an organizational structure review. This review, conducted by an outside consultant with an internal team, was designed to assist the unit in reorganizing in a way that would better reflect its future directions and needs. During the review, the need for pilot-testing and expanded information system support was identified and addressed. Thus, the case has two reports, one on the matrix design and one on its implementation.

The case questions are in three sets:

I Diagnosis
   What is the presenting problem?
   What systems are involved?
   Who are the stakeholders?

II. Approach
   What is your plan for action?
   What personnel are needed?
   How much time is required, and who has responsibility for the solution?

III. Impact
   What system changes are expected?
   What happens to the problem?
   What additional data are needed?

Along with the case analysis questions, consider the following:

1. Does a matrix structure make sense in social and technical terms?
2. What about the containing system—the whole organization?
3. Who would you use to design and implement this system?
4. What barriers would you expect to find?

Some general case facts are provided in Table 3.4.

Table 3.4 Case Facts: Church and Community Services Organization

1. Business: Children and youth services (religious and general)
2. History: Approximately 25 years old
3. Location: South-central Ohio
4. Products/Services: Provide nursing, social, and adoption services; home care; counseling; and education
5. Territory: Six county regions
6. Customers/Clients: Families, individuals, and congregations
7. Employees: 400
8. Ownership: Privately owned and operated, nonprofit
9. Revenues: $5 million to $8 million or more
10. Reason for consultation: Redesign for greater efficiency and effectiveness

Case Report: Matrix Design for Community Services Department

The purpose of this report is to identify a possible solution to one faith-based community service department's organization problem. Using a matrix organization design, the department addressed issues of how to manage current performance and how to plan for continued growth. The experience is similar to that faced by many nonprofit organizations such as county and local human service agencies including family services, addictions, counseling, mental health, criminal justice, and health service providers.

STRUCTURAL PROBLEM DIAGNOSIS

Recognition of this organization design problem has occurred elsewhere in Ohio. For example, a series of evaluations of 14 public health agencies revealed structural confusion. Interdisciplinary teams used a management consulting approach to achieve both evaluation and organizational development objectives. The similarity of problems and the general parallel nature of the agencies suggested a widespread concern about organization design issues across areas of specialty (e.g., addiction, mental health, criminal justice). Differentiation and integration issues were frequent topics of organization design debate.

For many agencies, the problem is not one of achieving organizational differentiation of programs and departments. Differentiation frequently is mandated by virtue of federal and state categorical program interests and following funds. How to integrate the diversity into a coherent system of services is the dominant question. Integration is difficult to achieve when many program types exist under a county agency umbrella (e.g., mental health/mental retardation with its hospital, residential, and day care programs) or when many diverse departments exist within one large nonprofit agency (e.g., an alcoholism treatment organization with its outpatient, detoxification, residential, and information/education departments). Efficiency and control often are elusive at best.

Public agency organization problems resulting from the diverse programs and funding seem to cluster around three points:

- The need to make maximal use of special technical knowledge
- The need to efficiently use organizationwide resources across programs
- The need to maintain control and coordination of the diversity

Discussion of these needs surfaces questions such as the following:

- How do you set goals and objectives for the differentiated organization—by program, by function, or by both?
- How do you develop and present information regarding organizational progress?
- How do you maximize current output and improve capabilities?

One way for a community services agency to answer the questions is to develop a matrix organization design—a structural solution.

Community Services Department Restructuring: Report 1

A description of the organization's purposes and activities provides the background. Church Social Services (CSS) is one of four faith-based social service agencies within the Central Region Affiliated Churches of America. The West Region has the responsibility of supplying social services for three districts—Wayne, North Wood, and Midville—comprising the geographical area of two counties.

CSS is an independent nonprofit corporation with its own board of directors. The CSS board consists of 32 members; of these, 14 are clergy, 9 are members-at-large nominated by the board, and the other 9 represent the three districts (3 members for each district) and are nominated by the districts. CSS is the community and social service agent for 70 congregations in the region. The agency provides both institutional services (nursing care) and community services (counseling, day care, volunteer coordination, and criminal justice). CSS is organized for the following purposes:

- To respond or assist in responding to needs identified by the congregations
- To identify emerging human service problems that will affect congregations, churches, regional institutions, and agencies
- To assist in the management and evaluation of community and social service programs for this region
- To develop lines of communication among congregations, churches, and institutional and community services agencies

Currently, the Community Services Department and the CSS organization are involved in a broad range of activities structured as a consortium of institutional and community services. The agency was incorporated in 1936 and has developed a variety of nursing, medical, and social programs since its founding.

Initial development of the agency focused on institutional services. Resources were committed to the development of the Thomas Nursing Home (98 beds) opened in 1960, the Springdale Nursing Home (105 beds) replacing an older facility in 1976, the Townhouse Retirement Apartments (150 units) opened in 1980, and the continuing development of cottage sites (120) during the 1990s. The majority of these resources are located on a 60-acre site in Ohio.

In addition, community and social programs, such as foster homes for the elderly and congregational counseling services, are available. Persons are accepted as participants and residents regardless of race, national origin, religious creed, ancestry, or political affiliation. For example, men and women 65 years of age or older, or persons under age 65 whose physical conditions call for resident nursing care, are eligible for the institutions.

The regional organization's constituents are the congregations-at-large, the various church staff, agency employees, and the communities in two counties. The service site has grown from a limited budget of $500,000 to a $25 million complex with an $8.2 million annual program budget.

The Community Services Department initiated development of a range of social programs including a Latin American Civic Association for Spanish Americans, a Retired Senior Volunteer Program, a minority group community input program, community seminars, a public committee for the humanities program, a prison counseling service, and a cooperative child care project.

To date, the organization has been involved in serving congregations and communities with a range of medical, nursing, and social services. It is concerned with serving special interests, such as the regional need for youth emergency shelter services, that have not been sufficiently addressed by programming. With a pattern of continued growth, the Community Services Department identified a need to address the organization design problem so as to meet both current and future needs. Four concerns were key: design of the structure, development and redesign of a management information system, unit performance, and future development.

Design of the structure. Several problems initiated the design action. The basic organizational choice was whether to organize by program or by function. Development in this department occurred over a period of years by program. The diversity in programs operated by the Community Services Department ensured differentiation but presented difficulties of integration. Internal and external personnel understood the individual programs but had difficulty in understanding the purpose, activities, and development of the department as a whole, that is, how it was integrated and focused on a common goal.

Second, the various staffs in different programs were working in professional and functional isolation. For example, the therapists in the offender program had no contact with other therapists for support, professional sharing, and development. Also, no career path by function existed. To advance, personnel had to leave the program and the agency.

In addition, there were concerns over the issues of client services versus marketing/program development, reporting priorities in terms of program versus functional allegiance, and the need to formalize the structure to prepare for the continued and future growth of the department. These issues were addressed through the creation of a matrix organization design.

The structure was outlined by a matrix with both program and functional areas represented in Table 3.5. Prior to matrix design, the power balance was solidly program oriented. Authority was vested in program personnel. The creation of the matrix design resulted in the following:

- An integrated view of the organization through program-function matching
- A matched view of the purpose, activities, and development direction (two ways: by program area and by function)
- An ability to develop dual planning strategies

Table 3.5 Service Area, by Function: Existing

Administration, Social Services, or Research and Evaluation

Function/Program	Management	Finance	Clerical	Public Relations	Program Development	Counseling	Casework	Psychological	Volunteer	Transportation	Research and Evaluation
Aging											
Retired volunteers											
Volunteers in the community											
Child welfare											
Day care											
Criminal justice											
Offender services											
Children and youths											
Shelter											
Drugs and alcohol											
Offender services											
Education											
Life enrichment programs											
Human development											
Life enrichment programs											

- The beginning of career ladders within functional areas along with interpersonal sharing and support in those functional areas
- Recognition of dual responsibilities in both program and functional areas
- An outline of the department to aid planning and development
- Creation of interdependence among specialized program units
- A resource allocation scheme

The matrix design provided a structure for ongoing operations as well as planning for future development. It provided a mechanism for organizing current operations and a framework on which to place future categorical program development opportunities offered by local, state, and county governments.

Development and redesign of a management information system. The expansion of the agency increased the need for reliable information. Reporting requirements increased with each new program. Combining church region with local, state, and federal information needs necessitated an updated and revised information system. The Community Services Department is required to make periodic reports concerning service activities throughout the region. The agency experienced difficulties because of inadequacies in the reporting system. Some difficulties led to unreliable data and invalid reporting. To ensure an efficient and effective information system, the agency initiated a study of its information requirements.

The staff examined three aspects of the agency information system:

- The lack of information needs assessment in the various service areas
- The absence of common definitions of activities among state and county officials and agency staff
- The use of reporting documents that do not satisfy current needs for information

The study group considered the need to address policy questions of whether to develop a large-scale or limited system, development of a data dictionary, and new or revised reporting forms.

In general, the process requires an assessment of the information needs of each of the programs, identification of key terms and their definitions, and a revision of the data-gathering forms. The critical individuals and agencies were as follows:

- Program staff
- State and county agency personnel
- Regional agency staff

To make the data meaningful for these people, critical terms were defined. The definitions were based on current and intended use by agency staff and by staffs of the federal and state bodies.

Information system design began with meetings with the staff and state agencies. Staff were asked for assessments of the current reporting system through meetings held at program and agency locations. The meetings were in-house sessions with directed discussion centering on the following five questions:

1. What are your information needs?
2. Who are the other significant users of the system?
3. What does each of these users need?
4. What problems do you see in meeting these needs?
5. From your experience, what problems do service personnel have with reporting requirements?

In addition, those attending were encouraged to provide any other comments that might be pertinent to the review.

Data gathered during the review led to four products: (a) a flowchart of the information process in the agency, (b) revised reporting forms, (c) a revised dictionary defining the key items on the forms, and (d) a statement of findings and recommendations for future system development. For example, the flowchart became a guide for identifying and ordering service process activities that need to be reported. The programs handle cases in very different ways, but the system flow model reflects a major portion of that activity.

Unit performance. How will the new matrix structure assist in increasing and improving capability? First, the organizational structure developed as a matrix leads to an information system design that focuses on both program and functional output. To monitor output, the organization must have a continuing supply of data on performance. Developing data on functional lines represents both a new source of information for management and a new view of existing data—a comparative one. Comparisons enhance short- and long-term performance because they allow program areas to be monitored in relation to each other and their respective markets (e.g., aging services vs. criminal justice vs. welfare). Although they are different services, a basic level of comparison is critical to an assessment of organizational performance. Matching program and functional activity with market needs allows for the reassignment of resources according to demand.

Second, staff meetings should be the primary means of formal communication for the organization as a whole. The meetings should involve all programs and both program managers and staff. With the matrix design, regular meetings were instituted among functional personnel. For example, counselors from all programs meet for joint consultation with an outside psychological consultant. Their performance as a functional group is enhanced both individually and collectively. They also function as a task force for development by meeting periodically to discuss how the counseling capability of the department could be expanded.

Third, the matrix enhanced communication in two ways: (a) by encouraging staff with similar functions in different programs to communicate and (b) by setting up a regular organizational structure to support and legitimize it. Output and capability improvement are assumed to derive from increased communication.

Fourth, the department developed relations across programs. The use of cross-program teams serves the purpose of improving capability by linking members with parallel skills. Their pooled resources strengthen the overall organizational capability in that skill area. Without the matrix design, there was no mechanism for developing relations across programs.

Future development. The organization of the department as a matrix outlined both the general direction and the scope of future development. Prior to the matrix, development thinking was one-dimensional; that is, growth was envisioned through new programs. With the matrix, functional growth was added, resulting in a dual development direction.

Development requires planning to define the scope, time frames, and specific objectives. The agency could now construct both project and functional development plans. To address the integration problem cited earlier, cross-project functional teams can be formed to construct short-, medium-, and long-range plans. Planning promotes internal relations among staff and develops consensus around development objectives.

Organizational change resulted from discussions of the new design. A list of program-oriented development topics was created. At first, they were viewed as autonomous units to be designed and operated independently. As a result of the matrix design, however, the new programs added their contributions to functional departments as well. A new program added to the matrix is a certified mental health clinic, defined by the functional departments (e.g., counseling, casework, consultation).

SUMMARY

This first report has described how one community service department responded to an organization design problem. The creation of a matrix form of organizational structure produces change in four areas: (a) basic design of the department, (b) development of a management information system, (c) improved performance and monitoring, and (d) new views of development possibilities and direction.

Implementation of New Matrix Structure: Report 2

INTRODUCTION

The Community Services Department reviewed its organizational design. The department decided to develop a matrix form of organization in response to the following problems:

- The need to integrate very different programs funded by a variety of public and private agencies
- The need to develop a departmentwide goals and objectives system
- The need to use departmentwide resources across programs
- The need to develop a department-management information system
- The need to maintain and direct department growth
- The need to maintain control and coordination of program diversity

These needs coincided with the presence of three conditions necessary for matrix thinking: (a) pressure for both program and functional focus, (b) pressure to process great amounts of information, and (c) pressure to share limited technical resources.

For example, whereas a variety of programs exist within the department (e.g., prison counseling, volunteer program), there also is a mental health counseling service that is a functional specialty. Second, the diversity in programs and the constantly changing environment (external influences) of each program (e.g., government funding situations) demand a strong information system. Third, the technical resources available to each program (e.g., counseling) are limited and should be shared for both service capacity and economic reasons.

Discussions of these problems and needs have taken place over the past year. The matrix design was chosen as a structural solution. This follow-up report represents a plan for developing a matrix design within the Community Services Department. Five steps are involved:

1. Establish the design and work plan.
2. Inform and educate staff.
3. Revise the plan and design.
4. Initiate pilot matrix behavior.
5. Evaluate pilots.

STEP 1: ESTABLISH THE DESIGN AND WORK PLAN

The first step was a departmentwide recognition of the basic matrix design. This section on design does not repeat the earlier report on restructuring, but it does focus on critical points that determine staff support.

Matrix picture: Community services. The matrix for the Community Services Department was developed and is presented in Table 3.5, with implied development direction presented in Table 3.6. Several questions are relevant. Are all programs and functional activities represented? Do staff support the two-dimensional thinking? Are the service development directions, as represented by the department, appropriate? Once basic design is understood, key changes in organizational structure must be discussed.

Power balance. A key aspect of the design is to develop a balance of power between the program and the functional sides of the department. Because this department has operated with program dominance, the program directors will feel the most direct change. As functional heads are appointed, program directors will need to begin a negotiation process that did not previously exist. New functional heads will have the problem of defining their jobs and working relations in a structure that is almost as new as they are. One of the first points for dispute likely will be authority.

Dual authority. Coincident with and supportive of the power balance is the dual authority structure. Under the existing system, authority is vested in the Community Services Department director and the program managers. Authority flows in pyramid fashion—from director to program managers to their respective staff. Now there will be a dual track in that functional department heads (e.g., counseling) also will be vested with authority.

Table 3.6 Service Area, by Function: Potential

Administration, Social Services, or Research and Evaluation

Function/Program	Management	Finance	Clerical	Public Relations	Program Development	Counseling	Casework	Psychological	Volunteer	Transportation	Research and Evaluation
Aging											
Child welfare											
Children and youths											
Commerce											
Community affairs											
Drugs and alcohol											
Education											
Energy											
Health											
Human development											
Humanities											
Justice											
Labor											
Mental health											
Mental retardation											
Transportation											

Community Services Department Director

Program Manager   Functional Heads

With dual authority systems, questions of direction and task and time scheduling will arise. For example, do counselors become involved in organizational planning, and if so, then for what period of time and at whose expense—the program or the functional department? Resolution of such questions will require confrontation and management of the dual authority issue.

Team concept. The matrix design is based on a team concept of management. The department has developed the management team over the past year. To date, only program managers are represented; once functional head appointments are made, however, they also should be included in team meetings. The first appointment might be a director of counseling.

The management team should operate the matrix. Jointly, the team members discuss and establish expectations, objectives, leadership, decision making, responsibilities, and problem resolution methods. Two examples of team activities during the past year are the goals/objectives sessions at the retreat and the decision-making review. Both activities helped develop the team, which would now approach those activities with a matrix orientation.

Task forces. To work on the integration problem and to begin the team building, task forces were appointed. The task forces worked on problems that have both program and functional impacts. Two task forces illustrate the process. The first was a counseling policy task force composed of the volunteer program director, the program development director, and the two counselors. The task was to develop goals, objectives, and policies that would serve both social services and the general counseling function. The group met every 2 weeks to review materials and make recommendations. After a period of approximately 10 weeks, the group submitted a report that was accepted by the Community Services Department director.

A second task force is just beginning. The information system task force is composed of the director, the program development director, a day care caseworker, the volunteer program director, two counselors, and the program development consultant. The group will review the information forms and reports now used and will make recommendations for new forms or for redesign of existing ones.

The task forces produced substantive solutions to the tasks (i.e., counseling policy and information system design). They provided an opportunity for team building through interaction of different staff members in work groups. In addition, they exposed work group members to general organizational problems—in effect, a management training experience.

Negotiation. Once the matrix is fully accepted, a constant process of negotiation is initiated. Because nearly all of the organization's activities will now have impacts on program *and* function, both dimensions of the organization will need to be represented. For example, the expansion of the emergency shelter program to include an abused children component would affect the design of the shelter (a program-level change). And because existing counselors are to be used, it also would affect the existing counseling function (e.g., its long-term plans for growth, its immediate plans for scheduling and job assignments). Program and function representatives will need to negotiate a series of "best fits" that satisfy both (using trade-offs to arrive at the best fits).

Staff meetings. The character of staff meetings will reflect the new two-dimensional thinking. Other people will be present to represent functional concerns. A natural inclination toward negotiation will come with the representation. Full staff meetings should be negotiation meetings only when substantial members of the group have an investment in the outcome. Two-party discussions can be held separately. Staff meetings will be used to constantly monitor the two-dimensional performance of existing efforts and growth in new efforts.

Time and scheduling. Implementation of the matrix will require 12 to 18 months given that it has already taken several months to consider development.

Costs and benefits. The costs and benefits of the program are identified as follows:

1. The matrix becomes a training and development opportunity for members of the organization, particularly the managers.
2. All staff involved in the matrix gain an understanding of all functions in the organization; traditionally, this is accomplished only through job transfer.

3. Managers must spend more time with the organization.

4. There are training costs associated with the new behaviors that managers must learn.

5. Group skills are sharpened.

6. Skills in planning, analysis of business problems, and decision making are developed.

7. For many staff members, personal development options in the organization are significantly broadened.

8. More individuals are given the opportunity to develop from technical or functional specialists into general managers. The organization increases the pool of people from which to choose its leaders.

9. The organization must create an increasing number of opportunities for the increasing number of generalists.

10. There are needs for adjustments in career paths, job evaluation systems, and human resource flows.

Although this listing is not all-inclusive, several of the most critical costs and benefits are highlighted. Outstanding among the costs are the management time, training time, and learning time needed to adapt to matrix ways. One of the chief benefits is the developmental opportunity for junior managers. Their understanding of the complex organization is increased, their horizons as to opportunities and possibilities are broadened, and their experience in many of the primary management activities of general managers (e.g., negotiations, human relations, experience with complex planning) is increased.

STEP 2: INFORM AND EDUCATE STAFF

This second step addresses the need to inform and educate staff about their role in the new matrix design through four steps:

1. Circulate background materials to introduce the new structure.

2. Hold initial discussion sessions with the primary managers, reviewing both the reading papers and the design paper developed to link matrix thinking with this organization (i.e., the matrix structure in Figures 3.5 and 3.6).

3. Distribute a brief summary of the changes required of the managers and the programs to adopt the matrix design.

4. Hold a series of staff meetings and one-to-one sessions in which the purposes and process of the matrix design are explained to other key staff.

The background materials for circulation include Galbraith's (1973) *Designing Complex Organizations* and an internally written adaptation for CSS titled *Matrix Organization Design for a Community Services Department.* The Galbraith publication presents an overview of the matrix organization design including the phases and steps required to combine functional and project forms. The internally written paper outlines the use of the matrix design in the CSS organization including four topics: (a) goals and objectives, (b) information systems, (c) maximization of output and capabilities, and (d) development direction.

The discussion should include any issues involved in both designing and implementing the matrix plan considered important by staff.

The process of going through and identifying common changes sets up, in essence, a matrix planning process. All managers in the organization have responsibility for spotting potential problems and for making changes needed to fully achieve the matrix design. In this organization, the matrix is developing in a division within the total organization. The final information/education step is bringing other staff and managers not involved so far into the process.

STEP 3: REVISE THE PLAN AND DESIGN

The informational and educational discussions will generate a series of comments on the original matrix plan and the design to be developed. This third phase is to incorporate comments and make any changes. If enough members have serious misgivings about the proposed design, then consideration of scrapping it or of developing an alternative certainly is relevant.

The CSS organization had been operating with a program design. The inclusion of a new functional area requires functional appointments. Subsequent problems may emerge. For example, some staff members might want salary increases for their new department heads or "chairmanship" identities.

A third part of the revision/design phase is consideration of the information required. At this point, the managers should begin thinking about the information system that will emerge with the fully developed matrix. Definitions of the information system elements will continue the learning process about matrix and lay the groundwork to keep all involved parties informed about progress. The information system is added at this point as information is necessary to evaluate progress on the implementation.

Because the Community Services Department has operated on a program basis, the information design will use that as a base. For example, although each of the programs records counseling session numbers, the matrix system requires an integration of the counseling session numbers across program categories. Counseling sessions must be defined in a standardized way, thereby enabling a "functional" count of counseling sessions across all programs.

STEP 4: INITIATE PILOT MATRIX BEHAVIOR

At this point, some understanding of the matrix concept has been achieved. This step begins the actual use of the matrix in planning and operations. Because this is a pilot phase of the matrix, two examples will illustrate.

The matrix requires several planning changes. First, it requires that the primary service activities of the department now be considered in terms of both program activities and functional activities (Tables 3.5 and 3.6). Second, the matrix requires that the budgets that previously were considered solely in terms of program centers now be considered also in terms of functional activities. Third, personnel decisions need to be made regarding, for example, who is involved, to what extent, with what time commitment.

Operations also are used for initiating pilot matrix behavior by including both program and functional representatives on task forces. Using matrix members to work on these task forces provides them with the opportunity to see matrix thinking firsthand. Over the time period when the matrix was being considered, a counselors task force was employed to construct a plan for the counseling department for the year 2000. A review of the purposes, processes, and outcome of this group illustrates how the matrix might work with various task force groups.

STEP 5: EVALUATE THE PILOT MATRIX BEHAVIOR

The purpose of the pilot matrix behavior project is to provide an opportunity for testing matrix ideas prior to full implementation. The evaluation ensures that the implementation plan is on track and helps leaders decide whether a partial or full matrix is more appropriate. Two areas of the project must be evaluated: (a) the progress of the first matrix efforts and (b) the results of the matrix behavior.

The matrix design is reviewed by feedback meetings held as a part of the regular management team sessions. These group discussions concern the members' understanding of how the matrix is progressing and whether or not they believe that the concepts and techniques are useful. These discussions include topics such as the number of meetings involved in the matrix, the sharing level that is developing between programs, and the overall increase or decrease in the workload as a result of the matrix. At some point, a questionnaire survey of staff within the organization may be used for diagnosis and feedback.

Evaluation also targets results of the new design. This outcome evaluation should be undertaken approximately 1 year after the start-up of the implementation plan. At that time, leaders may ask the following questions: Do we have increased commitment to the organization among staff? Do we have increased motivation to perform? Is there better general manager expertise? Do staff believe that there is enhanced integration of the organization and a greater understanding of the organization as a whole? Do we have an increased ability to design and develop our future, both in program terms and in functional terms?

The evaluation should be used as a mechanism for identifying strengths and needs in the plan. For example, if few negotiated linkages have occurred around new functional areas, then two programs could be deliberately asked to focus on that activity. If the volunteer program and the family emergency shelter find no apparent way of linking, then the program managers and the program development director could initiate a series of discussions on how counseling can be used for the benefit of families and for organizational growth in terms of the counseling function.

Once the evaluation is completed, matrix members need to review the findings and recommendations. If the findings are positive, then a carefully controlled expansion of the matrix to all parts of the organization is developed.

Case 3.4   A High School Merger in a Suburban School System

In this case, a public school system considers a new structure—the merger of two high schools. The following material is an edited version of a newsletter report of the merger proposal sent to parents, students, and citizens. As you read the presentation, consider the pros and cons of this structural solution—merging two high schools in your area. Students can develop the arguments for and against by using local high school data and Web sites. Two teams can develop competing structural designs and debate the rationale for and against the merger.

A Unified High School: Two-Building Campus Is Planned

- The district's newest high school building, not the oldest, will be renovated.
- The entire high school complex will be upgraded to the best learning environment in Ohio.

Under the new configuration, the 9th- and 10th-grade students will occupy one building on the current East High School campus, and the 11th- and 12th-grade students will be housed in the other building. What is now West High School will become the third junior high school. This new school, Oate Junior High, and R. W. Rose Junior High will feed into the new unified high school in the Suburban School System. The entire high school complex will be upgraded to the best learning environment in Ohio by Fall 2004.

No longer will we lag behind in computer or communications technology, science labs, or libraries. In this plan, we are spending money to improve the newest of our high schools, not the oldest. If we had chosen to renovate West High School, then we would have spent millions of dollars to update a 40-year-old building. The new high school campus renovates our newest high school and completely modernizes and transforms the building next door.

The current two-school model divides our total high school student body into two smaller schools for the 9th through 12th grades. In the unified high school, those students also will occupy two buildings. By the year 2005, the enrollment is projected to increase from 2,900 to 3,600 students. *This means that we must prepare to house 1,800 students in each high school building. That number is the same under both configurations.*

The difference in the unified high school is that the students will be divided by grade level. The students will be spending most of their time with peers in their own age group. They will not, however, be limited to their buildings. They will be able to travel back and forth for classes and activities. This model permits horizontal grouping by age and maturity level as well as vertical grouping by interest area and ability in academics or extracurricular activities. This means that underclassmen's participation with upperclassmen will occur in a controlled setting (e.g., orchestra, drama, accelerated classes, varsity sports). Upperclassmen will be able to develop and demonstrate leadership skills and positively influence underclassmen during organized activities such as clubs and campuswide student council, sports, and extracurricular activities.

LOOKING TO THE FUTURE

The construction option that the board chose was to enlarge and renovate the East High/junior high complex to unify the two high schools, housing 1,800 students in each building.

Another option considered was to retain the current system, but to enlarge and renovate West High School, a 40-year-old building with little surrounding land available for expansion.

Fiscal responsibility implies doing the right thing with the taxpayers' money. Both options cost essentially the same, but the first option (unifying the two high schools) involves a much lower cost by far over the long term. This plan allows for the future growth of our community. It solves the current over-crowding problem and looks to the future as well. It eliminates the need to re-draw school boundaries.

By making West High School into a junior high, we are preparing for the expanding influx of students in that age bracket over the next 10 years. Projections tell us that there currently is a "bubble" of students moving through the system. When this bubble of students reaches junior high age, it will not be necessary to build a fourth junior high or to expand existing junior high schools to accommodate them.

It is more difficult to project the number of elementary school-age children. Based on proposed building projects and continuing expansion within the district, however, it is inevitable that the elementary population will grow. Rather than spend millions of taxpayers' dollars on further expansion of elementary school buildings, 6th-graders can be moved to the junior high school, which will have sufficient space to comfortably accommodate them.

This plan looks to the future—for our children as well as our tax dollars.

CONSTRUCTION PHASE: A MINIMAL DISRUPTION

The first stage of the construction project will be to add classrooms to Oate Junior High School and R. W. Rosa Junior High School. There would be minimal disruption of the students in both buildings. When the buildings are expanded to their full capacities, students from West High School and Oate Junior High School will switch places between the two buildings.

West High School was built for 1,300 students and presently houses 1,600. This is expected to exceed 1,700 students for the 2000-2001 school year. Five classroom trailers have been purchased to accommodate the 100 additional students for the next year. These trailers would be located in the already too small parking lot. If the decision had been made to renovate West High rather than to unify both schools, then a minimum of 16 additional trailers would consume the rest of the parking area.

This would have had a definite impact on the current freshmen and sophomore students during their junior and senior years. Rain or shine, warm or cold, one third of their classes would be held in trailers on the parking lot. There would be an additional 5 to 10 contractor trailers on the site for the 200 workers involved in the renovations. *The board believed that this would not have been conducive to a quality education, especially for students who would not reap the benefits of a new facility.*

FUTURE GROWTH: ROOM TO GROW AT ALL LEVELS

The current system does not allow for adequate growth. Fully developed neighborhoods surround West High School. It might not have been feasible to add sufficient classrooms to meet the needs of the increased student population of the next decade, much less of the anticipated growth afterward. The building was not designed for the addition of a second story. The parking lot already does not accommodate all the drivers' cars.

The new unified system allows for growth. The possibility of acquiring land adjacent to the East High School campus complex allows for future expansion of the high school.

The combination of the two high schools and the use of the West High School building as a junior high *allows for the anticipated growth of the middle school population.* Not only would our three junior high buildings be able to absorb predicted population increases, but it also would make possible the transition to a true middle school model. Many of our educators believe that a 6th-through 8th-grade model is a more effective learning environment.

We could provide the best educational environment for our children during the early secondary years and enjoy the benefit of easing the overcrowding problem that our elementary schools eventually will experience. *This also will save future tax dollars by limiting the cost of additional elementary building projects.* This would not be possible with the current two-school configuration.

FEEDER PATTERNS TO BECOME MORE STABLE

A feeder pattern, determined by geographical boundaries, establishes where students will attend school within the district based on their locale. As communities expand and change, feeder patterns also must change. There are flaws in even the best feeder patterns. For example, in areas of our district, children starting kindergarten may be separated from their classmates twice. The first separation occurs when they graduate to different junior high schools. They are separated a second time when the junior high feeds two different high schools. *These separations will not occur after the high school unification.*

Students no longer will leave junior high school classmates behind; they will simply add new acquaintances in the unified senior high school. New classmates and friends join each other gradually in an age-appropriate way.

In the future Suburban School System, students will begin kindergarten with children from their neighborhood. That same group will join a larger group of children from the same geographical area for junior high school. Finally, students from the junior high school will join with students throughout the district in the 9th grade, always advancing to the next level with their classmates.

This transition is possible only through unification of the high schools and the extra capacity that will be available at the junior high school level.

Historically, even small changes in school boundaries have been very contentious. *The single high school model permits primary and secondary school feeder patterns to remain fairly constant over time and provides future school boards with more flexibility.*

Stability in feeder patterns enables children to maintain their friendships while gradually expanding their peer groups. *The progressive controlled exposure to larger groups of children from increasingly diverse backgrounds teaches adaptability and encourages cooperation.* The resultant social skills are valued in today's world and will help our graduates when they enter college or the workforce.

We all have been reminded that "bigger is not always better." This is an important issue for us to address. The Suburban School System is a large school district, but it is not the largest. A significant number of schools across the country have grown to the size of our district's projected high school student body. We are faced with the reality that our school district has two high schools that eventually must house 1,800 students each. The plan that we develop today not only must meet the immediate needs of our high school students but also should be a plan with enough flexibility to meet the future demands of a rapidly growing district. The one-campus concept provides that flexibility.

Many districts manage growing populations by dividing the student bodies into smaller groups. The "school within a school" concept, with theme-oriented curricula, also is gaining acclaim as school sizes grow. It preserves the ability for teachers to offer students individual attention, even within a large school setting. The unified high school option presents many excellent opportunities to develop concentrated courses, such as business and technology, that can be offered to all high school students.

The board will work diligently to ensure that all students are afforded the personal individual attention that they need and deserve. The teacher-to-student and administrator-to-teacher ratios will not change. Children will not "slip through the cracks" or "get lost in the crowd."

COLLEGE OPPORTUNITIES: ADMISSIONS AND SCHOLARSHIPS

More than 75% of our graduates go on to some form of higher education. Community members have expressed concern that a larger graduating class will mean that class rank will be lower and, therefore, that fewer students will be accepted into college or receive scholarships. That will not happen. College admission officials across the country are well accustomed to high schools of all sizes. They choose students based on SAT scores, grade point averages, and class percentages, not numeric ranks. It is completely different to be the 25th in a class of 100 than to be 25th in a class of 1,000. *If we double the graduating class size, then we double the number of students in the top 10% at the same time.* Colleges also give consideration to which classes students took to get that ranking. More advanced and diverse classes all contribute to making students more competitive for admissions or scholarships. In the Suburban School System's unified high school, with its expanded curriculum, students will be able to take more of those courses than ever before. Large competitive colleges see applicants with every possible combination of academics and extracurricular activities. With the future West High School's expanded extracurricular program, activities not available now will set our students apart from schools that cannot offer as much.

CURRICULUM IMPROVEMENT

The primary duty of our school system is to provide the best possible education for our students. In many ways, that is a result of the quality of the curriculum and its delivery. In considering unification, the board reviewed the curriculum offerings of similar-sized school districts across Ohio. Our review confirmed that districts our size with one high school offer significantly more academic courses than do districts with two high schools. It is our belief that a combined school improves the curriculum in three ways.

Increased breadth of curriculum. A combined school will have more efficiency of instruction, which can be converted into more course offerings. For example, right now there are at least 10 courses taught at the two high schools with an average class size of 20 students at West High and 7 students at East High. By joining the two schools, many of those classes can be combined, resulting in a more balanced average class size. This will free up several rooms and teachers to offer additional courses. This can be done without spending more money or increasing the teachers' workload or the average student class size beyond our designated limit. We can maintain our teacher-to-pupil ratio and still increase our course offerings. Entirely new classes in core areas such as math and science, or a new curriculum in an area such as business or computer science, can be offered.

Increased depth of curriculum. With children grouped by grade level, it is possible to offer more levels of each course. Freshman English, for example, could be deepened from three to five levels by adding courses of instruction for the advanced, middle, and struggling students. The goal is to challenge children to achieve their maximal potentials.

Increased curriculum specialization. If classes are offered more efficiently, then teachers can devote time to courses that are of particular interest to them and their students. This will improve the quality of instruction as well as the teachers' job satisfaction and morale. Specialized teachers will be available to all students at a single high school.

For freshmen and sophomores, the future participants in the new design, this means the following:

- A student who is progressing ahead of his or her peers will be able to take upper level courses at the building for 11th- and 12th-graders.
- A student who needs additional assistance will have a class specifically designed to push the student to his or her maximal potential.
- A student in step with his or her peers will have a larger selection of courses with *the same class size and teacher contact.*

For juniors and seniors, this means the following:

- A student who desires to take courses in any subject can have any of the teachers in the entire district who specialize in that subject.
- A student who wants to spend more of his or her elective time in a particular area of study will have more courses from which to choose.

- A student who chooses to broaden his or her education with a variety of electives will have more courses from which to choose.

In summary, combining the schools allows us to deliver a broader and deeper curriculum to every one of our high school students. *This is accomplished without changing the number of teachers, teacher workload, current class size, or student-to-teacher ratio.*

OPPORTUNITIES: EXTRACURRICULAR ACTIVITIES

There will be many opportunities for new extracurricular activities in a unified high school. *One advantage of consolidation is that any savings from combining some of the extracurricular activities will be used to introduce new programs that have not been offered before.*

A valid concern expressed by a number of parents and students is the potential decrease in extracurricular opportunities in a unified school. To some extent, this concern is real. There will be only one of each junior varsity and varsity team. The number of players who start on a team, assuming that no one plays two positions now, will be reduced. However, the teams do have the potential to be larger and stronger than they would have been in either school alone.

Every other extracurricular activity could be doubled in number or expanded into more specialized activities. A larger marching band would be impressive. Musicals and dramas could be performed in each building. Expanded clubs and groups would enrich and encourage the talents of more students.

A unified high school will help promote community identity. It will be "our kids" who produced the play or "our team" that won the championship. We all can share in the pride that was limited to half of the community in the past. Now the entire community can say, "Our high school is the best!"

- The unified high school will occupy two buildings, dividing students by grade level.
- Each building can house 1,800 students.
- The teacher-pupil ratio will stay the same.
- Course offerings will be increased.
- Educational opportunities will be increased.
- Extracurricular opportunities will be increased.

- Doubling the average class size also will double the number of students in top 10%.
- There is room for growth and expansion.
- Students can experience a transition to a true middle school.
- There will be significant future cost savings.

PARITY: THE BEST OF BOTH SCHOOLS

Having two separate high schools creates a never-ending battle for equality. No matter how hard we try, the two schools never would be equal. They have different facilities, different faculties, and different students. As a result, the same opportunities are not really available to all high school students. One school might have a better art program, whereas the other has a better drama department. One might have a better math department, whereas the other has a better English department.

In the new unified high school, we are combining the strengths of both schools to give the best we have to all the students.

Students in the class of 2003 will be entering a modern West High School during the fall of their senior year. They will be reunited with all of their grade school and junior high school friends. They will take an expanded curriculum from the best teachers in the district. They will have a school filled with new possibilities. They all will be a part of an exciting new West High School.

Case 3.5   Southwest Airlines Expands

In this short case, an airline considers the implications of dramatically expanding its route structure.

The structure of Southwest Airlines's market has been rather tightly defined since the airline's inception. The company began operating in Texas and has gradually expanded into different markets, primarily in the East. Both the size of its market and the potential growth were defined by the arbitrary but highly profitable structure. But the need to continue to grow and to compete with ever-larger airlines suggested a review of the airline's mission and market targets. How the company structured its "reach" would, in large part, determine its future prospects.

No one inside the company (or outside the company, for that matter) has suggested publicly that Southwest should expand into South America. But we could imagine a team charged with just that question. Should Southwest continue a merger with, or an acquisition of, a South American airline?

This somewhat challenging question is, at first glance, a structure and mission issue. This team would need to ask, "Are we a domestic airline or an international airline?" The company's history makes the answer quite simple—a domestic airline. But the environment is changing rapidly. The fragmentation of carriers, both within countries and across country boundaries, is fading into a consolidation of major international airlines—if not with outright mergers, then at least with strategic alliances. Thus, the structure question surfaces fundamental issues of "who we are" and "who we would like to be." The need to address the changing structure of the international and domestic market requires a team that can think both broadly and specifically. How would a South American acquisition change the company?

Using the Southwest Web site (www.southwest.com) as a starting point, pick a South American partner that would expand and strengthen Southwest's future.

Note

1. From F. E. Kast & J. E. Rosenzweig, *Organization and Management: A Systems and Contingency Approach.* Copyright © 1985 by The McGraw-Hill Companies. Reprinted with permission.

4

Solving Psychosocial System Problems

What we've got here is a failure to communicate.
—from *Cool Hand Luke* (1967 film)

We have discussed the nature of product/technology and structural systems and reviewed several cases illustrating each type of organization and management problem. The "psychology" of the organization also is fertile ground for problem development.

The Nature of the Psychosocial System

In our case of the Internal Revenue Service (IRS), problems of information system inadequacy, quotas for performance, and a poor divisional structure have been noted. But what do we do about the rude and abrasive IRS agents? Along with product/technology and structure, public and private organizations have a psychological dimension. This system comprises the "people" dynamics—individual characteristics and interpersonal relations—that becomes the "psychological climate." Sociotechnical thinking requires considering not just technical and product design elements (e.g., manufacturing production) or the effectiveness of medical therapies but also the social aspects of the production and delivery system. This subsystem is defined as follows:

> Every organization has a psychosocial subsystem that is composed of individuals and groups in interaction. It consists of individual behavior and motivation, status and role relationships, group dynamics, and influence systems. It is also affected by sentiments, values, attitudes, expectations, and aspirations of the people in the organization. (Kast & Rosenzweig, 1985, p. 114)[1]

Organization and management problems can develop as a result of the following:

- Personality and attitudes
- Perception
- Learning and reinforcement
- Motivation
- Communication
- Group dynamics
- Conflict
- Power and authority

The fourth area for organization and management problem solving is the psychosocial subsystem of the organization—people's individual attitudes and behaviors as well as their interpersonal relations.

Problem-solving actions in this subsystem rest on several crucial assumptions that already are well known in organization and management circles:

- Organizations are social systems.
- People solve problems.
- Organizations change when people change.

The actions needed to problem-solve in this subsystem assume that the organization is a human social system.

For example, a trade association of architectural professionals received a consulting group's report heavily critical of its communication activities. A first thought was to fire the chief executive officer (CEO) and the public relations vice president. The executive staff and board began to discuss the impact of this "firing" response to the "communication problem," but there was much uncertainty about action. Discussions with an outside consultant indicated that the communication problem in a professional society necessitates a wide-ranging review of the core of association work—communication with members, with the public, and with a variety of stakeholders. Using the interpersonal conflict as an entrée, this systems model helped the organization identify its communication strengths and needs. Eventually addressing structure, management, and missions, system thinking pushed the communication problem beyond psychological climate to a broader strategic context and toward organizationwide responses. The problem was surfaced by a generalized "psychological concern" about poor communication, but as in several of the cases in this chapter, it illustrates the interactive effect among systems.

Any organization, or any unit of an organization, that sets out to improve must address the psychosocial subsystem. Motivation, status and role relationships, group dynamics, and influence are factors in this subsystem, as are the values, attitudes, and expectations of employees and managers. Sometimes, psychosocial problems are individual in nature—one employee, one problem—that can be addressed mostly with attention to that employee. For example, not all IRS agents are abrasive. The employees with abrasive attitudes can be counseled individually. Or, the problem can be team- or organizationwide. The culture of the IRS rewards and reinforces a tough abrasive approach to citizens. The overlap with the managerial subsystem is evident in planning, goal setting, and leadership. The psychosocial subsystem emphasizes the psychological aspects of individual and group behavior, the "psychological climate" within which employees and customers act. Methods for solving these problems are different from those employed for problems of technology and structure. This chapter has cases of communication, morale, conflict, management style, and service by design.

Case 4.1   Fedstate Medical Center Morale Study

A hospital in the government health system, Fedstate Medical Center, was concerned about the morale of employees at all levels, from physicians to nurse's aides and administrators. The Fedstate hospital CEO was told that conducting a survey of employees was one effective way of securing employee input and providing data for problem diagnosis. By naming an internal team, the CEO showed that he believed that his managers had both the skills and the objectivity needed to address morale problems. And the hospital would incur no outside costs. The following material is taken from the survey and feedback process used in the public hospital and is presented through three memoranda.

The case questions are in three sets:

> I. Diagnosis
> What is the presenting problem?
> What systems are involved?
> Who are the stakeholders?

> II. Approach
> What is your plan for action?
> What personnel are needed?
> How much time is required, and who has responsibility for the solution?

> III. Impact
> What systems changes are expected?
> What happens to the problem?
> What additional data are needed?

Consider these questions and focus on the following additional issues:

> 1. Was the survey a useful approach?
> 2. Are the questions (content) appropriate?
> 3. What type of feedback process would you use?
> 4. Who should collect and analyze the data?

Some general case facts are provided in Table 4.1.

The following memorandum from the medical center director describes the survey process and offers a summary of responses.

Table 4.1 Case Facts: Fedstate Medical Center

1. Business: Health care, long term and acute
2. History: Opened during 1930s by the government
3. Location: Eastern United States
4. Products/Services: Health care; total facility includes 100 beds in nursing home-type unit and provides general medical and surgical services; 1,000 operating beds
5. Territory: Mid-Atlantic region
6. Customers/Clients: Poorer and generally long-term patients
7. Employees: 1,275 personnel
8. Ownership: Government owned and operated
9. Revenues: Unknown
10. Reason for consultation: Improve staff and employee relations

---

MEMORANDUM 1

FROM: Fedstate Medical Center Director

TO: All Employees

RE: Employee Morale Study

1. The long-awaited results of the employee morale study have been compiled and reviewed. There were several obstacles experienced in compiling the data. Compilation was especially complicated because the project was designed to consolidate results of individual questions not only hospital-wide but also by service, by age, by proximity to patient care, and by department level. Additional time also was necessary due to data processing problems. After the results were compiled, they were evaluated and plans were developed to take action on the results.

2. Participation in the project was excellent, with nearly 500 of the 1,275 employees responding.
   a. In general, the majority of employees participating responded positively on the following issues:
      (1) Staff courtesy to each other
      (2) Staff competency
      (3) Quality of patient care
      (4) Physical attractiveness of the medical center

(Continued)

b. Issues showing employee concern were as follows:
(1) Staffing and workload levels
(2) Quality of supervision
(3) Logistics (e.g., equipment, supplies, space)
(4) Communication
(5) Employee recognition
(6) Continuing education

3. We recognize that the data generated by the survey are dated (18 months old). It also must be recognized that there have been significant developments since the survey was conducted that may have affected several of the issues in question. For example, recent ward consolidations have enhanced staffing levels of various wards. The continuing education activity within the medical center has been significantly enhanced in terms of both volume and quality of in-service programs. Efforts to improve communication have been ongoing (e.g., expansion of the weekly news report, quarterly newsletter, efforts by management to make services more aware of communication breakdowns). And there were several developmental programs conducted to improve supervisory skills. However, even considering these developments, it is realistic to assume that many of the concerns reflected in the survey results remain current.

Using the preceding introduction to the survey process and the summary of results, evaluate the appropriateness and quality of the following survey and the survey process. If you were using a survey for this purpose in your organization, is this the instrument and process you would use?

<u>SURVEY</u>

Please list your service _____

Do Not Sign Your Name

MORALE STUDY

Instructions. The best rating of each statement below is your personal opinion. Use one number to rate each statement; fill in the left space with your answer. Apply the statements to your own situation or, if not applicable, to this hospital in general. Answer with the following: 4 = *strongly agree,* 3 = *agree,* 2 = *disagree,* 1 = *strongly disagree.*

___ 1. Despite the pace of daily routine, staff here are courteous and considerate to one another.

___ 2. This hospital can boast that the staff are competent in their field of work and training.

___ 3. The administrators of the hospital do not notice, support, or provide recognition to staff efforts.

___ 4. Staff at this hospital find professional opportunities available.

___ 5. Staff who I know are pleased with the quality of the direct supervision received from their supervisors.

___ 6. This hospital has enough staff in all areas to do the work necessary for quality performance.

___ 7. Despite careful work and dedicated efforts, staff are rarely, if ever, recognized for the excellent jobs done.

___ 8. Scheduling and distribution of staff seem to be well thought out and fair.

___ 9. Staff are expected to do more than is humanly possible, sometimes even the work of two people (by one person).

___ 10. Although there may be other concerns, hospital equipment is of good quality, is in good condition, and, like supplies, is readily available.

___ 11. Pay levels for staff are well up to standards.

___ 12. No matter what type of work, it seems that the level of work is evenly distributed among services.

___ 13. Staff are not provided sufficient money, time off, or other opportunities to pursue continuing education.

___ 14. Check one as it applies to your job at this hospital:

    ___ (1) I treat patients (e.g., physicians, nurses, social workers).
    ___ (2) I often interact with patients as part of my job (e.g., pharmacy workers, clerks, lab people).
    ___ (3) I seldom interact with patients as part of my job (e.g., typists, maintenance workers).
    ___ (4) I rarely, if ever, interact with patients as part of my job (e.g., personnel clerks, fiscal officers, computer specialists).

MEMORANDUM 2

FROM: Fedstate Medical Center Director

TO: All Employees

RE: Feedback Sessions

1. Findings of the morale survey indicated a need for better internal communication. In response to your comments, we will be initiating regular feedback sessions. These sessions—open to all levels of management and staff—will provide a forum where we can share ideas, voice opinions, ask questions, and solicit feedback.

2. The first feedback session will be held Tuesday, December 1, from 2:15 to 3:45 p.m. in the large conference room. Refreshments will be served, and all employees are encouraged to participate in this informative session.

3. Naturally, I recognize that not everyone will be able to attend given that our work of providing quality compassionate care must continue. However, I am asking that every department chief and/or unit supervisor determine the maximum number of people who can be spared from their areas. Then let the frontline staff decide among themselves who would like to attend.

4. To ensure that every employee has an opportunity to share his or her thoughts (even if he or she cannot physically be present at the feedback session), I have attached a brief questionnaire. Please complete and return it to the director of employee relations so that we can incorporate your feedback.

5. Thank you for your interest and input. Together, we can build an even better future.

FEEDBACK SESSION QUESTIONNAIRE

Please be sure to think in terms of organizationwide impacts (as opposed to specific persons or incidents) as you give your input.

List two (2) items you like best about the hospital and/or two (2) areas where you think we do well:

_____, _____, _____, _____.

List two (2) areas where you think the hospital could use improvement and/or two (2) items that you do not like about this facility:

_____, _____, _____, _____.

Name (optional): _____

Service (optional): _____

Thank you for your interest and input. Please return this questionnaire to the director of employee relations.

MEMORANDUM 3

FROM: Fedstate Medical Center Director

TO: All Employees

RE: Comments on Session

More than 80 employees in person, and more than 60 employees through written feedback, shared their feelings on major strengths and weaknesses at the feedback session. They are as follows:

(Continued)

STRENGTHS	WEAKNESSES
Good patient care	Insufficient staffing (8)
Friendly/Conscientious staff	Supervisors lack managerial/leadership/ communication skills (7)
Management communication improving	Lack of communication (7)
Employee services (e.g., credit union, library)	Low morale/Negative attitudes (6)
Good benefits	Lack of team concept (5)
Educational seminars	Insufficient employee praise and recognition (4)
Job security	Unfair pay scale (4)
Buildings/Grounds clean, well kept	Ineffective recruitment and retention (4)
Volunteer program	Decisions made without "grassroots" input (2)
Community outreach improving	No patient accountability (2)
Potential for growth and development	Insufficient equipment (2)
Management stronger and more capable	Little room for advancement (1)
Training	Unequal allocation of resources (1)
	Lack of smoking policy (1)
	Fear of repercussions
	Too many memos
	Tendency to "blame"

NOTE: Numbers in parentheses indicate the number of votes those items received when participants were asked, "If there was only one weakness we could work on right now, which one would you want to work on?" Employees indicated that, in general, the following were priority areas for improvement:

- Insufficient staffing
- Supervisors' lack of managerial/leadership/communication skills
- Lack of communication

These three areas will be the major topics of discussion at our next feedback session. Please come prepared to share your ideas and suggestions on how we can improve in these areas.

This was one hospital's attempt to create an internal diagnostic and planned improvement process to address the "psychological climate." Consider how the material presented succeeds or fails to assist the organization in moving forward. What alternative approaches or procedures could be used?

Case 4.2 Communication at the Airline Owners Association

One executive faced what he thought was an isolated problem of communication failure in his association. Believing that he and his executive staff were too close to the problem, he used consultation services to search beyond surface-level communication breakdowns for the root causes in the climate, structure, and management of the Airline Owners Association (AOA).

Consider these case questions:

I. Diagnosis
   What is the presenting problem?
   What systems are involved?
   Who are the stakeholders?

II. Approach
   What is your plan for action?
   What personnel are needed?
   How much time is required, and who has responsibility for the solution?

III. Impact
   What systems changes are expected?
   What happens to the problem?
   What additional data are needed?

Some general case facts are provided in Table 4.2.

An AOA executive was concerned that communication was "less than open and prone to breakdowns" and that it was adversely affecting labor-management relations. This was not a formal conflict in a unionized organization but, rather, a feeling that internal labor-management communication was not "as it should be." The executive secured outside assistance for a diagnostic phase designed to establish a preliminary understanding of the situation. The goal of the project was "to see what's going on."

Under the guidance of an outside consultant, the AOA engaged in a problem-solving process designed to assist the organization in continuous improvement. Recognizing the importance of adaptation to change, the AOA examined

Table 4.2 Case Facts: Airline Owners Association

1. Business: Legislative and member services
2. History: 47 years old
3. Location: Eastern United States
4. Products/Services: Education, legislative activity, regulatory reviews/guidance
5. Territory: Mid-Atlantic region
6. Customers/Clients: Owners of airline services companies
7. Employees: Approximately 50
8. Ownership: Nonprofit organization
9. Revenues: Approximately $3 million to $5 million
10. Reason for consultation: Increase level of communication and forward movement

its internal strengths and weaknesses and identified actions to guide its work during the next several years.

This report presents some of the results of periodic problem-solving sessions held over a 6-month period. The board and senior staff met in one-day sessions to consider current internal conditions and to begin to identify actions for future improvement, particularly with regard to communication and climate. Included here are the groups' views of the internal strengths and weaknesses of the AOA as it now exists as well as some needed changes for the future.

During these early diagnostic discussions, the executive concentrated on several key aspects of relations with the staff—the lack of new projects, low motivation, and poor communication. These were used as lead items to introduce a broader analysis of the organizational situation. A group of approximately 30 staff members in two different sessions assessed the organization's internal state including its technologies, structure, psychological climate, and management behavior. From this analysis came a set of corrective and developmental actions (e.g., personnel policies, regular staff meetings, more defined structure) that the organization pursued over the next several years. Problem-solving responses were multisystem based, recognizing the "whole" of the organization.

Believing that all organizations have strengths and weaknesses, board and staff members reviewed five major internal areas: programs/services, staffing, facilities and equipment, organization and management, and finance/funding. Their discussion is summarized in what follows (see also Table 4.3).

Table 4.3 Airline Owners Association: Internal Strengths

Programs/Services
  Seek/take advantage of opportunities
  Liaison to get into business (cut through red tape)
  Information source
  Bulletin service
  Health program
  Educational
  Data processing
  Political/Lobbying
  Purchasing (competitive pricing)
  People
  Information management

Staffing
  Wide variety of knowledge
  Use part-time help efficiently
  Stable length of employment (average 13 years)
  Young group
  Good working relationship
  Good placement/fit of jobs

Facilities and equipment
  Computer system
  Environment

Organization and management
  Freedom for creativity
  Freedom to express viewpoint
  Viewpoint sought
  Structure not rigid
  No barriers/Not afraid to approach

Financing/Funding
  Well managed
  Overall organizational perspective

In *programs/services,* a key strength is the AOA's information management, with strong programs in training, health care, and purchasing. Concerns involve little assessment of needs, complacency about past success, sporadic marketing and promotion of services, and a need to further develop the education program.

Staffing levels are considered appropriate, with a strong and committed staff at all levels, particularly at headquarters. Concerns include continuing training and development, function and numbers of field staff in regional offices, communication between and within groups, and a need for stronger customer-member contact.

Facilities and equipment are thought to be high quality, with the facilities viewed as excellent. Two concerns exist: expansion and storage space. Equipment concerns include Internet and telephone capabilities and the use of 800 lines.

The AOA is well *organized* and *managed,* with the current structure seeming to support both mission and operations. Strong support for creativity and personal involvement exist. Concerns include communication, continued support of innovation, possible managerial layering (illustrated by proliferation of titles), and a need to clarify committee purposes.

The *finance/funding* situation is very good, with the only concerns being the very real threat to revenues from the consolidation of the airlines and the unknown impact of the dues increase. The need to constantly search for new revenues also was noted.

The weaknesses are listed in Table 4.4. The staff generally focused on the communication problem, a common problem in many organizations. Discussion did surface the question of how open and participative the climate really was. Several staff members suggested that they have the rhetoric of openness but, in practice, there was very little communication about what they are doing and where they are going.

During the staff sessions, which were open meetings of 20 to 30 persons, communication was repeatedly raised as a problem. The staff viewed the current mechanisms for communication as including the following:

- External and internal newsletters
- Regular staff meetings
- Executive staff meetings
- Annual planning retreats
- 800 lines for members
- Web page
- E-mail
- Open-door policy for executives
- Legislative letters
- Complaint system

Table 4.4 Airline Owners Association: Internal Weaknesses

Programs/Services
    Complacency
    Educational program needs assessment
    Promoting political successes
    Marketing of association
    Overly cautious
    Continuing education of staff
    Motivation/Change

Staffing
    Communication changes
    Teams/Sharing
    Understaffed in field representatives
    Goals in conflict
    Motivation low at times
    Development of staff not taken seriously
    Transition of staff to new roles

Facilities and equipment
    Storage limited
    Phones always busy
    Computers outdated
    Fresh air intake deficient

Organization and management
    Reluctance to "try again"
    Take more chances/Fear of failure
    Lawyers burden flexibility
    Definition of responsibility by departments not clear
    Knowledge of activities and communication to department
    Distribution of information inadequate

Financing/Funding
    Future (where association is going)
    Dues too low?
    Overdependency on insurance revenues
    Real estate (overcommitment)
    Educational programming poorly funded
    Relying on associate business members for dues revenues

Even with the categorization of methods, the staff agreed that communication remained a problem. Detailed responses to the problem-solving effort were viewed as the responsibility of management. But the board and senior staff groups agreed that future program and action steps should include the following:

- A member needs assessment survey to ensure knowledge of airliner owner needs and to search for product/service opportunities
- Actions to continue to develop the strength and capability of the legislative program in response to expected demands
- Analysis and possible redesign of the health care insurance program to ensure a prepared response to the national and state health care changes (which will undercut association insurance revenues)
- Reviewing and acting on communication technology needs (e.g., Internet, computers, other support equipment).

Other programs and actions will be developed as a part of yearly operations planning, some of which will address communication more directly.

A follow-up committee was developed to address this specific problem. The AOA executive asked for advice from his two vice presidents regarding the follow-up work. His request made to them was as follows:

> Assume that you are structuring this problem-solving session for the association. Give me your suggestions on the following three design questions:
>
> 1. How would you prepare the executive team and the committee for the session?
> 2. What would be the content and process of the session(s)?
> 3. What would you do to follow up on these recommendations?

Case 4.3   Intergroup Conflict: National Pharmaceuticals

The vice president of operations at National Pharmaceuticals received a complaint from Barbara Anston in the product services department. Anston was concerned that customer demands were becoming too heavy. Customers were dissatisfied about the timeliness with which deliveries were made and questioned whether the company was being forthright in terms of its public positions. She complained that the salespersons were saying that products were available practically 24 hours a day. When customers called, they *expected* immediate delivery. When they had to wait several days, they were angry, to say the least.

Both the sales contract department and the product services director were aware of the problem. However, the two directors did not get along and were not even able to hold a discussion regarding the problem. Their last attempt at a meeting, which occurred some 4 or 5 months ago, quickly dissolved into a shouting match and was ended before any useful suggestions emerged. Anston only knew that, at her level, customers were unhappy. Even when she was able to address the customers' problems, they were dissatisfied because of the time delay (mostly an expectations problem, she believed). Anston could see that increasing dissatisfaction among customers would hurt sales and morale at the company at some point in the future.

Anston's vice president agreed to look into the case, suggesting that he would talk with other employees in both units before he talked to the respective department directors. He did this and found that the complaint was essentially valid. The obvious first action seemed to be to initiate a meeting of the two department directors with the vice president as a third-party mediator.

The meeting was held. Both directors at first expressed surprise over the existence of the problem. On assurance that it was fairly evident from the employees, they both admitted its existence. A 1-hour session probing possible solutions degenerated into a near shouting match. The vice president suggested another meeting to try to resolve it independently, without higher involvement. The directors agreed, but that meeting also was unsuccessful. Some possibilities for department changes emerged, but they could not be agreed on.

The vice president requested a third meeting, to which he invited their already informed senior vice president (after telling them he would do this). Both were emotional and somewhat stubborn, but they were able to resolve the conflict with the senior vice president present at the next meeting.

How would you structure this meeting? What are the expected outcomes for the individuals and organizational units? What could have been done to intercept this problem at an earlier stage?

Case 4.4 The Bad Bank Board Director at Community Bank

Community Bank was created to present an alternative to the regional and national banks that were rapidly consolidating across the country. The consolidation often meant a drop in service for small customers.

Tom Jameson was hired as the new president by the founding board. In his late 40s, Jameson had been in banking his whole career. His most recent position as senior vice president gave him operations responsibility for a multistate bank. This was his first start-up.

The founding board was a group of self-made millionaires and professionals (e.g., lawyers, doctors). Although very successful individually, the group members had been only lightly exposed to complex organizations. Their natural inclination was "to run things themselves."

One board member, Harold McShill, was the owner of a meat processing plant that he had founded. As the group turned to discussions of strategy and operations, McShill seemed to "blow up" at every meeting. The board had important start-up business to conduct—what kind of business to pursue, which markets, location of a second bank, and so on—but McShill sabotaged the meetings. Specifically, he attempted to dominate all discussions, would rudely cut off his fellow board members and the president, would not compromise on any issues, and was disparaging of his colleagues at the meetings. Jameson was frustrated.

Jameson decided to use several strategies that he hoped would improve the meetings over a 6-month period:

- Trying to be solicitous of McShill
- Using a highly structured agenda with time limits for discussion
- Developing elaborate preparation materials and sending them to the board before the meetings
- Confronting McShill about his "blocking"
- Using other board members to assist in controlling McShill
- Engaging in private diplomatic counseling with McShill about his behavior

With minimal to no progress, Jameson decided that he needed outside help. The bank was doing fine, but the psychology of the board meetings was ruining his work life and undercutting the quality of business decisions.

What kind of help does Jameson need?

Case 4.5   An Engineering Department's Problem

At one southwestern university, the Department of Engineering appeared to suffer from significant morale and internal conflict among its division and project groups. An outside team of two academics and a consulting engineer conducted a departmental review, offering the following report. The case illustrates the interactive effects of psychological climate, work standards, and leadership behavior—a natural bridge to the management cases to be discussed in Chapter 5.

Purpose and Objectives

Recognizing the changing national environment, the need for intradepartmental change, and the general discontent with the current situation, the chairman and the faculty of the Department of Engineering requested an "outside current status review." This review focused on the organization and management of the department and on some of the related scientific and professional issues that require attention from faculty.

This department has an eclectic mix of three engineering divisions: transportation, computer, and civil. The transportation division is working on the natural expansion of highways, both new construction and state-of-the-art maintenance—from highways to bridges to airport runways. The computer division was strongly engaged in software development but has picked up the theme of artificial intelligence and has, for the most part, been working on basic science concepts. The civil division is focused on major waterways projects for power generation and recreational use. The transportation and civil groups often share the support scientists—biologists, environmentalists, geologists, and so on—and have considered closer collaboration. Faculties are active in professional societies such as the American Society of Civil Engineers.

Engineering departments across the country are addressing the challenges presented by new teaching technology, globalization, and a great economy. Despite a favorable environment, many departments have realized smaller student pools, stagnant compensation, and increased workloads. Over the years, this department has established a strong reputation for applied research and teaching. Graduates have consistently performed very well on their board examinations and have been successfully placed in professional positions.

The objectives of this outside review were as follows:

- To collect the perspectives of faculty, administrative leaders, and staff, identifying both current status and possible actions for continuing development of the department

- To provide additional data for decision making by the chairman, faculty, and institutional leaders seeking to move the department into the future

While addressing a perceived crisis, the philosophy and spirit of the review were that of a constructive continuous improvement model. Faculty willingly gave their time to the interviews and provided written responses. All contributors seemed committed to the forward progress of the Department of Engineering.

Method, Data, and Limitations

The primary methods for learning about the department were through personal interviews and official documents. In consultation with the chairman, it was decided that all faculty were to be given the opportunity to comment. Related departments were represented as well. The 30- to 60-minute interviews included the following:

- Faculty of the Department of Engineering
- Deans of the university
- Department chairman
- Department scientists (e.g., biologists, economists, environmentalists)
- Administrative staff
- Related department representatives (e.g., medicine, business administration)

The interviews followed an interview guide that targeted the general status of the department, culture and climate, structure, level of university support, leadership, and recommended actions to move the department forward. In some cases, faculty members brought completed questionnaires and additional information to the interviews.

Other departmental materials included the following:

- History of engineering (departmental document)
- Annual report from 1998
- Curriculum vitae (CV) abstracts from the engineering program review
- Engineering professions white paper (description of department future)
- Supplemental material provided by the faculty and chairman

A total of 43 members of the faculty and staff were interviewed over a period of several days. Those who missed the interviews because of competing duties were given the opportunity for telephone interviews the following week.

Limitations. The combination of the interviews and the supplemental materials provides a good picture of the department. But the short time line for this review and the limited data sources (primarily faculty opinions) dictate that the report not be used as a "stand-alone" tool for decision making. The report is best used to support follow-up analyses and actions by the chairman, faculty, and deans of the university.

Findings

The need for this review has developed over the past year, a period in which some significant changes have occurred. In particular, the following changes have occurred in the department:

- Moved to a new building
- Hired new faculty
- Established joint degrees in business and information systems
- Established an associate chair structure
- Welcomed a new dean
- Established and funded research opportunities

Thus, this need for continued work on the climate and the organization and management of the department is not a surprise to dedicated successful faculty and to a chairman with a sincere commitment to departmental development.

The following findings of the visit are presented under three categories: (1) culture and climate, (2) primary scientific and professional activities, and (3) organization and management.

CULTURE AND CLIMATE

1. *Many faculty believe that commercial projects and applied work are devalued.* In the move to build a more academic department (a direction supported by the faculty and required by the dean), the "sent message" is now that basic research is the focus and that applied commercial project work is "to be

tolerated." This was not the intended message, but in a department with a very strong applied emphasis, this communication was strongly felt.

2. *High levels of interpersonal discomfort and conflict exist in the department.* Although some of this is related to the "forced change" that is occurring in universities across the country, there appears to be a lack of teamwork and a falling off of the "family feeling" and collegial support of years past. Faculty have a shared sense that "doom" prevails and that leaders are not aggressively attacking the problem.

3. *In general, morale is very low.* The combination of external changes in the engineering industry and the lack of consensus and perceived inaction with regard to various departmental issues have created a uniform assessment of an "extremely poor working climate." This situation has become steadily worse over the last 6 to 8 months, so that faculty now describe it as a "psychological crisis."

PRIMARY SCIENTIFIC AND PROFESSIONAL ACTIVITIES

4. *Faculty are experiencing great uncertainty over commercial project productivity and time demands.* The increase in commercial project requirements has abbreviated the "academic time" of the faculty and has led some to question whether "ceilings" have been established that protect both the newly academic orientation (time for teaching and research) and literally the quality of teaching. Some faculty have become anxious about burnout and have begun to question the levels of project assignments.

5. *There is a lack of a clear organizational model (e.g., ratio of engineers to support scientists and staff) including work boundaries and relationships.* This is not just a problem for this department; it also confronts other departments across the country. But there is significant uncertainty about the future. The creation of a departmental model is needed that would include differentiated responsibilities, roles, project assignments, compensation, and unique identifying characteristics of engineers in relation to project staff—biologists, economists, environmentalists, and so on.

6. *Weakening interest in the discipline of engineering from students has continued.* Faculty are visible and have continued to develop interest in the discipline. Significant steps to recruit and retain students and young faculty have been taken with some success. Current department morale could undercut this achievement.

7. *There is a lack of consensus regarding the emphasis on basic versus project research and on expectations regarding productivity.* In the move to create a more academic department, many faculty believe that basic research is the intended norm for the future. In particular, the computer engineering group has attracted much attention (and grant money) with its ongoing work on artificial intelligence. The dean wants that group to push further and into new work with NASA. Thus, there are questions about how many basic research scientists the department can support and whether this strategy is likely to be successful. The "intended future" was to include basic research and work on innovative approaches to teaching, but faculty members believe that the relative balance is not fixed at a level that will enable the department to succeed. And faculty research productivity is uneven across the group. Of 36 CVs reviewed, 23 of the faculty published only two or three articles during the past 5 years, whereas others were highly productive (12-20 papers).

ORGANIZATION AND MANAGEMENT

8. *An incomplete sharing of, and a lack of agreement on, vision exists.* At the time of recruitment of the new chair, the faculty and institution's leaders were in agreement that a more academic department was the desired future. However, now that the shift is under way, there is insufficient understanding and acceptance of what an academic department is. To some, an academic department is primarily a commercial project operation with teaching and limited basic research. To others, the department is a scholarly endeavor, with basic research and teaching emphasized and rewarded and with project services being the secondary means by which it is funded. But artificial intelligence and some basic space science research do not have immediate commercial application. Without pushing the shared vision further, the uncertainty and conflict will continue.

9. *Faculty seem to see a single-contributor cause for the departmental conflict.* Many faculty members believe that the leadership of the new dean and the new chairman is the primary cause of the difficulties. But the departmental climate is coproduced by leaders and faculty. The leaders have made contributions to the problems, but there are external environmental issues and some resistance to change as well (e.g., manpower analysis, new administrative structure).

10. *Compensation is eroding.* One of the contributing factors is the fact that project work demands are rising while comparative compensation is falling (rel-

ative to comparable university and private practice benchmarks). This would not build morale in any department in any discipline. The faculty are concerned that insufficient action is being taken by the department to define the boundaries now seen as a "free fall."

11. *Roles and expectations of the chairman are not well understood and differ.* A large part of the leadership conflict has to do with the orientation of the chairman to the role. He has taken actions that emphasize the development of the department through external relations (e.g., national recognition through involvement in engineering societies and commissions), delegating administrative duties. Faculty members believe that the issues facing the department are more internal and that these need immediate attention, so that although the leader is working hard, his efforts are perceived to be on the wrong tasks for this department at this time.

12. *The management behavior and style of the chairman have been different from those of the preceding chair and have contributed to the difficulties.* With many unresolved issues from preceding years, this past year was expected to be a time of open communication, fast decisions, and follow-up actions. The chairman has provided less communication than needed, taken a deliberate and thoughtful approach to decisions, and moved slowly on actions until he had the full support of the faculty (consistent with faculty governance). Unfortunately, this style has appeared to be too slow at a time of rapid change—seeming to paralyze the department. The conflict between commercial project leaders and basic science research teams is an example.

Recommendations

PRIMARY AND IMMEDIATE

1. *Resolve the leadership question.* Although this is early on in the tenure of the new chairman, a crisis exists. Engineering chairmen are hard to recruit and retain. There are two options: (a) start again with the support of the dean, faculty, and willing engagement of the current chair, forgetting as much as possible the difficult first year, or (b) select a new chairman knowing that there will be a new start-up period required and that many issues will still need to be addressed. To choose the first option, the department's faculty advisory board would need to be firmly supportive of the renewed start. The transformation would require 1 to 2 years.

2. *Address immediate project needs.* Consensus about meeting commercial and research project workload requirements must be attacked with a plan that is known to all. The plan must ensure that teaching needs are met and that the successful efforts of the research and project teams are protected. Despite some planning, workload review, and new hires, the faculty are still anxious. The development of some "ceiling" to commercial project loads also must be developed. A review of the major highway project might be warranted.

SECONDARY AND LONGER TERM

3. *Clarify the role of the associate chairman structure with regard to team management.* Many faculty suggested that the associate chair structure has begun to indicate a very hierarchical approach. Rather than "command and control," associate chairs (e.g., project, education, research) should be acting as coaches and coordinators, facilitating the smooth functioning of teams in their respective areas. A close working relationship with the chairman is a requirement because the chairman and associate chairs, in effect, co-manage the department.

4. *Secure agreement on the basic research versus applied commercial project strategy.* As the basic research is expanding, there needs to be clear and widely announced support for projects and educational research. Some faculty members are just not as interested in computer science as they are in space projects. Open discussions about a relevant balance would be very useful, perhaps generated as a part of the "vision of the future" discussions. These discussions could include both scientific themes and applied project possibilities.

5. *Develop a strategic planning process and a plan.* This process would be a forum for discussing the future and a means for building teamwork among the faculty. A good start would be to work with a subgroup such as the chair's advisory group (the three associates plus two faculty-members-at-large), defining external threats and opportunities, internal strengths and weaknesses, a vision of the future, and strategies and actions required. This strategic analysis would then be shared with the full faculty later in the process.

6. *Create study groups to address project coordination, education, and research development.* Led by each associate chair—transportation, computer, and civil—these groups would diagnose the current state of the department, create a brief targeted plan for continued improvement, stimulate and take ac-

tion, and conduct an evaluation of progress. The study groups would provide both analysis and team building, working within and across the divisions.

7. *Conduct a benchmarking study.* This study would help the faculty compare their workload, teaching approaches, and research productivity to those of other academic departments that combine both basic and commercial project work. The process can be both educational for faculty members and advantageous in its production of new ideas.

8. *Extend an invitation to other academic chairs to discuss models of academic departments.* Part of the "vision" problem has to do with limited information on just what an academic engineering department is. Invitations to visiting chairs (two or three carefully selected ones) would be the basis for an educational/informational forum. Appendix 4.1 contains some possible topics, but these should be carefully edited/expanded to fit the department's informational needs.

9. *Create a model that defines the relationships of engineers to scientists and support staff.* This is a problem across the country, and it is a point where this department could become a leader. Issues of site access, wetlands preservation, and economic impact are not purely engineering questions. Create and describe a model of collaborative practice with biological and environmental scientists and community and economic development planners that is then tested and evaluated. This could move the department to the forefront of interdisciplinary questions in the field.

10. *Create an annual "report card" that identifies the progress to the future in terms of project services, education, and research.* Once the department has pushed past the crisis point and a vision of the future has been developed, yearly progress must be visible and announced. An annual report card that briefly describes developments in project services, teaching, and research will give all members a sense of progress and will be an accountability tool. The report becomes increasingly more powerful as institutional leaders and the faculty look forward to yearly advances toward shared goals.

Summary

A talented faculty with a highly successful track record of commercial projects and applied teaching is being encouraged to conduct more basic research. The change has produced a problematic situation. The conflict seems to be over style and the deliberateness of approach, not management technique and wrong actions. The four leading concerns—basic research versus commercial project values, communication, decision making, and actions—can be addressed. But success will require some change in leadership style, patience and a willingness to "restart" from faculty members, and renewed support from the institution's leaders. Organizational "swamps" of this sort are best navigated with a series of practical actions that build a record and expectation of positive problem solving. An advantage is that both the chairman and the faculty are openly discussing the problem. Attacking the two immediate issues—leadership and project services support—will establish a base for addressing the other recommendations. Consistent attention will enable the department to say that it is better off 1 year from now.

Appendix:

Sample Agenda for Visiting Chairman

Scientific and professional topics
- Project/Academic delivery model
- Project/Academic productivity standards
- Project/Scheduling model
- Nonproject time for teaching and research
- Teaching requirements
- Student recruitment process
- Research expectations (federal research funding vs. commercial vs. nonfunded)
- Grant dollars (e.g., applied for, yield, types)

Organization and management topics
- Associate structure
- Role of chairman and associates
- Approach to planning
- Committee structure
- Compensation plan
- Annual performance review process
- Annual report model
- Required adaptation to departmental size

Case 4.6 Marriott and the Start-up Hotel

Tom and Susan met while they were students in a hotel and hospitality management program at the state university. They dated for several years, married, and took positions with a major hotel chain in an eastern U.S. city. After several years, they switched to small "boutique hotels" where they both believed that they could make more of a contribution to the hotels' management. And they both believed that their ultimate goal was to own their own hotel. As they had two children, they delayed their dream of ownership.

Their boutique hotels were not part of a national chain. When they traveled, they tended to look for a familiar name to ensure comfort, reliability, and security, particularly when the children were with them. Marriott Hotels were a natural; they were everywhere, and they were supposed to be "family friendly." As it turned out, they were.

Their first encounter was a trip to Washington, D.C., for a family wedding. Although the wedding was late in the afternoon, everyone was worried about being dressed and "ready." At the 11 a.m. check-in, the friendly desk manager asked where they were from and what they had come to see. He noted that the usual check-in was 3 p.m., but on hearing of the wedding plans, he quickly gave them a room, available immediately. As they wandered about the hotel, they were greeted by staff and asked whether they needed anything. An extra cot was delivered to the room before their bags were unpacked. Their first experience was a good one.

That winter, they were returning for a family reunion during a holiday. They again stayed at the Marriott, arriving a full day early to visit some of the city sights. By the evening dinner hour, both parents and kids were exhausted, and they chose to eat in the hotel. The dinner buffet sounded right. They were not expecting the waiter's graciousness or his offer. He asked how old the children were—3 and 5 years. He suggested that the parents just get them what they wanted from the buffet without charge. Tom and Susan were excited because they often paid from $8.95 to $14.95 per child, only to watch them eat two rolls and some applesauce. This was the case again that night: The cost to the hotel was about 60 cents, whereas the gain in customer satisfaction was quite stunning. The follow-up gain amounted to customer loyalty for life.

Some years later, Tom and Susan came into a small inheritance that allowed them to begin to plan for their own hotel (working name: "The Start-up Hotel"). Their plans included the intention to replicate the customer service and graciousness they received at the Marriott.

Using the Marriott's Web site (www.marriott.com) and other materials, a small group could create the architecture of a customer-friendly hotel. What would be included in the design?

Note

1. From F. E. Kast & J. E. Rosenzweig, *Organization and management: A Systems Contingency Approach*. Copyright © 1985 by The McGraw-Hill Companies. Reprinted with permission.

5

Solving Managerial System Problems

Leadership and learning are indispensable to each other.
—John F. Kennedy

In this five-system model, executives and managers are at the center of the organization, supporting production and distribution with structure while building a quality psychological climate. Some problems are rooted in the management system.

The Nature of the Managerial System

Organization and management problems can emerge from the behavior of managers and the design of the managerial system. If there are managerial problems at the Internal Revenue Service (IRS), how would we recognize them? Kast and Rosenzweig (1985) defined the managerial task as follows:

The managerial subsystem spans the entire organization by relating the organization to its environment; setting the goals; developing comprehensive, strategic, and operational plans; designing the structure; and establishing control processes. (p. 115)[1]

In an integrated view, managers carry out duties that can be described as follows:

- Planning and design
- Organizing and stewardship of resources
- Developing systems and educating personnel
- Evaluating and controlling performance

They complete these activities through a set of roles. One perspective, developed by Mintzberg several decades ago, depicts managers as acting out their responsibilities through these roles.

Mintzberg (1994) indicated that the leader's work can be described by sets of behavior related to positions. In his view, there are three interpersonal roles (figurehead, leader, and liaison), three informational roles (monitor, disseminator, and spokesperson), and four decisional roles (entrepreneur, disturbance handler, resource allocator, and negotiator). These various roles can be illustrated by our IRS case and its group of leaders.

Interpersonal roles. The IRS commissioner (*figurehead*) greets visiting political science faculty to discuss taxation policy. The commissioner (*leader*) exhorts subordinates to increase tax return processing so as to meet this year's improvement goal. The chief information officer (*liaison*) meets with the chief of software design at lunch to see whether the new specifications will be ready on time.

Information roles. The IRS legislative director *monitors* federal legislation to determine what impact it will have on IRS policy and funding. The IRS deputy for operations *disseminates* information in staff meetings so that it will reach appropriate subordinates. The chief of the audit division (*spokesperson*) testifies before the Senate Tax Committee to lobby for authorization to provide expanded services that require more staff.

Decisional roles. Top IRS managers are now involved in *entrepreneurial* tests of new division structures and training in adaptation to changing conditions. For example, legislation required rapid and responsive changes watched over by congressional oversight committees. As much as managers try to plan, act on, and control activities in a rational and straightforward manner, a significant amount of their time is spent in *handling disturbances.* When a taxpayer complaint of abusive treatment during an audit makes the front pages, IRS managers must investigate and react quickly. The commissioner acts as a *resource allocator* when he balances the number of audit programs proposed by department directors with the anticipated flow of revenues for the coming year. The *negotiating* role can involve negotiations with several department managers and staff over the relative emphasis on speedy tax claim processing versus careful auditing when suspicions arise.

The combination of the traditional view of managerial activity (planning, organizing, developing, directing, and controlling) with the roles perspective (informational, interpersonal, and decisional) defines the managerial subsystem and becomes a "potential problems matrix" (illustrated in Table 5.1). In a recent view presented in a popular text, these core activities and roles are successfully handled if leaders have seven "competencies": managing self, managing communication, managing diversity, managing ethics, managing across cultures, managing teams, and managing change (Hellriegel, Slocum, & Woodman, 2001). And these "missing" competencies can be the source of management problems.

Let us return to the IRS case. The commissioner believes that there are technology problems (e.g., responding to computer breakdowns and updates) and structural problems (e.g., restructuring into business units, individual taxpayers, small businesses, large businesses, and nonprofits). Staff morale is low. Taxpayers are experiencing abrasive and abusive behavior by IRS agents (psychosocial). Because leaders ultimately are responsible for technology, structure, and psychological climate, there are implied management problems. For example, using the matrix (Table 5.1), we can ask managers whether they have *planned* for computer currency by acquiring information about the breadth and depth of the problem and by making decisions about how to address it (*informational* and *decisional* roles). Because no management systems are perfect, we can expect to find opportunities for continuous improvement (mapped by the matrix).

Table 5.1 Management Problems Matrix

	Role		
Function	*Interpersonal*	*Informational*	*Decisional*
Planning			
Organizing			
Developing			
Directing/Leading			
Controlling			

Managers are responsible for coordinating and integrating the other sub-systems—culture, structure, product/technology, and psychology. Both managers and consultants find problems in the managerial subsystems, as the following cases illustrate.

Case 5.1   Medical Department Strategic Planning

An anesthesia department chairman in a medical school responded to a request that he develop a strategic plan including a vision of the future and the path leading to that future. This case presents a report describing the outcome of the consultant-assisted process used to solve the manager's problem.

The case questions are in three sets:

I. Diagnosis
What is the presenting problem?
What systems are involved?
Who are the stakeholders?

II. Approach
What is your plan for action?
What personnel are needed?
How much time is required, and who has responsibility for the solution?

III. Impact

What systems changes are expected including interactions?

What happens to the problem?

What additional data are needed?

The case facts available to the team are provided in Table 5.2.

Why should physicians and organized medicine plan? There are many reasons. Without a clear vision of their desired direction and future, what physicians decide on a day-to-day basis—at the individual practice level, at the group practice level, at the academic and clinical department level, at the college level, and at the national level—does not much matter. A future will be created, but it will be created *for* physicians and organized medicine, not *by* them.

In a presentation on the purpose and process of planning, Ackoff's (1981) subtitle to his book, *Creating the Corporate Future,* is *Plan or Be Planned for.* Environmental influences on physicians are changing, with significant analysis and a vision of a shared future being important requirements (Ziegenfuss, 1987b). Government regulators, corporations, and some patients are concerned about physician and medical care costs. They have in mind a future that *they* most desire—involving close control and limitations on care and cost.

The question for physician managers is a reactive to proactive one: Have physicians designed a desired direction and future, and have physicians tried to establish ways of getting from where they are now to where they would most like to be?

The changing pressures on the Johns Hopkins School of Medicine and the Johns Hopkins Hospital led both institutions to create new visions of the future, to establish alternative structures, and to move aggressively to create a future beneficial to both institutions (Heyssel, 1989; Ross & Johns, 1989). Determining the department's future is an organizational problem. A case example of planning in a medical school clinical department is presented to demonstrate a manager using the strategic planning rationale in practice, the process used, and some benefits and actions to date.

Introduction: The Need for Planning

Many reasons define why individuals and organizations engage in planning.[1] Ziegenfuss (1989) identified five reasons as leading points of the rationale:

Table 5.2 Case Facts: Medical Department

---

1. Business: Provision of anesthesia services
2. History: Approximately 25 years old, founded with new medical school
3. Location: Mid-Atlantic region
4. Products/Services: Clinical anesthesia, research, and medical student education
5. Territory: Regional and national
6. Customers/Clients: Regional patients, national/international clients for research, and national board of students
7. Employees: 28 faculty
8. Ownership: University
9. Revenues: Approximately $20 million
10. Reason for consultation: Planning for further development

---

- Few organizations currently have a vision of a desired future. Some believe that an easy extrapolation of the past will do.

- During recent years, organizations might have relied on a single executive and a single vision of the future, but this too no longer is adequate.

- Organizations are increasingly searching for ways of involving employees at all levels, improving productivity and performance, and improving the quality of working life.

- Organization futures must be designed openly and consciously as a way of generating excitement about where the organization is going. Neither executives nor managers and employees have enthusiasm for the mindless extension of what they currently are doing into the future.

- Managers need guidance in their day-to-day decision making. How will they know which decisions make sense if they have no defined future?

Who would dispute that, like Alice in Wonderland, physicians have entered a forest of competing interests, problems, conflicts, and uncertain directions? Strategic planning is a process by which physicians and organized medicine can begin to identify a path through the forest including the forks in the road. For a successful strategic plan, the chairman of the anesthesia department needs the following:

- A vision of the desired future
- The ideas and contributions of many individuals

- To involve many constituencies (e.g., providers, patients, citizens) in design
- To generate optimism and excitement
- To engage in strategically oriented day-to-day decision making

All must be addressed by the department leader as a part of his primary role.

The purpose of a strategic planning process is to assist the organization or organizational unit in identifying changing external conditions, in identifying internal strengths and confronting weaknesses, and in defining a desired future that the organization members can strive for and achieve.

How? The Strategic Planning Process and Case

The anesthesia department chairman at the university college of medicine engaged in strategic planning in response (a) to recognition of changing external trends and (b) to the creation of a universitywide strategic planning process. Departmental-level strategic planning was designed to be integrated with an all-college strategic planning process that was, in turn, linked to an all-university process. Department members believed that they needed to engage in a creative proactive process that would best prepare them for the universitywide changes.

The department began to plan by recognizing the following needs and desires:

- The need to identify the department's mission and its position in the greater organization (which was engaged in planning)
- The need to respond to rapidly changing external conditions
- The desire to adapt the organization to fit the needs of the discipline, the faculty, residents, patients, and students
- The desire to involve faculty and staff in designing the organization's future

The incentive to initiate planning was both external and internal. There was outside pressure from rapid changes in the medical and health fields (e.g., cost, quality, delivery system developments). There also were internal incentives given that both the medical school and the university were beginning to plan more formally but without much physician participation.

Context: The university strategic planning process. The department planning was conducted in the context of a college- and universitywide strategic planning process with the following elements:

- Appraisal: Including external and internal assessment in relation to mission
- Matching: Linking program quality and need
- Setting priorities: Defining resource requirements and developing alternative strategies
- Implementation: Creating action plans

Within this universitywide framework, there was space to tailor make college- and department-level processes with the requirement that individual plans could be "translated" and linked to the general universitywide effort. This department created its own process, relating its plan to the university system at the implementation step. Physicians in this department wanted to be proactive within the university, not reactive to other departments and to the administration.

Department-level planning process. In response to the medical college dean's charge to initiate department-level strategic planning, the anesthesia department developed a planning process. The summary of the plan represents the integrated work of the department's planning team and the review by all faculty with regard to external and internal analyses, future direction, and program actions.

The planning process was designed to generate participation from department faculty through a representative model. Planners met in four group sessions (approximately 4 hours per session) led by a planner-facilitator. Along with the chairman, the department's planning team included five senior professors—clinical, education, and research directors representing the major areas in the department.

A successful planning process requires an individually tailored design. Following general design guidelines, the planning process was characterized by these nine points (a design coproduced by the chairman and the consultant):

1. The strategic phase was to involve a small working group with only departmental leaders involved. (size)
2. Participants were chosen carefully to represent all division and major departmental activities. (involvement)

3. The process was to be informal but with regularly scheduled meetings and a formal output. (formality-informality mix)
4. Qualitative data and professional judgments comprised the database. (nature of information)
5. An external planner was engaged to assist in design and to facilitate the process, with the department chairman and secretary coordinating the processes. (process support)
6. No computer support or formal data analysis was used in this stage. (analytical approach)
7. The process was expensive in terms of both consultant costs and faculty time expenditures. (cost)
8. The strategic first phase of the process was implemented in 30 days. (time)
9. Periodic updates of progress toward implementation were to be held beginning with a full department review at a day-long retreat. (follow-up)

Four steps defined the procedure in the first strategic phase, with further involvement of additional department members occurring at a retreat some 3 months later.

Step 1: *Current scenario.* This was an analysis of the current situation including (a) an external scan defined as a review of critical issues outside the college-hospital and outside the department (within the medical school) and (b) an internal scan defined as a review of strengths and needs within the department. The internal review considered the following: What does the department do well, and what needs to be done or needs to be done differently?

Step 2: *Creative redesign.* This was a scenario of how the department would be redesigned if it could be redesigned in any way it wanted. This was a creative view of the desired future. The mission for the "future department" was defined and elaborated.

Step 3: *Comparison of future to present.* This was a comparative analysis of the current scenario with the redesign. What are the gaps, problems, and issues?

Step 4: *Strategies and actions.* What strategies and actions must be taken to move from where the department is now (current scenario) to where it would like to be (desired future)?

After these steps were completed, the strategies and action plans were converted to program plans as identified in the university strategic planning process. A report or "white paper" was developed with several parts—an internal and external review as well as a creative redesign of the department with a statement of primary mission, definition of needs, and strategies and actions to take the department to its desired future. The white paper was distributed to the full faculty.

The plan. An executive summary of the plan is presented in Table 5.3 to provide a sense of both the issues and the directions proposed by the planning group.

The summary includes points that encompass each of the steps of the process—external and internal review; mission statement; desired future; and strategies, programs, and actions. The report was both a summation of the first phase and a milestone in the continuing planning work.

The framework enabled the chairman and the physicians to confront the changes in the medical field and the developments occurring within their own university, hospital, and clinical field. Combining external and internal analyses with discussions of mission and future generated the first fully dynamic discussions about the department's future. Discussions were both thoughtful and intense as the faculty and division chiefs began to consider their stake in the future and the degree of fit between the department's emerging direction and their own personal objectives and interests.

Most important, the design led to stimulating and sometimes differing thoughts about what the future should be and how to get there. This rarely is done in an open and participative way that allows planning team members to *co-design* their *joint* future with the chairman. Debates involved the extent of effort to be devoted to research versus education versus clinical work. Did the department want to be large or small? Should research be directed toward themes for maximum impact departmentwide, or should any research topic be acceptable and supported? In short, the thinking and debates established by the structure were the essence of planning; success was defined as people engaged in purposeful design of a joint future.

Continuation and Planning Benefits and Actions

The strategic white paper reported on the first round of planning with key departmental leaders. A continuing planning process was developed as a follow-up. After the first planning steps were completed, the strategies and actions were converted to program plans as identified in the university strategic planning process. The general findings from the first phase appeared in the report, which was reviewed by the full department at a 1-day retreat session.

Table 5.3 Strategic Planning Report: Executive Summary

The medical department engaged in a strategic planning process designed to assist both the department and the institution in preparing for the future. Recognizing the importance of adaptation to change, the department considered its mission and philosophy, future, external and internal issues, and status and identified strategies and program actions to guide its work.

The department's *primary mission* is to advance the science and practice of anesthesia through the integration of medical education, graduate education, research, and clinical service in a single academic community. This mission requires teaching, research, and clinical work of the highest quality for international, national, and local consumers.

The department's *desired future* requires change in four directions: (a) continued development of teaching, research, and patient care organization (to include additional resident fellowship year and additional academic degree, new molecular neurobiology research programs, and new clinical programs); (b) general increases in support services for educational and managerial work such as a full-time faculty educator and a professional business manager; (c) increased planning and coordination of clinical services, facility use, and physical and programmatic development directions both within the medical department and in the surgery and medical center administration departments; and (d) design of systems for maximum flexibility and innovation and for minimum bureaucracy (e.g., within the university system).

Critical *external issues* were identified as location, medical/political, and emerging opportunities. Within the hospital-college-department, key *internal strengths* included the institutional image, the department's national reputation, and a strong financial base.

Critical *needs* included increased external monies, long- and short-range planning, coordination, and service support, all of which are considered inadequate for high-quality teaching, research, and clinical care.

Four leading *strategies* were selected to guide the department's decision making: (a) a growth and development strategy to capitalize on increasing size, innovative services, and new groups of patients; (b) a financial strategy to drive the search for external monies such as endowment, grants, and contracts; (c) a competitive/collaborative strategy combination to account for institutional battles for patient referrals and the simultaneous benefits of joint ventures; and (d) a reorganization strategy to consider department redesign stimulated by integration in one physical location.

Program *priorities and actions* were defined for the four major divisions: education, clinical anesthesia, intensive care, and research. In the education division, resident and undergraduate education programs are to be enhanced, and a transitional year program will be instituted along with an additional fellowship year and a new master's degree.

In the clinical anesthesia division, pain management and regional anesthesia are to be enhanced. Cardiovascular anesthesia and operating room administration are to be maintained at their superior levels.

In the intensive care division, the adult program, involvement of anesthesia staff and residents in overall patient management, and the nursing home ventilation program are to be enhanced. Addition of a hyperbaric chamber is proposed.

In the research division, the cardiovascular program is to be maintained at its superior level. The neuroscience program is to be redeveloped in a molecular biology direction. Epidemiology, computerization, and bioengineering programs are proposed for development.

All 28 physicians and research members of the department were in attendance at the retreat. A second report recorded the comments and suggestions of group members in their review of the strategic white paper. Six topics comprised the follow-up report:

- External review
- Strengths and needs
- Mission
- Education issues
- Medical student education
- Third-year residency program characteristics

Actions. As a result of the initial planning and the follow-up retreat, several actions have been taken, including the following:

- Initiation of a medical student education program planning process using the Delphi technique to solicit further faculty input
- First design of the 4th-year residency program, also using the Delphi study method
- Commitment to development and participation in a Thursday evening seminar series to promote educational activities
- Creation of a study group on quality assessment
- Further awards of external funding and active recruitment in the molecular neurobiology field
- Establishment of an administrative/business manager position

These actions are directly derived from the priorities and strategic directions presented in the original plan. Further planning retreats will focus on clinical services and research with one half day devoted to each for full department discussion.

Discussion and Implications

This case example presents one demonstration of strategic planning for a physician merger in a college of medicine. It illustrates how one department attempted to create a vision of its most desired future. This process helped physicians be proactive through the following:

- *Issue identification:* The group focused on critical issues likely to affect the department's future success and achievements.
- *Dialogue:* The process fostered a strong dialogue about external and internal changes within and without the department.
- *Education:* Faculty and division chiefs were educated about the department's strengths, needs, and personal objectives.
- *Psychological sensitivity:* Department members became psychologically attuned to the internal and external change pressures in medicine and within this organization.
- *Interdepartmental needs:* The process identified the need for interdepartmental planning at the medical college level given that the future is a joint venture of several departments.
- *Consensus building:* Planning helped to generate consensus on the key issues and the need to focus resources.
- *Alternate visions:* The group was forced to think about its future and the alternatives available.

The physician group benefited from a strategic planning process that encouraged self-analysis and the proactive definition of a desired future.

Note

1. This case was formally presented as an article published in *Physician Executive* (Biebuyck & Ziegenfuss, 1992) and is presented here as an edited version with permission.

Case 5.2   Labor-Management Needs Assessment

In this case, the Winchester Area Labor-Management Council (WALMC) sought information from management and labor regarding the barriers to and supports for economic development in the community. An outside team bringing both "extra hands" and objectivity was selected to facilitate the council's work and to conduct the study.

The case questions are in three sets:

I. Diagnosis
  What is the presenting problem?
  What systems are involved?
  Who are the stakeholders?

II. Approach

What is your plan for action?

What personnel are needed?

How much time is required, and who has responsibility for the solution?

III. Impact

What systems changes are expected including system interactions?

What happens to the problem?

What additional data are needed?

Along with the case analysis questions, consider the following:

1. How does this study contribute to community development?
2. What action implications are apparent from the study?
3. Are the needs identified by management and labor primarily social or technical in nature?

The case facts that were available are provided in Table 5.4.

Table 5.4 Case Facts: Winchester County

---

1. Business: Primarily manufacturing
2. History: Incorporated as a city in 1895
3. Location: Arizona
4. Products/Services: Diversified but mostly manufacturing
5. Territory: City/County population 44,619
6. Customers/Clients: City/County residents
7. Employees: 1,691 Winchester County employees
8. Ownership: Public
9. Revenues: Unknown
10. Reason for consultation: Address the needs of workers for jobs and the needs of management for workers

---

Business and labor leaders were concerned about the future economic health of their community and about the considerable labor-management conflict. Several members of the leadership council read the following newsletter piece about communitywide labor-management committees:

An Overview of Community-wide Labor-Management Committees (Chisholm & Ziegenfuss, 1986a)

Many communities have begun to realize that their economic problems are so extensive that they cannot be solved without a cooperative effort that involves organized labor, business and industrial leaders, and local government. Cooperative efforts often take the form of community-wide labor-management committees (LMCs). The principal concern of an LMC is to promote a healthy local economy by retaining, strengthening, and expanding existing business and industrial enterprises and by attracting new ones to the community.

Community-wide committees go beyond the traditional collective bargaining process by undertaking cooperative efforts to minimize negative aspects of the relationship between management and labor and to generate a positive one through collaborative programs. Such programs aim to improve both productivity and the quality of working life by giving workers a greater voice in the decision-making process. Most LMCs were initially started as a reaction to crises; in recent years, many of the existing committees have also moved to improve the community's economic health through labor relations.

Committees are customarily established through the initiative of a key leader or a small group of leaders who are concerned about their community's economic problems. Leadership to form a committee can come from any sector of the community—government, industry, or labor. However, in order to be effective, the committee must have broad-based community support and participation. LMCs may be of any size; there is no predetermined number of members that guarantees success. The most important size factor is that all interested groups be represented. Typically, committees have an equal number of representatives from labor and management with co-chairs from each group.

Ideally, a committee's structure reflects its function. In a community where the committee's primary function is to bring about and maintain a good labor-management climate, the committee's structure is relatively simple. A committee with more ambitious goals is likely to have a more complex structure. Full committee meetings and executive board meetings usually are held on a monthly, quarterly, or ad hoc basis. Subcommittees and task forces tend to meet more frequently. Labor and management representatives alternate in chairing the meetings.

(Continued)

Most committees attempt to work closely with local government while at the same time maintaining their independence. By functioning independently, the committee is less affected by political changes in the community. In some situations, however, the LMC can be a formal part of the governmental structure. Because labor-management committees are composed of volunteer members who hold full-time jobs, a small professional staff usually is considered to be vital to a committee's success. Duties of this staff can be strategic, developmental, and administrative. Some LMCs also employ professional consultants who have experience in organization development, labor relations, and other related areas. The size of an LMC's staff depends not only on goals of the organization but also on the availability of financial resources. Funds to support a staff and to pay for programs come from a variety of sources including municipal government, member organization dues, regional or federal agency funds, and fees for services rendered. Funding can be a continuous problem for LMCs, yet stable financing is required for a committee to have a chance of success.

Although LMCs usually are formed to respond to immediate problems, they often evolve to develop more general objectives. These objectives usually include improving overall communications between labor and management, establishing worksite committees, stimulating industrial development, improving the work skills of employees and managers, and improving productivity and the quality of employees' jobs and the work environment.

As a result of their discussions, the business and labor leaders commissioned a future planning study. The study report included an executive summary, as presented in Table 5.5.

Winchester Area Labor-Management Council Future Planning Study

STUDY PURPOSE AND PLAN

The WALMC initiated a broad-based labor-management relations survey of organizations in Winchester County. The four purposes of this survey were (a) to increase the council's knowledge of the Winchester labor-management situation, (b) to increase labor and management participation throughout the

Table 5.5 Winchester Area Labor-Management Council Future Planning Study:
Executive Summary

The purpose of the Winchester Area Labor-Management Council (WALMC) is to promote and improve the business climate of Winchester County through specific targeting of labor-management relations. The WALMC was founded by representatives of labor and management interested in maintaining a strong economic base for future community development. In broad terms, the council intends to assess labor-management relations in Winchester, participate in planning for an improved economic future, take positive actions to continue labor-management development, and evaluate progress toward the desired future.

The future planning study has several purposes: (a) to increase the council's knowledge of the Winchester labor-management situation, (b) to increase labor and management participation community-wide, (c) to generate additional ideas and activities that would build positive labor-management relations, and (d) to set an agenda for the future. Two faculty members from a university Center for the Quality of Working Life were hired as consultants to conduct the survey. The survey questionnaires were distributed to 600 labor and management representatives in a wide variety of organizations in Winchester County. Major findings of the study (based on 108 responses) include the following:

1. The general view of labor-management relations is skewed slightly in the negative direction. Although respondents do not see an impending crisis, they express an overall attitude that is somewhat more negative than positive. Respondents also give a higher number of negative examples than positive ones to illustrate their views of existing labor-management relations.

2. Management attitudes and labor attitudes are identified most often as major factors that influence labor-management relations in Winchester County. Respondents also view the condition of the local economy as a major influence on these relations.

3. Results indicate that labor and management each must become more cooperative, change attitudes or perceptions of the other party, improve communication, and increase productivity. Changes by government (e.g., economic policy, attitudes) and the media (e.g., become more positive and objective) also are required to improve relations between management and labor.

4. Large proportions of respondents identify several activities that would help develop labor-management relations. Key activities cited include holding conferences and seminars on labor-management cooperation, establishing joint in-plant committees, educating the community on labor-management problems, providing a forum for discussion of common problems, sponsoring a health care cost containment project, and training displaced workers.

5. A fairly high level of support is expressed for WALMC activities. More than half of the individuals state a willingness to serve on council committees or task forces, and about half indicate that they would join the council.

---

community, (c) to generate additional ideas and activities that would build positive labor-management relations, and (d) to begin to set an agenda for future council action.

The need for the study was based on several assumptions from which these purposes are derived:

1. It is necessary to have detailed information about the nature and scope of the labor-management situation (beyond a surface understanding).
2. Communitywide labor-management relations, by definition, must involve full participation of both labor and management to be representative and to have the basis for communitywide change.
3. The scope of the task (positive development of labor-management relations) is beyond the reach of a small group; ideas and activities are needed from the whole set of labor and management organizations.
4. The small group of labor-management leaders stimulating this work wants to develop a participatively derived plan for action over the next 5 years (not a centrally controlled one).

With this set of assumptions, a survey with both a participative and idea-collecting motive was determined to be a good starting point. The survey would simultaneously provide data on the nature of the problem, generate communitywide participation, and provide suggestions helpful in creating an action agenda for the future.

METHODOLOGY

The idea for the survey was first raised at a council planning session. The planning discussions were used as a means to determine the council's views regarding (a) who should be surveyed, (b) what the appropriate survey topics are, (c) when and how the survey should be distributed, and (d) analysis and distribution of the results. From the start, the approach assumed that this would be the first of a series of ongoing data collection efforts involving surveys, interviews, and additional information from corporations and unions. These data would be analyzed as a whole to establish the "facts" of the situation in Winchester County.

As a result of the planning and review, the faculty developed a questionnaire that was revised and subsequently approved by the council. The mailing list was developed from members of the Manufacturers Association, labor union lists, attendees at the WALMC kickoff breakfast, and several other sources. This mailing list was used to send approximately 600 questionnaires to organizations throughout the county. A total of 71 responses were received. A follow-up letter, together with another questionnaire, was sent to organizations that had not responded by that time. This follow-up produced an additional 37 responses.

Profile of responding organizations. Table 5.6 gives a breakdown of the organizational representatives who responded to the survey. As this table indicates, a total of 108 organization representatives returned questionnaires before the final cutoff date. Questionnaires generally were filled out completely. The individuals answering the questions appeared to do a conscientious job of providing information. Overall, a total of 33 industrial firms responded to the survey, compared to a total of 27 labor organizations. In addition, 16 representatives from educational organizations and 15 representatives from government organizations (federal, state, or local) returned questionnaires. The remaining 17 responses came from organizations in wholesale and retail trade, finance, insurance and real estate, or other miscellaneous organization types (3 came from organizations that did not identify primary activities).

The bottom portion of Table 5.6 gives a breakdown of the size of responding organizations. As these data indicate, the largest number of responding organizations (50) have between 100 and 499 employees. In addition, 20 organizations have fewer than 50 employees, and only 17 organizations are clearly in the moderate to small range.

This distribution of responses is considered to be representative of the organizations in the Winchester community. The sample size is sufficiently large to make the comments generalizable to the set of union and management representatives in Winchester. As with all surveys, however, there are inherent limitations in the survey process (e.g., fears of confidentiality, specific situations, more or less informed individuals), necessitating consideration of survey data as only one of multiple sources of information for labor-management planning.

RESULTS

The results of the survey are presented in a set of tables in the following pages, accompanied by descriptions of responses. There were seven areas of respondent comments:

- Indicated willingness to support council activities
- Current labor-management relations in Winchester County
- Factors that influence labor-management relations in Winchester County
- Examples of labor-management relations in Winchester County

Table 5.6 Profile of Respondents

	Number of Responses	*Percentage of Responses*
Primary activity of respondent's organization		
Industrial firm	33	30.6
Labor union	27	25.0
Educational services	16	14.8
Government (federal, state, and local)	15	13.9
Finance, insurance, and real estate	4	3.7
Trade (wholesale and retail)	5	4.6
Others	5	4.6
No response	3	2.8
Total	108	100.0
Size of responding organizations		
1 to 9 employees	5	4.6
10 to 49 employees	15	13.9
50 to 99 employees	10	9.3
100 to 499 employees	50	46.3
500 to 999 employees	8	7.4
1,000 to 1,999 employees	7	6.5
2,000 or more employees	10	9.3
No response	3	2.8
Total	108	100.0

NOTE: Percentage totals may vary slightly from 100% due to rounding.

- Changes required to improve labor-management relations
- Activities to develop labor-management relations in Winchester County
- Labor-management problems in responding organizations
- Top issues for WALMC

Each of these response areas provides some part of the information needed to develop an action plan for Winchester County. The following response descriptions will be used for initiating the planning process.

Indicated willingness to support council activities. The survey asked respondents to indicate their willingness to participate in council activities. Table 5.7

Table 5.7 Indicated Willingness to Support or Participate in Various Activities

Activity	All Organizations	Labor	Industrial Firms	Government	Education	Other[a]
Number of respondents	108	27	33	15	16	17
Attend seminars/ conferences						
Number of responses	83	26	25	7	13	12
Percentage of respondents	76.9	96.3	75.8	46.7	81.3	70.6
Donate funds						
Number of responses	30	14	7	1	3	5
Percentage of respondents	27.8	51.9	21.2	6.7	18.8	29.4
Serve on task force/committee						
Number of responses	58	19	19	4	8	8
Percentage of respondents	53.7	70.4	57.8	26.7	50.0	47.1
Join as member of council						
Number of responses	42	15	18	4	2	3
Percentage of respondents	38.9	55.6	54.5	26.7	12.5	17.6

a. "Other" category includes finance, insurance, and real estate; trade (wholesale and retail); others; no response.

presents the responses to this question. The largest number of respondents (83) indicated that they would attend seminars or conferences on labor-management relations. In addition, 58 respondents indicated that they were willing to participate by serving on a task force or committee of the council, 42 individuals stated that they would become members of the council itself, and 30 persons indicated that they would support council activities by donating funds.

Findings suggest two points: (a) that a fairly high level of expressed support exists among individuals who responded to the survey and (b) that as the demand for time and financial resources increases, the willingness to participate in activities declines (e.g., 42 would join as council members, whereas 83 would attend seminars).

Labor union leaders and managers of industrial firms generally expressed greater willingness to become involved in various council activities than did representatives from government, education, and other types of organizations. Also, labor leaders expressed a greater overall level of support than did respondents from industrial firms. For example, more than 51% of labor union respondents indicated a willingness to donate funds, compared to approximately 21% of the representatives from industrial firms. More than 96% of the labor leaders surveyed also indicated a willingness to attend labor-management conferences and seminars; the comparable figure for managers of industrial firms was approximately 76%. Despite differences of expressed support, there is both labor and management willingness to get involved.

Current labor-management relations in Winchester County. The first survey question asked individuals to provide an overall evaluation of the climate of labor-management relations in Winchester County. Individuals were asked to assess relations on a 10-point scale (1 = *worst possible,* 10 = *best possible*). The top two lines of Table 5.8 summarize the results of responses to this question for all organizations. Results indicate that the vast majority of individuals see labor-management relations as somewhere in the moderate range (4, 5, or 6 on the 10-point scale), as 60% of the individuals placed labor-management in these three categories. By contrast, 15% of the respondents placed labor-management relations in the bottom three categories (1, 2, or 3), and 13% rated relations in the top three (8, 9, or 10). The average rating (mean) was 5.3.

Overall, 56% of the individuals who responded placed labor-management relations in the bottom five categories (1 through 5), and the remaining 44% placed relations in the top five categories (6 through 10). Thus, respondents' general ratings of labor-management relations are skewed slightly toward the negative side. This does not suggest that people see an impending crisis; it merely indicates that the prevailing view is slightly more negative than positive.

A breakdown of overall responses by type of organization reveals different response patterns by members of various organizations. Members of government organizations and labor unions view labor-management relations least favorably (means = 4.3 and 4.6, respectively). By contrast, individuals from educational organizations and industrial firms see labor-management relations more positively (means = 6.5 and 5.7, respectively). Thus, a different overall view of labor-management relations exists between labor leaders and their management counterparts in industrial organizations.

Table 5.8 Current Labor-Management Relations in Winchester County

| | (Worst) | | | | | | | | | (Best) | |
	1	2	3	4	5	6	7	8	9	10	(Mean)
All organizations (N = 108)											
Number of responses	1	3	12	18	26	21	13	13	1		5.3
Percentage of respondents	1	3	11	17	24	19	12	12	1		
Labor (n = 27)											
Number of responses			1	4	7	9	5	1			4.6
Percentage of respondents			4	15	26	33	18	4			
Industrial firms (n = 33)											
Number of responses		1	2	6	6	8	5	4	1		5.7
Percentage of responses		3	6	18	18	24	15	12	3		
Government organizations (n = 15)											
Number of responses			1		4	2	5	2	1		4.3
Percentage of respondents			7		27	13	33	13	7		
Educational services (n = 16)											
Number of responses			1	1	2	3	3	6			6.5
Percentage of respondents			6	6	12	19	19	38			
Other (n = 17)											
Number of responses		1	1	2	4	3	4				5.6
Percentage of respondents		6	6	12	24	18	24	12			

NOTE: Percentage totals may vary slightly from 100% due to rounding.

Examples of labor-management relations climate. Another part of the question asked individuals to give two examples of why they rated labor-management relations as they did. A total of 99 respondents gave first examples, and 83 gave second examples. Table 5.9 indicates the response categories derived from the answers given and displays the response frequencies by type of organization.

The category for negative comments about labor-management relations was mentioned by the largest number of respondents (n = 30, 27.8%). Higher proportions of labor leaders (51.9%) than managers of industrial firms (30.3%)

Table 5.9 Examples of Labor-Management Relations

Type of Example	All Organizations	Labor	Industrial Firms	Government	Educational	Other
Number of respondents	108	27	33	15	16	17
Negative labor-management relationships						
Number of responses	30	14	10	2		4
Percentage of respondents	27.8	51.9	30.3	13.3		23.6
Positive labor-management relationships						
Number of responses	28	8	7		9	4
Percentage of respondents	25.9	29.6	21.2		56.2	23.6
High strike levels						
Number of responses	20	2	8	6	1	3
Percentage of respondents	18.5	7.4	24.2	40.0	6.3	17.6
Low strike levels						
Number of responses	19		6	4	6	3
Percentage of respondents	17.6		18.2	26.7	37.5	17.6
Negative comments—management						
Number of responses	19	10	4	1		4
Percentage of respondents	17.6	37.0	12.1	6.7		23.6
Negative comments—union						
Number of responses	16	1	7	5	1	2
Percentage of respondents	14.8	3.7	21.2	33.3	6.3	11.8

cited negative examples. In the category for positive comments, a slightly higher percentage of labor respondents, compared to industrial managers, also gave examples of positive labor-management relations (29.6% vs. 21.2%).

Virtually equal numbers of respondents identified high strike levels ($n = 20$, 18.5%) and low strike levels ($n = 19$, 17.6%) as examples of their overall rating of labor-management relations. Managers of industrial firms (as opposed to union leaders) gave more examples of both high and low levels of strike activity

Table 5.9 Continued

Type of Example	All Organizations	Labor	Industrial Firms	Government	Educational	Other
Specific organization mentioned						
Number of responses	11	1	3	2	3	2
Percentage of respondents	10.2	3.7	9.1	13.3	18.8	11.8
Negative comments regarding community/economy						
Number of responses	11	5	2	2	1	1
Percentage of respondents	10.2	18.5	6.1	13.3	6.3	5.9
Local comments regarding economy						
Number of responses	10	2	4		3	1
Percentage of respondents	9.3	7.4	12.1		18.8	5.9
Strike mentioned						
Number of responses	10		5	1	3	1
Percentage of respondents	9.3		15.2	6.7	18.8	5.9
Winchester Area Labor-Management Council mentioned						
Number of responses	4	2	1		1	
Percentage of respondents	2.5	7.4	3.0		6.3	
Ratio: negative examples/total examples	106/178	32/45	36/57	17/23	6/28	15/25
Percentage of negative examples	59.6	71.1	63.2	73.9	21.4	60.0

NOTE: Representatives from educational institutions listed the largest number of positive examples ($n = 9$, 56.2%).

($n = 8$, 24.2%, and $n = 6$, 18.2%, respectively) than did those from government organizations ($n = 6$, 40%, and $n = 4$, 26.7%). In the opposite direction, the largest percentage of education respondents cited examples of low strike levels ($n = 6$, 37.5%).

Negative comments about management and unions make up the two categories of examples identified most frequently to explain individual ratings of overall labor-management relations. Union leaders were about three times as likely as industrial managers to make negative comments about management (37% vs. 12.1%). By contrast, more than five times as many managers from industrial firms (as opposed to union leaders) gave negative comments about unions (21.2% vs. 3.7%). However, the highest proportion of negative comments about unions came from government respondents ($n = 5$, 33.3%).

The final line of Table 5.9 summarizes the ratios of negative comments to total examples given. The overall ratio provides general support to the overall rating of labor-management relations reported in Table 5.8: Respondents gave more than 59% negative examples of the total number of examples listed. As noted previously, this percentage approximates the 56% of respondents whose ratings fall in the bottom half of the scale range (1 through 5). Government respondents (73.9% negative comments) and labor leaders (71.1% negative comments) have the highest negative/total comment ratios. These findings fit with the relatively low ratings of overall labor-management relations given by these two groups in Table 5.8.

The position of the industrial managers' ratio as somewhat above the total respondent ratio also is congruent with the overall rating by this group reported in the previous table. Thus, the profile of ratios for the various groups provides additional support for the subjective ratings of current labor-management relations in Winchester County described in the previous segment of this section.

In short, neither union nor management representatives believe that the situation is a crisis. However, the clearly negative perspectives suggest that some action is desirable and that there is room for improvement.

Factors that influence labor-management relations in Winchester County. Table 5.10 summarizes responses to a question on the factors that affect labor-management relations in the county. Respondents were requested to check the three most important items. Large numbers of responses indicated that management attitudes (74) and labor attitudes (73) are important factors that influence labor-management relations. Many individuals (61) also believe that the condition of the local economy is important in influencing labor-management relations.

Holding labor-management discussions outside the normal collective bargaining process is the next most frequently listed factor (32). In addition, 29 persons indicated that newspaper, television, and radio presentations have an important influence on Winchester labor-management relations. National organization or union policy was cited by 26 respondents, and governmental policy was cited by 28.

Table 5.10 Major Factors That Influence Labor-Management Relations in Winchester County

Factor	All Organizations	Labor	Industrial Firms	Government	Education	Other
Number of respondents 108		27	33	15	16	17
Government policy						
Number of responses	28	17	8		1	2
Percentage of respondents	25.9	63.0	24.2		6.3	11.3
Local economy						
Number of responses	61	14	15	12	12	8
Percentage of respondents	56.5	51.5	45.4	80.0	75.0	47.1
Labor attitudes						
Number of responses	73	13	28	10	9	13
Percentage of respondents	67.6	48.1	84.8	66.7	56.2	76.5
Management attitudes						
Number of responses	74	21	27	5	8	13
Percentage of respondents	68.5	77.8	81.8	33.3	50.0	76.5
Media						
Number of responses	29	8	5	2	7	7
Percentage of respondents	26.9	29.6	15.2	13.3	43.8	41.2
Labor-management discussions outside bargaining						
Number of responses	32	8	6	8	6	4
Percentage of respondents	29.6	29.1	18.2	53.3	37.5	23.5
Transportation						
Number of responses	2	2				
Percentage of respondents	1.9	7.4				
National organization or union policy						
Number of responses	26	2	8	10	3	3
Percentage of respondents	24.1	7.4	24.2	66.7	18.8	17.6

NOTE: Respondents were requested to check the three most important items.

The breakdown by type of organization reveals several differences that deserve mention. To begin, in comparison to members of other organizations (e.g., industrial firms, 24.2%), labor union respondents (63.0%) indicated that governmental policy has a greater impact on labor-management relations. Second, in comparison to respondents from other types of organizations (e.g., industrial firms, 84.8%), labor respondents attributed less importance to labor's own attitudes (48.1%) Third, both labor and management view management attitudes as highly important (77.8% and 84.8%, respectively).

The suggestion here is that labor and management attitudes must change if there is real interest in changing the perceived negative situation in Winchester County.

Changes required to improve labor-management relations. Table 5.11 provides the responses to a question about actions required to improve labor-management relations in Winchester County. As these results indicate, the largest number of respondents believe that some change in either the management or labor approach is required. A total of 67 people indicated that change in some aspect of labor's approach needed to occur, and 66 indicated similar kinds of changes are needed in management's approach. Types of changes required for labor include cooperating more with management, being more aware of management's position, improving communications, and increasing productivity. Suggestions about changes for management include changing attitudes, improving communications, cooperating more with labor, and increasing productivity.

A total of 39 people indicated that some change is needed in media coverage of labor-management relations. Of these respondents, 21 indicated that newspaper, television, and radio must become more objective in reporting labor-management appearances. In addition, 15 respondents indicated that the media need to become more positive.

An additional 39 responses suggest that some aspect of government (e.g., economic policy, laws, attitudes) must change to improve labor-management relations.

A total of 34 persons volunteered comments indicating the need for some change in the local economy. The need for industrial development was the most common response in this general category. In addition, 28 individuals suggested that national organizations or unions should provide greater local autonomy to the organizational units located in Winchester County.

Table 5.12 presents the suggested changes for improving labor-management relations by type of responding organization. Although the numbers in the categories are too small to make definitive interrelationship statements, several in-

Table 5.11 Changes Needed to Improve Labor-Management Relations

	Category Total Suggestions	Percentage of Total Suggestions
Government	39	13.9
Economic policy	16	
Laws	11	
Attitudes	10	
Other	2	
Local economy	34	12.1
Industrial development	17	
Improved local economy	9	
Other	8	
Labor	67	23.8
Cooperate with management	14	
More aware of management position	13	
Change labor-management relations	11	
Improve communication	9	
Increase productivity	8	
Other	12	
Management	66	23.4
Change attitudes	26	
Improve communication	18	
Cooperate with labor	15	
Increase productivity	5	
Other	2	
Media	39	13.8
More objective	22	
More positive	15	
Other	2	
National organization or union policy	28	9.9
Greater local autonomy	14	
Broaden perspective	11	
Other	3	
Other miscellaneous changes suggested	9	9	3.2
Total changes suggested	282	100.0

teresting differences between labor union and industrial organization respondents appear.

Table 5.12 Changes Needed to Improve Labor-Management Relations, by Type of Responding Organization

	Labor	Industrial Firms	Government	Education	Other
Number of respondents	27	33	15	16	17
Government					
Economic policy					
Number of responses	2	7	1	2	4
Percentage of respondents	7.4	21.2	6.7	12.5	23.5
Laws					
Number of responses	7	3			1
Percentage or respondents	25.9	9.1			5.9
Attitudes					
Number of responses	6		1	2	1
Percentage of respondents	22.2		6.7	12.5	5.9
Local economy industrial development					
Number of responses	3	4	3	4	3
Percentage of respondents	11.1	12.1	20.0	25.0	17.6
Improve local economy					
Number of responses	3	2	1	1	2
Percentage of respondents	11.1	6.1	6.7	6.3	11.8
Labor					
Cooperate with management					
Number of responses	3	7	1	1	2
Percentage of respondents	11.1	21.2	6.7	6.3	11.8
Aware of management position					
Number of responses		6	1	3	3
Percentage of respondents		18.2	6.7	18.8	17.6
Change labor-management relations					
Number of responses	2	3	3	1	2
Percentage of respondents	7.4	9.1	20.0	6.3	11.8
Improve communication					
Number of responses	3	3		1	2
Percentage of respondents	11.1	9.1		6.3	11.8
Increase productivity					
Number of responses	1	1	3		3
Percentage of respondents	3.7	3.0	20.0		17.6

For example, labor representatives believe that changes in the laws and the attitudes of public officials have the greatest potential to influence government. On the other hand, managers believe that economic policies stand to have the greatest effect. It is not surprising that more managers of industrial firms than

Table 5.12 Continued

	Labor	Industrial Firms	Government	Education	Other
Management					
Change attitudes					
Number of responses	5	6	2	1	4
Percentage of respondents	18.5	18.2	13.3	6.3	23.5
Improve communication					
Number of responses	5	6	2	1	4
Percentage of respondents	18.5	18.2	13.3	6.3	23.5
Cooperate with labor					
Number of responses	5	6	1	1	2
Percentage of respondents	18.5	18.2	6.7	6.3	11.8
Increase productivity					
Number of responses	1	3	1		
Percentage of respondents	3.7	9.1	6.7		
Media					
More objective					
Number of responses	9	4	2	6	1
Percentage of respondents	33.3	12.1	13.3	37.5	5.9
More positive					
Number of responses	5	3	1	3	3
Percentage of respondents	18.5	9.1	6.7	18.8	17.6
National organization or union policy:					
Greater local autonomy					
Number of responses	1	4	3	3	3
Percentage of respondents	3.7	12.1	20.0	18.8	17.6
Broadened perspective					
Number of responses		3	5	1	2
Percentage of respondents		9.1	33.3	6.3	11.8

labor officials believe that greater union cooperation with management and greater awareness of the management position would be beneficial to industrial relations.

Nearly equal proportions of union and industrial firm representatives indicated that changed attitudes, improved communications, and greater cooperation with labor by management will improve relations. By contrast, labor and management views diverge regarding the desirability of changes by the media, as labor representatives expressed a need for the media to become more objective and more positive to a considerably greater degree than did managers of industrial firms.

Table 5.13 Activities to Develop Labor-Management Relations in Winchester County

	All Organizations	Labor	Industrial Firms	Government	Education	Other
Number of respondents	108	27	33	15	16	17
Seminars on labor-management cooperation						
Number of responses	71	23	19	7	11	11
Percentage of respondents	65.7	85.2	57.6	46.7	68.8	64.7
Health care cost containment						
Number of responses	54	18	11	11	7	7
Percentage of respondents	50.0	66.7	33.3	73.3	43.7	41.2
Established in-plant labor-management committees						
Number of responses	65	15	19	7	10	14
Percentage of respondents	60.2	57.7	57.6	46.7	62.5	82.4
Training for displaced workers						
Number of responses	50	19	8	9	6	8
Percentage of respondents	46.3	70.4	24.2	60.0	37.5	47.1
University education/training						
Number of responses	25	6	7	4	3	5
Percentage of respondents	23.1	22.2	21.2	26.7	28.8	29.4
Special skills training						
Number of responses	36	8	10	5	7	6
Percentage of respondents	33.3	29.6	30.3	33.3	43.8	35.3

Activities to develop labor-management relations in Winchester County. The survey also requested that individuals indicate which of the items on a list of activities would contribute to improving labor-management relations in Winchester County. Table 5.13 summarizes answers to this question. Conferences and seminars on labor-management cooperation were indicated by the largest number of

Table 5.13 Continued

	All Organizations	Labor	Industrial Firms	Government	Education	Other
Information distribution						
Number of responses	31	10	10	3	1	7
Percentage of respondents	28.7	37.0	30.3	20.0	6.3	41.2
Long-range planning						
Number of responses	42	15	8	9	5	5
Percentage of respondents	38.9	55.6	24.2	60.0	31.2	29.4
Information research						
Number of responses	41	14	13	5	5	4
Percentage of respondents	38.0	51.9	39.4	33.3	31.2	23.5
Combined in management						
Number of responses	42	14	10	8	3	7
Percentage of respondents	38.9	51.9	30.3	53.3	18.8	41.2
Educate Winchester on labor-management problems						
Number of responses	59	19	16	8	6	10
Percentage of respondents	54.6	70.3	48.5	53.3	37.5	58.8
Provide labor-management issues forum						
Number of responses	56	18	17	7	6	8
Percentage of respondents	51.9	66.7	51.5	46.7	37.5	47.1

individuals (71) as a desirable type of activity. Substantial proportions of representatives from all types of organizations identified conferences and seminars as a contributor to enhanced industrial relations (range = 46.7% to 85.2%).

The establishment of in-plant labor-management committees received similar broad-based support from labor and various types of organizations (range = 46.7% to 82.4%). A total of 65 respondents indicated that establishing in-plant committees would be beneficial. Educating the Winchester community on the nature and problems of labor-management relations was cited by 59 respondents. Again, substantial support from members of different types of organizations is evident. Providing a forum in which it is acceptable for management and labor to discuss communitywide issues was identified by 56 individuals as making a contribution to improved relations.

Sponsoring a health care cost containment project and providing training for displaced workers were the next two items mentioned most frequently. Other items mentioned by at least 40 individuals include long-range planning, providing a resource for information on labor-management cooperation, and combating unemployment.

Overall, these results indicate that respondents see a wide array of possible tactics to improve labor-management relations in the county. These tactics vary from general education of the community to providing guidance in specific areas such as health care cost containment and specialized skills training. In general, the activities selected most frequently are identified as important by a substantial proportion of representatives from all types of organizations.

Labor-management problems in responding organizations. The survey asked respondents to identify three labor-management problems or difficulties within their specific organizations. Persons also were asked to rate the difficulty of each problem as slight, moderate, or great.

Response categories were developed from answers to this question. Table 5.14 summarizes the numbers of responses that fell in these categories. A total of 34 individuals made comments regarding either labor or management. Comments about or references to management included the following: "management doesn't listen," "management's dislike of union employees," "management's callous attitude," and "management prejudice." Examples of comments about or references to unions included the following: "union doesn't understand economics," "labor not cooperating," "union politics," and "labor not aware of problems." A total of 32 individuals identified some aspect of the collective bargaining process as a problem (e.g., "contract language," "contract interpretation," "poor bargaining leadership," and "unfair labor practice"). Attitude problems such as "antagonism," "lack of trust," and "apathy" were listed by 27 respondents. An additional 26 comments covered labor-management communication and cooperation (e.g., "little communication," "poor communication," and "little cooperation"). Other problem areas identified included economic/cost/finance issues (21 mentions), awareness/understanding/perceptions (15), and personnel problems (14).

Table 5.14 Labor-Management Problems in Responding Organizations

Type of Problem	All Organizations	Labor	Industrial Firms	Government	Education	Other
Number of respondents	108	27	33	15	16	17
Comments—management on labor						
Number of responses	34	10	15	3	3	3
Percentage of respondents	31.5	37.0	30.3	20.0	18.8	17.6
Collective bargaining						
Number of responses	32	3	7	8	10	4
Percentage of respondents	18.3	11.1	21.2	53.3	62.5	23.5
Attitudes						
Number of responses	27	9	10	5	2	1
Percentage of respondents	25.0	33.3	30.3	33.3	12.5	5.9
Communication						
Number of responses	26	10	7	2	6	1
Percentage of respondents	24.1	37.0	21.2	13.3	37.5	5.9
Economic/Cost/Financial						
Number of responses	21	1	11	1	6	2
Percentage of respondents	19.4	3.7	33.3	6.7	37.5	11.8
Awareness/understanding						
Number of responses	15	2	4	2	6	1
Percentage of respondents	13.9	7.4	12.1	13.3	37.5	5.9
Personnel						
Number of responses	14	2	6	2	1	3
Percentage of respondents	13.0	7.4	18.2	13.3	6.3	17.6

NOTE: Respondents were asked to identify the top three labor-management relations problems/issues in their organizations.

As indicated in previous responses, the issues often focus on labor and management attitudes, the need for education and greater communication, and an enhanced mutual awareness of labor and management purposes and positions.

Labor-management council. The final section of the questionnaire asked individuals to identify the top two issues for the future work of the WALMC. Table 5.15 identifies the categories used for the open-ended responses. As these data indicate, some aspect of maintaining or developing the local economy is identified as most important ($n = 52$, 48.1%).

The second most important item identified was the improvement of labor-management relations (cited by 40 respondents). Education, mentioned by 21 individuals, was identified as the third most important issue. Image/media relations (12), employee benefits costs (10), and training (5) followed by order of importance.

Labor respondents gave improving labor-management relationships greater importance than did representatives of industrial firms (40.7% vs. 27.3%). By contrast, industrial managers identified local economic development as more important than did labor leaders (48.5% vs. 29.6%). Both groups believe that education is a fairly important issue for future council work.

SUMMARY AND CONCLUSIONS

The survey results presented here indicate that the various purposes of the action have been accomplished. First, greater knowledge of the nature of the labor-management problems has been generated. Second, both labor and management representatives were engaged in the process and will continue to be involved in subsequent analyses and follow-up action. Third, valuable ideas and suggestions for action were offered by the representatives. Fourth, the data will be useful in program planning for activities in future years.

Major findings of the study, based on 108 responses, include the following:

1. The general view of labor-management relations is skewed slightly in the negative direction. Although respondents did not see an impending crisis, they expressed an overall attitude that is somewhat more negative than positive. Respondents also gave a higher number of negative examples than positive ones to illustrate their views of existing labor-management relations.

2. Management attitudes and labor attitudes were identified most often as major factors that influence labor-management relations in Winchester County.

Table 5.15 Top Issues for Future Work of Winchester Area Labor-Management Council

Type of Problem	All Organizations	Labor	Industrial Firms	Government	Education	Other
Number of respondents	108	27	33	15	16	17
Maintenance and development of local economy						
Number of responses	52	8	16	6	10	5
Percentage of respondents	48.1	29.6	48.5	40.0	62.5	29.4
Improve labor-management relations						
Number of responses	40	11	9	2	9	4
Percentage of respondents	37.0	40.7	27.3	13.3	56.2	23.5
Education						
Number of responses	21	7	7	3	2	
Percentage of respondents	19.4	25.9	21.2	20.0	12.5	
Image/Media relations						
Number of responses	12	4	1	1	2	4
Percentage of respondents	11.1	14.8	3.0	6.7	12.5	23.5
Costs of employee benefits						
Number of responses	10	1	2	1	2	3
Percentage of respondents	9.6	3.7	6.1	6.7	12.5	17.6
Training						
Number of responses	5		1	1	1	1
Percentage of respondents	4.6		3.0	6.7	6.3	5.9

NOTE: Respondents were asked to identify the top two issues.

Respondents also viewed the condition of the local economy as a major influence on these relations.

3. Results indicate that labor and management each must become more cooperative, change attitudes or perceptions of the other party, improve communication, and increase productivity. Changes by government (e.g., economic policy, attitudes) and the media (e.g., becoming more positive and objective) also are required to improve relations between management and labor.

4. Large proportions of respondents identified several activities that will help develop labor-management relations. Key activities cited include conferences and seminars on labor-management cooperation, establishing joint in-plant committees, educating the community on labor-management problems, providing a forum for discussion of common problems, sponsoring a health care cost containment project, and training displaced workers.

5. A fairly high level of support was expressed for WALMC activities. More than half of the individuals stated a willingness to serve on council committees or task forces, and approximately 50% indicated that they would join the council.

These data will be used to create a program plan for developing labor-management relations in Winchester County. They also will be used as the basis for discussions about specific actions (e.g., educational program planning, study groups, plant-by-plant responses) and will serve as the first survey in a continuing series of surveys that report on the status of labor-management relations. In effect, this collection of information on the extent and nature of the problem is one of the first action steps leading to a more desirable future for labor-management relations in this community. Using this as one tool, the council can increase involvement of a wide range of groups and individuals in this developmental process.

Case 5.3   Clinic Merger Case

Three community-based medical clinics were told by funding officials that a merger would enhance organizational survival. In this case, the board presidents and the executives requested outside assistance to facilitate the merger discussions and to provide additional data for decision making.

The case questions are in three sets:

I. Diagnosis
   What is the presenting problem?
   What systems are involved?
   Who are the stakeholders?

II. Approach
   What is your plan for action?
   What personnel are needed?
   How much time is required, and who has responsibility for the solution?

III. Impact
   What systems changes are expected including system interaction?
   What happens to the problem?
   What additional data are needed?

Along with the case analysis questions, consider the following:

1. Should the consulting team be "outsiders," and who should have been included?
2. Is the report comprehensive?
3. What data are missing or needed in addition to those provided?
4. Do you believe that the merger is a good idea?

The case facts that were available are provided in Table 5.16.

An outside team of three consultants was engaged to study the problem of a possible merger. After 3 months of study, the consultants submitted the following report. The executive summary is presented in Table 5.17.

The Clinic Merger: An Analysis of Potential and Pitfalls

PROBLEM STATEMENT: STUDY QUESTION

The merger idea originally was proposed by the primary funding and coordinating organization, the Maryland Clinic Consortium (MCC), a group of 45

Table 5.16 Case Facts: Clinic Merger

---

1. Business: Health care
2. History: Approximately 30 years old
3. Location: Mid-Atlantic region
4. Products/Services: Health care services
5. Territory: Six-county region
6. Customers/Clients: Men, women, and children of all ages
7. Employees: 60
8. Ownership: Not-for-profit, nongovernmental
9. Revenues: Varies for each center, most $2 million to $4 million
10. Reason for consultation: Consider merger option to open future growth and development

---

clinics. The MCC was responding to a fear of reduced federal funds, following the direction of recent federal policies. The threat of reduced federal funding has not materialized, but MCC members realized that there may be other reasons to consider merger of their individual organizations. Specifically, the organizations identified the following five reasons for exploring merger:

- An interest in designing their own future
- A defense against future loss of federal funds, even though that threat was somewhat diminished
- An interest in maintaining and increasing the quality of services provided to clients
- The promotion of efficiencies through economies of scale
- The building of a cohesive supportive network throughout Maryland

The study question was, "Does the merger of the three agencies help accomplish these goals?" After nearly a year of study, a merger team (composed of board members and executives from each of the organizations) decided that a second opinion would be useful. They sought a substantive outside analysis of merger-related issues with recommendations on how to proceed—either to continue with more aggressive action toward a merger or to discontinue merger discussion if that seemed appropriate. The consulting team was composed of three persons, the first with expertise in health systems, the second in organization behavior, and the third in finance.

Table 5.17 The Clinic Merger: An Analysis of Potential and Pitfalls: Executive Summary

The board committee has been engaged for approximately 1 year in a study regarding the potential benefits of a merger for the three organizations. The merger idea was proposed 1 year ago because of potential cutbacks in federal funding and the advantages in economy provided by a merged organization. With a reduction in the threat of federal funding cutbacks, however, the organizations began to consider the potential of merger for other reasons.

The organizations are now discussing merger for five reasons: (a) in terms of enhancing the ability to *decide* their own *future,* (b) as a defensive strategy against the potential loss of future federal funds, (c) with an interest in maintaining and increasing quality of services to clients, (d) with interest in the promotion of efficiency, and (e) for the intention of building a cohesive supportive network of organizations providing these services through the state. With these interests, the study question was, "Does the merger of the three organizations help accomplish these goals?"

Consulting advisers were engaged to collect additional data, to analyze the data already collected and studied by the board and executive staff merger committee, and to present further analysis of both. Using a structured interview guide, the consultants conducted in-depth personal interviews of board members and staff at each of the organizations. In addition, we collected budget and official record data from each of the organizations to analyze financial and program operations. The results of this data collection and analysis are presented here. The interviews indicated that board members and staff are supportive of the merger idea. Program data and the financial review indicated feasibility for the merger.

It is the recommendation of the consulting team that the three organizations continue to move forward toward a merger. The merger would, in our opinion, provide benefits of the kind identified by the participants, for example, a defense against federal limitations, an ability to actively design a linked and successful future, and opportunities for sharing staff expertise that can maintain and increase quality of services. There also will be possible efficiencies through economies of scale and the continuation of the development of a cohesive network of providers.

It is the recommendation of the consulting team that a participative, task force-dominated process be used to effect the operational planning for the merged agencies. In addition, a governance structure is recommended that includes a continuation of advisory boards at each of the three community locations and the development of a consolidated board to guide overall agency operations. It also is recommended that both financial and legal advice be secured for the merger process, with these advisers assisting the respective task forces.

Finally, it is our recommendation that each organization's board decide whether to proceed with the merger in principle, simultaneously identifying a management team that would be able to lead this effort. Detailed operational planning can then proceed from that base to the full creation of a merged entity.

This study emerged from an already existing group of board members and agency executives. For the consulting team, this was particularly important. It indicated that the organizations already were substantively involved in merger planning and merger analysis and that there already was a degree of openness and trust established. It also meant that there was some significant degree of interest in continuing a thoughtful analysis of the benefits to be gained from merger. It was in this context of (a) already engaged individuals (b) who have collected significant data for (c) designing their own future that the merger consulting team began the project.

PROCEDURE

The procedure selected by the consulting team was an interactive one in which the team would continuously identify issues and data and feed them back to executives, board presidents, and the merger group on a regular basis. This procedure ensured that there was a degree of openness to an analysis that is potentially discomforting to those already deeply involved in the process. It was intended that the merger consultants would be able to continue the strong planning work that already has been initiated by the boards and executives.

The merger consultants began with data supplied by the executives detailing their analytical work to date. This work was reviewed and discussed at the first of several group meetings among the board presidents, executives, and merger consultants. From this initial review and the group session, a number of data needs were identified that were to be systematically explored through in-depth personal interviews of board members and staff. A series of questions were identified that would help gain an understanding of the position of board members and staff with regard to merger. Table 5.18 lists the 13 questions that were used as the basis for personal interviews of board members and staff at each of the organizations.

Each of the executives was asked to select board members and staff who could be interviewed by the merger consultants. They were asked to identify a cross section of staff at various levels involved in both management and clinic operations. They also were asked to identify board members who they believed would be open to questioning the merger process. The intent of the interviewing was to identify any of the potential benefits or concerns about the merger that might exist on the part of board members or staff. The interviews were designed to elicit strong discussion of the merger concept and were not designed to produce a strict quantitative count of "pro and con." In effect, the interviews were viewed as stimuli for discussion and analytical purposes.

As the interviews were completed, additional group sessions were held with the executives and board presidents to provide feedback on board and staff member positions (not individual opinions but, rather, an aggregate sense). New issues were identified for further investigations at that point. Along with

Table 5.18 Personal Interview Guide

---

1. What do you know of the merger/linkage plans?

   How would you rate the amount of information you have received about the merger plans?

   (no information)   (complete information)

   1 -10

2. What do you think of the idea?

3. What are the advantages of a merger? (benefits)

4. What are the disadvantages?

5. How would a merger affect your job?

6. How will others react?

7. What questions/concerns do you have about the merger?

   What questions/concerns do you think others will have?

8. If people resist the merger, why will they?

9. How would you like a large organization?

10. How would you describe _____ [the organization where you work now]?

    What images come to mind when you think about _____ [the organization]?

11. To what degree do people in your position support the concept of a merger?

    (no support)   (total support)

    1 -10

12. If the merger were to go ahead, what would help its progress?

13. Any other comments or suggestions you would like to make?

---

the merger materials already developed by the agencies and personal interviews of board members and staff, detailed financial data, including annual audits of each of the organizations, were requested. A financial analysis was conducted that was based on the audits and current budget projections.

In addition, the merger consultants examined several recent articles related to mergers and materials on the merger in other areas of the country. These materials provided reviews of the pros and cons of mergers in nonprofit organizations including the pitfalls to be avoided once a merger decision was made.

This was the procedure and database for the analysis. Table 5.19 identifies the number of board members and staff interviewed from each agency. The group of board members and staff interviewed is considered to be a representative group. Care was taken to ensure that any additional persons who had a desire to talk to the merger consultants could do so. Those interviewed are not identified by names, nor are any comments made by individuals to be released to the boards and executives. All interviews were conducted in confidence.

Table 5.19 Interviews Conducted

Agency	Board	Staff
A	5	8
B	4	8[a]
C	5	8

NOTE: Interviews conducted were exclusive of joint meetings with executives and board presidents.
a. Group session of 4 persons included.

RESULTS

In this section, we identify the results of our analytical work concentrating on three particular types of data.

- A review of the merger material collected and provided by the board and staff merger committee
- Interviews of board members and staff in each of the three agencies
- Financial data derived from budgets and revenue projections submitted by each of the three agencies

These materials, as well as additional readings and knowledge of organization and management systems, are the basis for the conclusions and recommendations presented later in this report.

Merger study materials. The team found the board's merger study materials to be complete and comprehensive in the identification of the issues that needed to be studied. These included the following:

- A comparison of affiliate organizations
- An identification of advantages and concerns regarding merger
- Some beginning financial documentation
- Consideration of headquarters and sites
- Administrative organization
- Community impact
- Public affairs and public relations
- Governance issues

The team believed that board members and staff studying the question had identified the critical topics for consideration. The task was not focused on uncovering new topics that had not yet been addressed; rather, it was focused on pushing further the analysis in each of these areas. In addition, there was a need to clarify and focus some of the concerns within each topic area. We also regarded our analysis as a process by which the already completed analytical work of the merger committee could be confirmed or disconfirmed. That is, we did not feel compelled to "find" alternative interpretations of the data. We believed that we had an obligation to clearly support the points in which we felt the merger committee already had discovered the facts of the situation. We found that this was true in most cases; the merger committee had identified the critical issues.

Interview findings. In this section, we report the findings of the individual and group interviews conducted with the board members and staff of the three agencies. In most cases, we conducted individual interviews of approximately 20 to 30 minutes in length. In several cases, however, it was possible to conduct a group session with several employees (e.g., the clinical managers meeting). This was regarded as an opportunity to get a "collective perspective" of several staff members simultaneously. Sometimes, the interactive effect of responding in the presence of others produces additional insight. The interview data are presented following the personal interview question schedule (Table 5.18).

Question 1: "What do you know of the merger/linkage plans?" In general, staff and board members of the three agencies considered themselves reasonably well informed of the current state of the merger/linkage plans. Few board members or staff were willing to state that they had complete information. However, no one identified that he or she had a complete lack of information about the current situation. We believed that, in general, the knowledge of merger/linkage plans matched pretty closely the current state of the process. That is, the merger committee was unclear about where it was, and this was reflected in the amount of information that board members and staff apparently have. This was regarded as appropriate at this point. We believe, however, that there is a clear need for additional information as the work proceeds. We thought that it would be useful to identify the actual data. We asked board members and staff to identify, on a scale from 1 to 10, the level at which they were "informed." The following is their estimations on such a scale:

Board members: Average (6.8)
Staff: Average (4.6)

Staff are less informed, consistent with higher board involvement to date. Following are some representative comments:

"They really keep you informed—we have received all information"
"Know a lot, have been at several meetings where the merger had been discussed"
"Have received minutes of some meetings and the tome on the Southwest merger"
"How much more can I know?"
"Not much, only who is involved and that's about it"
"Not very much—only that we are [merging] or probably will merge and which clinics are involved"
"Don't know much; have heard that _____ is resisting some—on again, off again"
"Everything—management team knows all"
"Don't know too much; one staff meeting in which general information was provided—more pros than cons"
"Only contact was that at the last staff meeting several months ago—mostly heard positives and not negatives"
"Absolutely nothing"
"A little bit—don't know much"
"A little"

Question 2: "What do you think of the merger idea?" In general, board members and staff indicated that there were significant benefits to be gained, and both were attracted to and excited by the idea. Few persons expressed outright hostility to the merger. Nor were board members or staff willing to identify a significant negative (or "nightmare") that might result from merger. We believed that board members and staff were generally supportive of the concept, with some regarding it as exciting and attractive. Following are some representative comments:

"Fine idea, especially if _____ is going to run the show"
"Don't feel threatened but don't know enough to be"
"Understand that no staff job will be affected, only management"
"Have positive reaction"
"Run the gamut: first, do we need, [and] what do we gain/lose?"
"If you expand into our hospital areas, there will be war"

"Have become more and more positive but remain concerned regarding loss of turf from the donor perspective"

"Very mixed reactions—have been analyzing and wonder if I am being too parochial"

"Am not closed but have some nagging questions"

"It's a great idea; I have been involved for a long time; it is necessary to survive over the long run"

"Travel—will we have to travel to cover for others?"

"Exciting—if it goes right, would strengthen our position"

"Like the idea; it's a good one"

"Very positive—understand potential benefits"

Question 3: "What are the advantages of the merger?" This was an opportunity to have the board members cite political support, enhanced size and program capability, and the ability to expand and develop the service providers in Maryland. Some of the specific advantages listed by board members and staff are these:

"Less concern about financial picture—don't know much about the administrative effects"

"More uniform care, bulk buying, equalization of pay, possibly be able to be open all week"

"Stronger financially and connections to agencies, which will stimulate ideas from them"

"Long-range planning and implementation—additional viewpoints and new ideas"

"More efficient—public affairs, buying power, education, more clout"

"Increased ability to provide services"

"Sharing ideas with other clinics"

"Chance for staff to grow"

"Development would be greatly strengthened"

"Education—if we have a large number of educators, we can improve services"

"May be better benefits, e.g., pay, fringe benefits, better job in agency"

Question 4: "What are the disadvantages?" We also were interested in what board members and staff considered was the "downside" of the merger. That is, what are the disadvantages from the perspective of board members and staff? In general, they indicated that the growing size and the potential loss of a "close-knit family atmosphere" would be a concern. They also frequently mentioned the concern for additional travel and some concern about how program activities would be linked. Some disadvantages cited by board members and staff are listed here:

"Board involvement—it's hard to find members"

"Medical profession may view the merger as increased competition; but if they want to compete, let's compete"

"Donor interest"

"Possible diffusion of image in community; we currently have a history and image in the local community"

"Service"

"We're kind of a family—our patients are ours; how would this be affected?"

"What will the structure be like locally?"

"Am I going to have a job?"

"We're not a business, not a bank—we're a social agency; everyone is saying we'll save dollars, but show me"

"How to get the strengths from each community (individuals with real commitment) on boards"

"Distance—when you get bigger, you may lose some; have had some of that occur as we have gotten larger"

"How would it affect fund-raising?"

"What's going to happen to my job?; decreased importance—is there someone better qualified for it?; will I be stuck in some God-forsaken place?"

"The larger the organization, the most chance for snafus"

"With small population and rural area, might decide it isn't worth it"

"Damned the employees, make a buck"

"Travel—if staff had to travel, members of clinic aren't free to"

"Communication—in larger organizations, you frequently don't get information or are the last to know"

"Job losses?; permanent transfers?"

"Community reaction—church paper if abortions occur in another location"

Question 5: "How would merger affect your job?" This question was directed at both board members and staff to gain an understanding of whether board members considered that their affiliations and involvements might shift. For staff members, the question asked that they consider the possibility of having a significantly different job in the future.

We found that board members were aware that their jobs would shift. Some of them would become part of a consolidated board, and others would remain involved in an advisory board capacity focusing on fund-raising, local community, and public affairs and public relations contact.

Staff members felt very secure in their expectations about retaining the basic nature of their jobs. They did not seem to be very anxious about significant changes. They believed that the new program and organizational designs would enable their basic work activities to remain intact. Some of the concerns about the job redesign were as follows:

"Feel pretty secure since I have been here a long time and know things that others don't—don't know how it will affect my job"

"Possibly lose my job if an RN [registered nurse] is required to do it; I currently have job based on previous experience"

"New rules and regulations and new job descriptions"

"Don't know, _____ said it would help, but others have said they may want to centralize this function in _____."

"Not sure"

"Depends on the management system—think they would still need clinic managers, but whether they need me, I don't know"

"An expansion of current duties to broaden role—but I'm not sure that I'll get the job; I may end up being someone else's assistant"

"More to do, busier—help develop programs elsewhere"

"As a management person, I am one of the people most at risk"

"I don't know where I'll be shuffled in or if there will be something desirable for me to do"

"I'm concerned about career development and how my next position would look to potential employers"

"Not sure where decisions stand on structure—possible concern about the potential influence on key decisions"

"Have no idea—only know that they said in the beginning there won't be any layoffs"

"Concerned about the possible need to drive long distances, effects on job—don't see any as long as I still have my job"

Question 6: "How will others react?" This question was designed to help in surfacing concerns by asking board members and staff how others would react to the same sort of merger uncertainties. In general, board members and staff did not identify expected negative reactions. Instead, they seemed to believe that other board members and staff would continue to support the agency with both voluntary board activities and staff work as they have in the past. They did *not* believe that participants would lobby heavily against the agency or quickly begin to search for other jobs. Following are some predicted reactions that were identified:

> "I'm not really sure; we have a hard core of six to seven dedicated people on the board, and the others tend to fall by the wayside"
>
> "Appear to be inexorably rolling toward it without a clear expression of support from the board"
>
> "We started in an odd way because we had to, and now the merger process has taken on a life of its own"
>
> "Really not sure due to the fact that we don't really have strong opinions one way or the other"
>
> "May take time to break down some subgroup barriers; some people are picky and don't like new people in their territory"
>
> "Sort of a lackadaisical attitude—has more committed board members, [and] they are interested because of possible contribution to increased autonomy; however, they don't know much about it"
>
> "No one on the board is upset about it"
>
> "Some of them feel threatened, and this probably depends on how much knowledge they have—the more they know, the less threat"
>
> "The management team is all in favor"
>
> "I don't know enough to respond, and most of the staff won't know a thing"
>
> "Generally viewed as a good thing; however, the final reaction will depend on the effects on hours, salary, etc."
>
> "Some positive, some negative—staff currently is concerned about whom they can go to talk with about problems"
>
> "Management really doesn't listen to you"
>
> "Board is somewhat volatile in approving steps—haven't really reached a decision one way or the other"

Question 7: "What questions or concerns do you have about the merger?" This question was a bit redundant from the earlier focus on disadvantages. It was another attempt to identify what the critical concerns were. The concerns seemed to be focused on distance between the organizations, potential need to travel, and ability to link the organizational cultures (ensuring that the close-knit group feeling that currently exists within each of the agencies would be carried over to the new larger organization). There were also some concerns about size as an organizational variable. That is, will a larger organization be the same as the smaller organizations? We found these concerns to be appropriate—and quite a natural part of the process. Additional questions and concerns that respondents identified included the following:

"Regarding self: what are all of the disadvantages?; would the job be reclassified?; it almost seems to good to be true—and why are board members reluctant?"

"Salary levels differ from one area to another—would be an advantage if everyone here got increases"

"Possible big changes that would cause staff to leave"

"Will I still have a job, and will I have to travel?"

"Will there be a chance for advancement into upper levels?"

"Will we be taken up by the larger organization versus continuing to be relatively autonomous?"

"The jobs remain unchanged, and relationships with colleagues remain the same"

"Relationships with other agencies (how will we operate?)"

"Will new framework be one in which everyone can be open?"

"How will it affect me?; how will it change what I do, where I go?"

Question 8: "If people resist the merger, why will they?" This was an attempt to identify what potential blockages would exist if the agencies decided to proceed with the merger. The most significant was a general resistance to change. In general, board members and staff did not cite "problems" that they thought would occur as a result of resistance. They suggested that, in the main, it would be a preference for the status quo and a resistance to change that all people in all organizations experience as they undergo development. Some specific resistances were identified as follows:

"Fear of the unknown, job security and nature of new job, fear of salary cuts"

"The bigness of it—hard to get decisions made; for example, will it be harder to order supplies due to cumbersome procedures?"

"It's new and different and afraid to go for it"

"Finances—a threat to current salaries, hours worked, etc."

"Weren't involved in the beginning or haven't been kept informed"

"Questions about distance—self-supporting?"

"We're a fairly tightly knit group both work-wise and social-wise; the merger constitutes a threat to this cohesiveness"

"New policies and procedures with less input; possibly work [with] people who don't share our philosophy"

"Maybe not enough information"

"How the merger is handled and announced; are the people included in the process?"

"Need to tackle 'we versus they' feelings, especially on the part of other affiliates"

"Local identity—what's the community going to think?"

"Will it work?"

"Travel if required."

Question 9: "How would you like a larger organization?" This question was intended to have the board members and staff address the question of size. Because size is a critical organizational variable, it is imperative to have board members and staff think through the size differential right from the start. Would they be discomforted by a larger organization? Board members and staff in general said no. However, there was repeated reference in other questions, and indirectly in this one, to an interest in retaining the close-knit family atmosphere that often is related to size as a variable. It seems important to explore, right from the beginning, mechanisms to retain individual size and culture at each of the locations so as to enable the closeness of staff and board relations to continue. Some other comments about size were as follows:

"Would feel okay—have worked in a large organization before"

"Feel small; where do I fit in?"

"If not involved with merged board, would need some real sense of what is going on—direct linkage to decision-making process, not just reports"

"Feel comfortable with it—see it being done in Arizona and other parts of the U.S."

"Really wonderful thing for education—an opportunity to work in the schools, with parents, etc."

"Will help overall"

"If I'm part of the process and have a worthwhile role, it is very exciting"

"Don't know how it will affect me directly"

"Strong sense of identity as the best; what happens if others don't share the same sense of pride in work?"

"Not as well as I like a small organization; have no fears as long as the job situation doesn't get worse—people are always unsure now"

"Feel comfortable; started in a larger agency, and that was okay—may be more pressure, but overall would be positive"

"No problem as long as the people are still involved in decision-making process"

"Where will the board meetings be held?"

Question 10: "How would you describe [the organization where you work now]?" This question was intended to identify the nature of the culture at each of the organizations. Because it often is difficult to mesh organizational cultures, it was important to identify any significant differences. In general, it appears that all of the organizations have close-knit caring cultures that tend to generate a strong team spirit. This is a significant advantage to the organizations individually but may offer some challenge in creating one whole organization from the three tight-knit individual units.

The board members and staff also suggested that the organizations operate with a minimum of bureaucracy and paperwork, focusing on service and people-oriented concerns. Informality was identified as an organizational characteristic as opposed to formal bureaucratic thinking and acting. Some descriptive comments of the organizations included the following:

"Sensitive to people's needs—caring"

"Image equals a happy feeling—like to come to work"

"Strong, unified team (clinic staff)—cooperative; sees a need and tries to handle it based on individual skills and knowledge"

"It's a team effort"

"Image—Ajax white tornado, rapid pace and getting the job done"

"Image—helping hand"

"Almost like being with a family for 8 hours—we work and play together and even though it's stressful, it's a great place to work"

"Image—clown with traditional sad face"

"Family—relentless, extremely professional; we do a darn good job, and when we don't, we take a look at it"

"If there is a real problem, can call director"

"Always being speared and reacting to [the] MCC, federal government, federation, own board, medical director; our leader buffers a lot of things"

"Let's be first, and let's be best"

"Dedication to care of service and quality; we also care about each other and have a professional image"

"Flexible, progressive, intellectual (examine ideas)"

"Image—a strong boat that can weather most storms; flag might be tattered, but we get through and learn from experiences"

"Not settled in feelings of satisfaction—have a sense of the need to improve constantly"

"Assertive, intelligent, open women culture"

"Dedication to women's health"

"Astonishing amount of community support across a broad political spectrum"

"Financial concerns—are we paid enough for what we do?"

Question 11: "To what degree do people in your organization support the concept of the merger?" This was a question designed to ask directly how much support for the merger is present in the agencies. Interviewees were asked to identify their level of support on a scale from 1 to 10. In general, there is medium to very strong support for the merger present throughout the board members and staff. No one interviewed strongly resisted the merger, and many people suggested that they believed quite strongly that it was a useful action. The following data indicate where the board members and staff placed themselves on the scale (supportive of merger):

Board members: Average (6.6)

Staff: Average (6.2)

Question 12: "If the merger were to go ahead, what would help its progress?" This was an attempt to identify what tools, methods, and activities would be helpful to the boards and to the executives if they decided to proceed with the merger. The item most often suggested was clear and open communication. This communication should include the steps in the merger process, the current situation, the decision dates, and the way in which major decisions about organizational design, work activities, employee selection, and so on would be made in the future. In short, board members and staff in these organizations, as in all organizations, want to be intimately involved and knowledgeable about decisions that affect their future work lives. Some board members and staff suggested the following to help the progress of the merger:

"Keep people more informed"

"Keep people involved in decision making"

"Meet with people from other agencies and find out their concerns and expectations"

"Recognize that as the merger process proceeds, tension will arise and needs to be dealt with effectively; have already been some differences regarding name [and] structure, and we need to develop processes to deal with these differences"

"More interaction among the local boards, e.g., joint finance committees"

"Will require the effort of everyone on the board to get behind it, attend meetings, and keep informed"

"Keep regular communications (bimonthly) and let the staff become part of the decision-making process; we have not been [doing so] recently"

"Sense of celebration—this is a birth, not a death"

"Allow us to get to know other people"

"Get everyone in the same position together and discuss how it's going to work—involvement"

"Now that it's coming, I wouldn't miss it for the world (a possible downside is donor's reluctance to have funds raised locally go outside the community)"

"A 1-day retreat, which would allow us to meet co-workers and share ideas"

"Information—complete and total information, even if it appears trivial"

"Education"

"Information—and give employees a chance to influence what's happening"

Question 13: "Are there any other comments or suggestions you would like to make?" In general, not much that was new emerged from this question, although several points were made that reinforce earlier concerns. The following comments are illustrative:

"It would have been nice to have had a presentation on the merger"

"Give staff a chance to meet with board members—exchange ideas and concerns; what's it like to be in the clinic on crazy days?"

"Better communication between staff and administration [so that administrators] really understand staff needs and concerns before the staff give up on administration"

"Educational piece—hope we can spread the work; the most important thing is getting into the schools"

"What have they been doing up to now?"

"A good chairman and nominating committee—people who really know the community"

"Would be very surprised if staff members of other agencies don't resist"

"Approaching the community"

"How to put the merger together with the service concept—can't put in the perspective of costs-benefits"

DISCUSSION AND CONCLUSION

In this section, we present the concluding discussion of the data reviewed and the issues related to the merger of the three organizations along with recommendations and suggested actions. We begin with a review of strengths to highlight the favorable attributes that each agency brings to the process. The uncertainties and difficulties associated with change usually are better handled when groups simultaneously recognize and rely on their strengths.

Strengths. There were several identified strengths that would strongly support a merger, some of which also support the continued viability of the individual agencies:

1. The staff commitment in all three agencies is very high.
2. There is clearly the energy and enthusiasm to merge. It is not unwanted or forced.
3. There is a "sense of excitement and enthusiasm" about the potential of the new agency formed of three individual organizations.
4. All parties are open to the merger discussion and are participating in good faith.
5. The recognition of the potential of a merged agency is a future orientation, evidence of the need to be adaptive to a changing environment.
6. Staff are secure about their positions, even in an "insecurity-generating" merger discussion.
7. Board and staff participants in the merger discussion have a "create the future" orientation (proactive rather than reactive).
8. Each agency has a reasonably solid financial position.
9. The staffs of the boards and agencies have conducted a significant and thorough study of the possible merger.
10. Board members and staff are informed about the state of the merger decision process. Although they express a need for more information, that information has yet to be collected.
11. Consolidation can work financially. Historical data show that revenues will support expenses on a consolidated basis.
12. Administrative expenses for each agency are 20% or less of all expenses. Conversely, program expenses comprise 80% of total expenses. This indicates that no agency is top-heavy administratively.

In summary, the board members and staff of the three agencies are a committed and interested group willing to work to explore alternative futures. This is a necessary base for undertaking a merger.

Concerns. The study has surfaced the following merger-related concerns. They are expressed both as statements in need of comment/thought and as questions that require planned responses.

1. Program/service opportunities that are available *only* if the merger takes place should be identified (e.g., are there many/few?).
2. Physician support for the merger must be systematically tested and developed.
3. The physical distance between agencies is an obstacle for many reasons, as evidenced even by the merger planning process (e.g., by limited board participation from an agency).
4. Data system decisions should follow the merger decision, not precede it.
5. A management and staff selection system for the merger must be discussed and designed.
6. Does the current financial situation provide sufficient strength to assume the costs and risks of a merger?
7. What is the MCC's position relative to the merger?
8. What is the desired relationship between the proposed merged agency and the MCC?
9. In general, board members of the three agencies still need to be convinced of the desirability of merging. What process should be used to provide the information needed and to facilitate the decision making by the boards?
10. What level of autonomy, and what functions (e.g., fund-raising, public relations, program needs assessment), should remain with the local boards?
11. What actions can be identified that will enable the local organizations to retain identity in each community while gaining the benefits of the merged agency?
12. Mechanisms are needed to communicate with clinical staff and middle management about their questions and concerns regarding the merger. They are supportive but lack information and have justifiable concerns (e.g., about job security, job redesign, and future working conditions such as travel).
13. A stated goal of the agencies is to become less dependent on governmental sources of revenue. Although the agencies are moving in that direction, they remain dependent on government to the extent of 75% of income.
14. Fund-raising efforts have been successful, but there are major problems in generating contributions.

In general, these concerns and questions assume some high degree of implicit support for the concept of a merger. But more than one concept has foundered on the realities of operational detail.

Implementation is key. Along with the concerns we have expressed, the challenges of a merger will present the boards and management with "potential problems" in the human resource areas. Because people are the key to an organization, the following problems might be useful for thought-provoking and prevention-oriented discussion. Merger can result in the following:

- Reduced productivity among employees at all levels because of the psychological effects of unexpected change, uncertainty about the future, and (sometimes) a sense of betrayal by top management
- Staff reductions, transfers, and other cost consolidation efforts without a systematic approach to retaining the "right" human resources needed to achieve the goals of the new organization
- Unwanted turnover, especially among the most competent (and most mobile) managers and professionals who leave for more stable career environments or because the early retirement offer is too lucrative to turn down
- Unexpected costs of employee benefits, such as underfunded pension plans, that create either large financial obligations that had not been anticipated or employee relations problems that possibly include lawsuits if such plans are terminated
- Dysfunctional leadership struggles in the new organization because succession plans and other aspects of management development have not been thought out, formalized, and communicated to managers early enough in the merger process
- The "wrong mix" of human resource skills and talents because of superficial or incompetent analyses of people and their jobs and the new requirements of work in the merged organization

People problems are the least desired and the most troublesome to solve. Some of our recommendations address avoidance initiatives, but first we need to consider the second most important area—finance.

Financial analysis. A comprehensive analysis of the financial conditions of the three agencies was undertaken. On a consolidated basis, the results of operation for the 2 recent fiscal years would have resulted in profits of $198,913 and $153,972, respectively (two agencies). Combining these figures into three agencies leaves a net income of $101,044 for 1 year and $107,561 for the 2nd year (given the third agency's losses).

The preceding findings also are presented on a percentage basis. When consolidating the information, revenues equal 100%. Program expenses and support services use 75% and 20% of revenues, respectively. The remaining 5% is excess of revenues over expenses (at the first agency). The second agency "breaks even" by consuming the entire revenues with program expenses (83%) and support services (17%). But in actual expenditures, it looks as though for every dollar earned in revenues, 69 cents is used for program expenses and 23 cents is used for support services. The profit margin is 8 cents on the dollar (or

8%). The third clinic uses 79% of its revenues for program expenses and 18% for support services. The remaining 3% is net income.

The revenue category was broken down into governmental unit reimbursement, program, title, and nongovernmental categories for 4 years. For every year except one, the nongovernmental revenues were larger than governmental revenues. On a consolidated basis, the governmental and nongovernmental revenues each contributed approximately 50%. But in 2 of the years, the nongovernmental revenues were higher than governmental sources of income. Also noted was the high governmental revenues, ranging from 40% to 30%.

A detailed analysis of the individual program services and support services also was conducted. Looking at the program services reveals that salaries and benefits are the largest expense in each of the three agencies; donated services totaled $95,467.

The agencies rely heavily on donated services. In an effort to make the financial analysis more meaningful, a question-and-answer format is used:

Q. Does the merger make sense financially?

A. Yes. The revenues of the agencies can support their expenses on a consolidated basis. In fact, the merged agency would have generated a 5% profit margin in the fiscal year.

Q. Are the individual agencies operating in the "black" or in the "red"?

A. The recent fiscal year showed all three agencies with more revenues than expenses (i.e., in the black), with profits of $88,000, $10,000, and $1,000.

Q. Will costs increase as a result of the merger?

A. Initially, yes. There will be additional costs as a result of the merger. Some of these include the following:

- Salary upgrades for administrative staff and others assigned new responsibilities

- Professional fees (legal and accounting) incurred to complete the merger along with training and development costs

- Increased travel, transportation, and telephone costs as a result of necessary site visits

Q. Are there cost savings anticipated?

A. Yes. Savings in certain costs will result from the merger including the following:

- Centralized purchasing, allowing savings from bulk buying

- Improved services through specialization and reduction in duplication of effort

- Possible future personnel savings through normal attrition (although no lay-offs will result from merger)

Q. Will revenues increase as a result of the merger?

A. The revenue situation is uncertain. With the ever-present threat of the loss of federal and state subsidies, a stated objective has been to become less dependent on governmental sources of revenues. It is hoped that additional fund-raising, contributions, and in-kind services will be received by the agencies, and they will work toward that goal.

Q. To what extent do the agencies rely on governmental subsidies?

A. On a consolidated basis, the breakdown of governmental funding comprises one half of all revenues. For recent fiscal years, however, the budgeted figures show less dependency on governmental income. Only 40% of all revenues is expected from government, and only 35% of all revenues is expected from governmental sources after the merger.

Q. What agency relies most on governmental subsidies?

A. Historically, one agency receives 75% of its income from government-related subsidies. The second receives only 40%, and the third has been at the 50% mark.

Q. Are administrative expenses similar among the agencies?

A. Yes. Administrative expenses among the agencies comprise 20% or less of total expenses—20%, 17%, and 16%—and do not appear to be excessive.

Q. How much of the money collected is spent for program services?

A. On a consolidated basis, 75%. Among the three agencies individually, 67%, 79%, and 83%.

Q. How solid is the financial condition of the agencies?

A. On a consolidated basis, assets exceed liabilities by $1,115,000, and investments exceeds bills and other payables (including a mortgage) by $650,000. This is evidence of a good financial position. Individually, all three agencies have maintained cash and investments necessary to pay all bills three to five times over.

Q. Will the accounting system need to be changed?

A. Yes. The accounting system will need to be revised to capture the financial information necessary to prepare financial statements, management reports, tax returns, and other government filings.

Q. Are there other concerns regarding the consolidation of the financial reporting?

A. Yes. The system of internal control will need to be reviewed. The objective of internal accounting control is to provide reasonable assurance of the safeguarding of assets against loss from unauthorized use or disposition as well as the reliability of financial records for preparing financial statements and maintaining accountability for assets.

Q. Will this be a costly change?

A. The concept of reasonable assurance recognizes that the cost of a system of internal accounting control should not exceed the benefits derived and also recognizes that the evaluation of these factors necessarily requires estimates and judgments by management.

Recommendations. We offer the following recommendations as "data" for the consideration of the three boards in their decision of whether to merge. The three options presented were reviewed at the monthly meeting of the merger committee. Our favored recommendation—merge the three agencies—is followed by a set of additional suggestions.

Option 1: Do not merge. This option ignores the numerous merger advantages that are compelling (e.g., enhanced program viability, strategic positioning for the future, increased political power, and professional and career development). Its major advantages are low risk and maintenance of the currently successful status quo.

Option 2: Merge three agencies. This option is attractive because it will enhance future potential, increase political power, increase program options, and provide benefits such as career development within an enlarged agency. However, there are several negatives that could be very troublesome— physical distance between agencies with limited board participation of one agency, financial dependency of the three agencies on federal funds, and uncertainty about acceptance by critical stakeholders (e.g., physicians, federal representatives, and the community).

Option 3: Merge only two agencies. This option supports a linkage of only two agencies because of geography, size, program comparability, and so on. A disadvantage is that the third agency is willing, is interested, and was "started" by one of the other two (a humanistic rationale consistent with a service mission).

We believe that Option 2 is possible. We think that it will gain consensus as the three agencies jointly address the advantages. But the following concerns also are critical:

- Physical distance between agencies
- Leadership
- Financial viability
- Time frames
- Full participation

- Communication to boards and staffs
- Design of future relationships

Lead and supportive recommendations. We begin with Option 2 and add suggestions that we believe will assist in implementation:

1. Merge the three agencies.
2. Create a management team and a work plan to guide the future merger work.
3. Secure legal and financial advisers to assist in the merger process.
4. Retain local advisory boards to assist in fund-raising, public relations, and local needs assessment.
5. Increase and maintain high levels of communication with boards and staff regarding the merger process.
6. Use task forces to involve employees and boards to take advantage of their expertise (e.g., in finance and in clinical affairs).
7. Involve MCC representatives in the merger process.
8. Develop a plan for monitoring the progress of the merger work.

Following a decision to merge in principle, the agencies must address organizational structure and design as well as a plan for action.

Organizational structure and design. The "Questions to Be Addressed" section of the original project description contains four questions that deal with the overall design and internal structure of the merged agency. Discussion of agency design and structure is organized around these questions.

The first question is one of *quality.* Would a merged organization maximize the overall quality of the medical and educational services?

The basic design and structure of the organization, plus the day-to-day style with which the merged organization is managed, will determine whether or not the merged organization contributes to the improvement of overall service delivery. At the moment, the most important strength of the three agencies is the high level of motivation and competence of the clinical staffs. These staffs comprise the "technical core" of the organization, delivering services that are the primary mission of the agencies. In addition, because clinical staff are in daily contact with clients, they have the best fix on client reactions to services and the quality of service delivery. It is imperative that the merged organization retains this basic feature by continuing to allow staff to have a major impact on key decisions and by not encumbering them with greatly increased control from above.

Often, when a new organization is formed with personnel in new roles in the headquarters office, these headquarters personnel have many ideas about what they would like the new organization to accomplish. Certainly, many of these new ideas and insights may be "on target" and should serve as inputs for consideration. On the other hand, they should not be imposed unilaterally on the clinical staff. Instead, the staff should have direct involvement and a real chance to participate in key strategic decisions. It would be deadly for the merged unit to become a "top-down" type of organization in which the head-quarters staff propose new ideas and the clinical staff merely carry out these dictates. It is desirable that a collaborative relationship focusing on problems and issues should exist between headquarters staff and clinical staff. This approach would allow for open discussion of new possibilities and joint planning of the future so that decisions are owned by the individuals who implement them. This approach also will help ensure that new programs and services are attuned to client needs and are adapted to differences that may exist among the various clinics. In brief, the process would involve open sharing of ideas and mutual influence.

The second question is one of *presence and standing.* Would the merged organization have a greater presence in the areas of public affairs, public relations, and development?

Again, the answer to this question rests on the basic design of the organization and how decisions are actually made within the new organizational structure. The role of headquarters staff and clinical staff is crucial. Higher levels of professionalism probably result from having staff groups in the headquarters organization who specialize in areas such as public affairs and public relations, development, and fiscal management. This higher level of knowledge and skill results largely from having individuals whose primary role is to keep abreast of the latest developments within their field. These individuals also become a storehouse of knowledge about what has worked in other nonprofit agencies and the current status of programs within the total merged organization. This increased knowledge can help contribute to the development of appropriate programs and services for the agency as a whole and for local community needs.

The critical decision revolves around the type of relationship between the staff in the headquarters group and those in the local agencies. Having the staff groups assume primary responsibility for the design and execution of programs and services in each local community would cut off the local agencies' responsibility for providing critical information about their locales and for actively participating in the organizational design. A top-down approach, over the long run, would have a negative impact on the overall functioning of the organization.

By contrast, using the staff groups as a central source of information and the local agencies as program/service designers would result in higher quality service that directly reflects the needs of each community. There may be general educational and public relations programs that make sense for all local agencies. But it is important to guard against the assumption that what makes sense in one community necessarily makes sense in another. It also is crucial to give the staff in each local agency a chance for real input into the decision-making process.

The third question is one of *board structure*. What type of board structure would be more effective? Would local advisory boards promote a sense of ownership to the larger organizations?

It seems essential that each agency retain a local board of advisers. These boards should be actively involved in maintaining their knowledge of the communities and in making recommendations concerning programs and services that reflect the actual needs of clients within these communities. They also should retain the primary responsibility for local fund-raising. In short, the local boards must retain real clout in decision making. It would be dysfunctional in the long run for local boards to become mere "window dressing." Again, the role of a local board is to provide continuous active linkage between the local agency and the community regarding the needs and perceptions of existing services and those new services that the agency might provide in the future. Local boards also must make recommendations regarding what is useful for the local agency's development.

A certain number of members from the boards of the local agencies would serve as representatives to the overall board. As members of the larger board, local board members would serve as linking pins between their clients/communities/agencies and the larger organization. They also would serve as decision makers regarding policies for the development and management of the new organization. It is important that they understand their role as representatives of local community needs and clients. At the same time, these representatives must transcend individual agency concerns to make decisions for the long-term viability of the entire organization. At the outset, however, it seems very important to retain a bottom-up orientation instead of a top-down one. If local advisory boards become little more than rubber stamps for key policy decisions and programmatic decisions that have been made from above, then these local boards will not have a sense of ownership and commitment to the new organization. Local advisory board members will feel ownership and commitment only if they have some influence on key decisions (e.g., budget allocations, development of new programs, and agency policies).

The fourth question is one of *shared services*. Are shared services an alternative to merger? A valid answer to this question rests on clear definitions of *shared services* and *merger*. So far, the definition of these terms is unclear, and in fact the proposals regarding organizational design are attempts to answer them. In general, however, it does not appear desirable to create a new organization in which there is merely a sharing of certain services (e.g., purchasing).

The key to the success of the merged organization lies in deciding which functions should be centralized and which should be decentralized and to continue to allow local professional staffs and advisory boards to make decisions in these areas. At one extreme, it seems clear that centralized purchasing of pharmacy products will result in economies for individual agencies. Therefore, there probably will be no difficulty in getting local agencies to agree to such centralization. At the other extreme, it seems necessary to allow latitude to professional staff and local boards on how to run their clinics on a day-to-day basis. In between, there are a host of activities on which decisions must be made regarding operations management. The general approach recommended is to take considerable time at the formation stage of the proposed new organization to think through and decide what functions to perform and how to perform them. This process must be a participatory one that gives local board members and staffs a chance to determine their own future as well as the future of the overall organization.

One general issue runs through the discussion of specific points on overall organizational design and internal structure presented heretofore—the basic roles of the top staff of the new merged organization. So far, three top-level positions have been endorsed by the merger committee: president, vice president–finance, and vice president–program development. But it is appropriate, at this stage of the merger process, that the roles of these positions have yet to be developed.

Outlining the general activities within each of these roles rests on defining the mission and goals of the new organization. What is it that the new organization is uniquely capable of doing? How does the mission of the overall organization mesh with, support, and facilitate the delivery of services by local agencies and satellite clinics? What roles at the upper echelon contribute to fulfilling the basic organizational purpose and enhancing local service delivery? The answers to these three questions are determined by following through on the design process described in the "Plan for Action" section to follow. But it is important to emphasize that managing the merged organization will involve new top-level roles and will require development of a new organizational system (e.g., finance and communication).

Coordinating the activities of three geographically dispersed agencies, each with its unique history and culture, is a different type of managerial function from managing a local agency. The emphasis of top-level staff is on how to create and maintain an internal climate that fosters human development, creativity and innovation, and continuing pride in work. Thus, a reorientation in and careful development of top-level staff roles through involvement of both external and internal constituents is needed.

The complete array of functions to be performed by top-level management is unclear at this point. However, available information does enable us to make a tentative recommendation about the senior positions. We believe that four positions are crucial for merger start-up: (a) president and chief executive, (b) vice president–clinical services, (c) vice president–finance, and (d) vice president–program and business development. These four positions will ensure that overall management and the three critical areas—clinical, finance, and development—are covered. Other positions would be addressed by this senior team.

PLAN FOR ACTION

Our view is that the plan for action toward merger implementation should be *participative, comprehensive,* and *creative.* First, it should actively involve board members and staff in their areas of expertise (e.g., finance, clinical services). This will foster involvement in the future organization and a sense of joint ownership. Second, because the new organization will be "new" in all facets of operations, the implementation planning must be comprehensive as well. The new organization will be new in all phases of operations—some more dramatically than others. Third, board members and staff should take the opportunity to create new approaches, systems, and methods. Some will be needed to make the new organization "work." Others will surface as participants begin to think about basic "givens," such as finance and facility, in the context of a new agency. In short, many new alternatives will emerge.

To assist in the implementation process, we suggest a five-phase process with participative tasks as a key component. The following is a starting point with "adaptation to fit" expected.

Phase 1: Merger implementation start-up. The first phase will require about 1 to 2 months and involves organizing the merger implementation and development process.

1. Identify the general task for all participants—the development of a new health service organization from the individual agencies.

2. Select an advisory group of about 18 individuals (the new board) and recruit task forces of 6 to 8 board and staff persons each (task force titles: clinical services, personnel, finance, organization and management, external relations, facility and equipment, and program development).

3. As a whole group, initiate discussion to identify specific problems associated with implementation of the merger (e.g., changes in services, services reimbursement, compensation, location, facilities).

4. Develop consensus on the objectives such as the following:
   - To define the existing situation in each area
   - To identify problems and changes likely to occur in the areas during and after merger
   - To develop a vision of a desired system—the new system
   - To compare the existing elements of organization to the merged agency design
   - To create a plan for managing the change

5. Develop a work plan with procedures, schedule, and so on with an executive committee of the whole (advisory group–new board) in the lead role and with appropriate staff support.

Phase 2: Current organizational description. In Phase 2, comprehensive analyses of the current organizations are undertaken to lay the groundwork for change needs and development opportunities.

6. Identify the aspects of each area of the organization that will be the focus of the study (e.g., service systems, personnel, finances, management, and external relations).

7. Identify what information is available (e.g., merger study materials) and review methods for collecting additional required data. That is, analyze existing service data and consider collection methods (e.g., questionnaire survey and telephone interview) and research responsibilities.

8. Review the information that is needed to analyze these areas.

9. Using the data, write a report describing the current organization with respect to the task force areas such as services offered, personnel, finance, and system integration and development issues.

Phase 3: Other organizational analysis and comparison. Phase 3 is designed to encourage the merging groups to search for other organizations that can be models for their desired future.

10. Identify other merged organizations similar in character, and secure data on the relevant areas of the task forces—personnel, finance, and so on.

11. Identify and analyze relevant state and national literature relevant to the effects of development.

12. Compare the current organizational situation to that of other merged situations so as to estimate possible and desirable changes resulting from merger implementation.

Phase 4: Plan development. In Phase 4, a plan for the full development and implementation of the merger is created using the task force data as a base.

13. Identify needs for change and preparation, if any, and the order in which changes and preparations should occur.

14. Create a comprehensive plan for development including assistance required and strategies for dealing with noninvolvement and resistance to merger including the following:
    • What is to be done
    • The rationale for activities and positions
    • Person(s) or group(s) responsible
    • Dates by which activities are to happen
    • Establishment of an action schedule and method for proceeding

Phase 5: Study summary and continuation consideration. Phase 5 evaluates the progress of merger implementation.

15. Review the process and results of the implementation planning to determine (a) whether the objectives were accomplished and, if so, (b) whether they were accomplished in the manner intended.

16. Consider continuation of the procedure for other topics with new task forces (Figure 5.1). Task forces are developed in these areas. Each task force could follow a four-step procedure:

Step 1: Assess the agencies in their content area (e.g., finance and services), and create a current scenario.

Figure 5.1. Task Force Planning Group Structure

Merger Implementation Advisory Committee
(consolidated board)

|

_____ Six Task Forces _____

Clinical Services	Organization and Management
Personnel	Facility and Equipment
Finance	Program Development

Step 2: Create a "vision of the future" in that subject area (e.g., finance) in the consolidated organization.

Step 3: Compare the present (output of Step 1) to the desired future (Step 2 output) to identify gaps.

Step 4: Create a set of activities/steps to go from the present to the future (a plan of action for each area).

Case 5.4 Branches for Citibank

Many bankers continue to face the question of what to do about their branch operations. Cost-cutting leaders believe that the branches are too expensive, duplicating services that could be offered at central locations and/or through telephone and Internet connections. Holding up the quick demise of branches throughout the country is the fact that banking customers still like them. They persist in wanting to talk to bank counselors, tellers, and loan officers about their needs. This is not unusual, but they want to do these things in person.

Citibank has not made a public statement about its efforts to address this problem. But I am guessing that it has become part of their vision for the future. If it has not, then it should be. The reader should think about this as a management problem—a challenge for leadership visionaries.

In this case, we can push along the challenge. Using information from the Citibank Web site (www.citibank.com), develop a team to attack this issue— "What to do about the branches?" To add a wrinkle to the task, address the opportunity to move the bank's branches into grocery stores. In some states (e.g., Pennsylvania), grocery stores such as Giant and Weis are increasing the square footage of their stores. The stores are getting ready for possible expansion to

Internet order and delivery, expecting that they will need to become "super stores" with significant warehouse space. But some store executives have considered a vision of the store as a destination site for meeting numerous customer needs including pharmacy (long established), dry cleaning, movie rental, fast food, and (finally) banking. Sites already are developed.

What would the study group advise Citibank to do about this opportunity to put full-service bank branches in grocery stores in Pennsylvania?

Case 5.5   Motorcars and Leadership Development

Leaders of many companies recognize that it is their responsibility to develop the next generation of leaders. It is not a surprise that this task presents a problem for many management teams. What do we teach our up-and-coming managers, and how do we teach them? These questions are quite transferable across industries, and they are now very much a concern of the auto industry.

Think of the innovation and design success of recent years—the invention of the Chrysler family van (and then the sport utility vehicle), the reliability of import cars such as Honda and Toyota, the style of Jaguar, and the overall performance of BMW's 3 Series cars. How do we develop the next generation of managers to continue the industry and, indeed, to improve its capability to deliver high-concept cars with great reliability and stingy gas usage? Just what do we teach them?

If we go to a current text, then we can find a recommendation for managers/ leaders to master seven competencies: managing self, managing communication, managing diversity, managing ethics, managing across cultures, managing teams, and managing change (Hellriegel et al., 2001). We can add information on roles (Mintzberg, 1975) and key responsibilities (Senge, 1990) and engage in a spirited debate about the content and process of management development efforts. We have one quite outstanding model—General Electric. For decades, the company has taken executive development as a source of pride, as a core competency, and as a competitive advantage. Much has been written about the current chief executive officer, Jack Welch, including his approach to development. How does this affect the motorcar business?

Imagine that you are part of the executive team at the relatively new Daimler Chrysler company. You and several colleagues have been assigned to a team to develop the new leadership program of the company. You have a rather significant budget—starting at $1 million with no visible ceiling. You may use any internal or external resources you choose, freely adding expertise from both Daimler and Chrysler, from university schools of business, and from specialty firms focused on leadership. Your executive calls the first meeting to charge the team with its mission. He first gives a rousing presentation about the critical contribution of this work. Then he assigns the team the responsibility for answering the following six questions:

1. What are the objectives of our leadership development effort?
2. What will be our philosophy and approach to leadership development during the next 15 years?
3. What is the "core curriculum" (the content of the program)?
4. What will be the teaching methods, broadly defined from seminars, to job rotation, to feedback sessions?
5. Who will be the "faculty," including inside senior managers and relevant outsiders?
6. Who will evaluate the performance of our leadership development program, both short term and long term, both formatively (for development) and summatively (for judgment of success/failure)?

The report is to be submitted in 8 months in written form with oral presentations to the senior executives and the board.

Using the Web site for General Electric (www.generalelectric.com) as a starting resource and the Web site for Daimler Chrysler (www.daimlerchrysler. com) as the subject company, think about how you would structure this team's work and the eventual model it will offer to the company.

Case 5.6 Charter Schools: Organization and Management Development

As part of its strategic futures planning, one nonprofit organization requested an outside review of its organization and management. No crisis was apparent; the effort was designed to be proactive, helping the executive staff and board to continue development. The consulting group met with board members and staff, reviewed official records, and talked with clients. A summary of its report is included here.

Organization and Management of Washington Charter School Consortium: Current Status Assessment

INTRODUCTION AND PURPOSE

Education systems across the country are confronted with the need to change. The pressures for redesign affect both large and small organizations, from public schools to private academics. The Washington Charter School Consortium (WCSC) has initiated a review of its organization and management structures and processes for several purposes: to continue organization development, to respond to changes in the environment, and to foster a participative collaborative approach to designing the WCSC future.

The WCSC has developed an impressive track record over its short 5 years of operations, marked by growth in schools and increasing sophistication of education system process and managerial controls. It was founded in, and continues to be supported by, a larger university academic education center. Thus, it is based in an organization dedicated to teaching, research, and delivery system innovation. The WCSC currently is a consortium of 14 schools that receive state and federal funding as private charter schools. They are offered as an alternative to public schools in troubled districts and are operated as private nonprofits. The WCSC is the funding and management services conduit for the members. Beginning with a focus on specialized science and arts schools, the WCSC has broadened its efforts to include an expanded range of schools. The WCSC has six divisions: program curriculum, facilities, personnel, finance, legislative affairs, and management.

The objectives of this outside review were as follows:

- To collect the perspectives of board members, staff, and school directors, identifying the current status and possible actions for continuing development of the organization
- To provide an "outside opinion" to facilitate decision making by executives, board members, and staff seeking to move the WCSC into the future

While addressing the perceived need to change, the spirit of the review was that of a constructive, continuous improvement model. Board members, staff, and school representatives willingly gave time to the interviews and were quite helpful in their contributions. All persons interviewed seemed committed to the progress of the organization. The intent of the report is to integrate internal and external suggestions with an outsider's perspective, offering a thoughtful and action-generating review.

METHOD, DATA, AND LIMITATIONS

The primary method for learning about the WCSC was through official records and personal interviews. In consultation with the executive, it was decided that selected senior staff members, board members, and school representatives were to be given the opportunity to comment. Two whole group staff sessions and 35 one-hour interviews were conducted with the following:

- Executive and senior staff members
- 6 advisory board members
- 25 teachers and school directors

The interviews followed a structured question guide that targeted strengths and weaknesses of the current system, relations with the member schools, regulatory and control systems, diversity of program and service activities, and the organization's future.

Other WCSC materials reviewed included the following:

- Brochures and annual report
- Student data summaries
- Organization charts
- Member contracts
- WCSC history
- Education program evaluation protocol

Limitations. The combination of the interviews and the supplemental material provides a good picture of the WCSC. But the short time line for this review and the limited data sources (primarily interviewee opinions and some official records) require that the report not be used as a "stand-alone" tool for decision making. The report is best used to support follow-up analysis and actions by the director, advisory board, and staff, as many of the individual recommendations could be of report length by themselves.

FINDINGS

The findings of the study are arranged in three categories: technical and professional, organization and management, and culture and climate.

■ *Technical and Professional*

1. *Growing diversity of activities has emerged.* From a narrow founding focus on specialized academics, the organization has been diversifying its activities to include full teaching services and programs. The "new" services—both managerial and curricular—are within the broader theme of educational systems development and are foundation and government supported.

2. *Core competencies exist in management and systems development.* Staff have developed strong capabilities in a range of management and control systems, program development, and program evaluation (helped by the strong institutional environment of the academic center). The skills are transferable across academic fields.

3. *Static per pupil revenues appear to be a trend.* Although the stable levels represent data from just the last 2 years, this indicates the potential for significant reductions (with continuously rising costs). Although marketing refinements may "stem the tide," by adding some students, it is difficult to see the opportunity for market share growth with the current schools configuration (and the very strong local competition from newly invigorated public schools). Something will need to change. School operations probably can be made more efficient, but the greater public and political environment is a significant contributor to the reduction.

4. *Fewer resources from traditional foundation and governmental streams are expected.* We are in a political period of careful conservation in many governmental programs. The expectancy will be for tighter budgets and limited expansion, if any, unless the support for charter schools changes suddenly.

5. *Public school backlash will change referral patterns.* The move to revitalization and the growth of more private schools will push students in new referral directions. As public funding through experimental vouchers becomes available for low-income students, some faith-based schools will aggressively pursue students that they formerly avoided.

6. *Historical low-cost advantages might not hold.* Competition will push contractual costs for student services to new lows, threatening the advantages that academically based schools have had. And "new competitors" often will have higher quality physical plants, creating a double-track attack on existing markets. Students will have choices that they might never have had before.

7. *Reimbursement may be "underbilled" using current methodology.* In some cases, the cost of per-pupil services is being set to reflect the expected low reimbursement levels set by regulation. But the setting of low levels eliminates the ability to bill at higher levels. Public/private billing could possibly be increased by using a comparative rate, and some opportunities to bill for related health services are being lost. Improvements could be documented, and they may be a substantial source of gain within the existing system.

8. *The vulnerability of the existing service system has surfaced.* Developed during a period of academic center activism and social and public service, the WCSC will find its core services increasingly vulnerable to education system reform—reform that is directed by public-private competition.

■ *Organization and Management*

9. *Strong skills at systems and network building are present.* Staff at the WCSC have been able to develop financial, information system, and program evaluation models that effectively span school boundaries and program domains (across academic fields). With years of experience in relationship building and collaborative action, there is a strong capability for success in creating integrated education delivery systems (e.g., K-12 plus community college and 4-year programs). The competitive strengths of a network—quality teaching, concern for students, diversity, geographic distribution, health promotion, individual student learning plans, and quality assessment—seem to be in place.

10. *Perceptions of a strong bureaucracy of regulatory requirements prevail.* Whereas many requirements were developed through foundation and federal mandates, others have resulted from management thinking. The summation is a "perception" that teachers and member school administrators are plagued by requirements that undercut the charter school efficiency agenda.

11. *Pressures to become lean and efficient will be enormous.* The private and public "competition" will force reductions in reporting, monitoring, and

data acquisition as the competitors begin to provide school services without some of the regulatory baggage (at least for a period of time).

12. *An evolving "new" vision is partially complete.* The board and staff have been working for some years now to broaden the vision and mission of the organization. The addition of new services such as internships and scholarship searches is evidence of success. But more work is necessary to complete the vision, and this work is made more critical by the fiscal crisis facing member schools.

■ *Culture and Climate*

13. *Strong loyalty and support from board members and staff is evident.* All of those interviewed are committed to the mission and values of the WCSC. This can be relied on as a primary asset in moving through a change period. "Working as a team" is an established pattern.

14. *A "social service and academic teaching" ethos still predominates over a "business climate."* Although the distinction is shifting, the dominant values are those of support rather than the "survival of the fittest." A greater emphasis on the business tasks of building markets, reducing costs, and inventing new educational products and services will be required. Setting performance targets and achieving business objectives will need to become the operating mandate in a more competitive educational market.

15. *School member relations are historical and challenging.* Vigilant attention to the member relations is a somewhat dysfunctional artifact of the history of the WCSC. The school alliance partners now contribute 70% of the overall revenues. Managing the relations is a requirement for survival, meaning that troubled schools are a liability. Consortium partners will need to feel that an expanded vision and mission will offer them "future strengths" as well; otherwise, they will resist the change. The joint task force that produced the joint purchasing initiative appears to offer great potential as a model for a more collaborative approach with member schools, one that is more task focused.

16. *Further culture change is expected.* The "business environment" in education will become more competitive, not less competitive. Attention to new business, to streamlined operations, and to "new members" will be a survival necessity.

RECOMMENDATIONS

Recognizing that some actions are under way and that others have been discussed, the following suggestions may help the forward progress by confirming assumptions and urging action. The changes suggested represent the use of three somewhat "faddish" approaches; however, they are descriptive of the need to adapt in different ways.

- *Continuous quality improvement:* Incremental refinement of existing administrative practices such as billing and reimbursement
- *Reengineering:* Dramatic and radical changes in a process such as teaching computer and technology skills
- *Visioning:* A scenario of a significantly changed and desired future such as an extension of the WCSC into the management of a wide-ranging set of school-related services

■ *Immediate and Primary*

These first seven recommendations are viewed as needing priority attention:

1. *Reject expansion into the direct ownership of charter schools.* It does not seem that this is a currently active option. The WCSC's skills in management and development provide the member schools with services. But there are no immediately visible advantages to direct ownership.

2. *Establish a "design group" to create a scenario of the WCSC future.* Now is the time to address an expanded vision. In the group sessions, we discussed a "hub and spoke" concept. The hub is the WCSC expertise in management (e.g., curriculum development, information systems, finance, evaluation), and the spokes represent the expanding school memberships. The design group would be asked to elaborate on the concept, identifying its "other future spokes" to be developed over the next few years (e.g., joint purchasing, specialized private academies). The organizing theme may remain *education* but incorporate a much expanded set of services. Outcomes of the work would include a scenario, several important stretch goals, and a sense of how to capitalize on strengths such as the school network.

3. *Consider the benefits of conducting a benchmarking study.* A review of similar but further developed (and probably older) academic and nonprofit cen-

ters would be helpful in pushing the vision forward. Studying three to five organizations that manage a range of education and human services would provide data on revenues, structure, staffing, culture, and other characteristics. The objective is to generate further information on the range of possible products/services, revenue streams, approaches to organizing, and performance review systems. Other organizations can provide "design options" to craft a unique model for the WCSC of the future. The Independent Sector based in Washington, D.C., would be a starting point for identifying suitable organizations.

4. *Increase the formality of relations with schools/partners as part of an "enlarging organization design."* As the WCSC moves forward, existing schools/partners will be part of a larger group, one that crosses programs and fields. To successfully manage the diversity of program and reporting requirements to state and federal governments, the contract and monitoring will need to be even more quantitative. And it will need to be defined in terms of both public and business objectives. Some of the "management by personal relationship" with member school directors will be lost as the WCSC shifts from a sense of the academic community to a network of business contracts and relationships.

5. *Redouble efforts at new business development.* The development track record is outstanding. The work needed in the future will be somewhat different—a new emphasis on private giving and revenue-generating activities. The government program development and the research work would be expanded to include feasibility studies for new educational services, contract management opportunities, and (for example) a model for managing charter schools in other regions. Other potential services include day care, seniors programs, and information systems design and management.

6. *Develop demonstrations of reengineered teaching processes and curriculum.* The "process of processing students through the schools" already has become cumbersome. Long forms and significant data requests are common at several points in the process. Without quick and radical reengineering, competitors will further erode the student base by making the "customer experience" with admission, registration, and tracking easier, quicker, and less intrusive.

7. *Develop alliance and partnership "experiments."* Education is moving into (or already is in) a period of rapid consolidation marked by partnerships, alliances, and the building of integrated delivery systems. A successful future without linkages is unlikely. Because of the stakes involved in "partnering," an experimental approach is needed. Identify pilot opportunities to learn

from and build on. For example, rather than committing the whole organization to a multiyear alliance with one large powerful foundation or with educational districts, the WCSC could "try out" 1-year contracts with several systems in different parts of the WCSC network. With this experimental approach, expectations about referral streams, costs of teaching services, and revenue gains all could be tested before larger, longer term commitments are made.

■ *Secondary and Operational*

These additional recommendations are offered as important but less pressing concerns and, in several cases, are operational in nature:

8. *Redesign school director's meeting.* It appears that the alliance partners' (school directors') sessions are not meeting the needs of participants as currently designed. This is an opportunity for continuous quality improvement—diagnosis of the current meeting purposes and functioning, with the intent of generating improvement in expectations and outcomes of the meetings for WCSC staff and school directors.

9. *Establish a pilot site for new curriculum and school management testing.* To compete in the future, schools will need to do some things differently. A model school holds potential. Perhaps a site could be identified to serve as the focus for innovation and redesign. Depending on the nature of the changes, there might even be some funding available for "demonstrations." And the WCSC might use the site to examine both curricular and management initiatives.

10. *Explore further savings in group purchasing.* The WCSC already is involved in group purchasing; it is not jointly purchasing supplies. A stronger statewide linkage would provide even greater leverage with vendors. One issue to consider would be the addition of janitorial and food services to the joint contracts. There are many group purchasing resources in the area (e.g., through the hospital networks).

11. *Convert quality assurance activities to continuous quality improvement philosophy and practice.* The current teaching-oriented quality control work seems to be oriented toward the policing and inspection of historical approaches to accreditation. Continuous quality improvement transfers the responsibility from external inspection teams to teachers and administrators, ask-

ing them to document their progress toward higher quality in every aspect of their school day, from teaching to administration.

12. *Create a staff leadership development plan.* An examination of the senior staff tenure and the organization chart reveals that the WCSC has been fortunate to recruit and retain an extremely capable team. For personal and professional reasons of all sorts, however, teams do not stay together "forever." Executives and board members should consider development of a plan and process for ensuring that the WCSC maintains the same quality leadership it has enjoyed.

13. *Review the future governance structure to reflect changes in vision.* The board representation also may reflect the focus on curriculum and methods reform that has both historical and operational attention. As education activities are further diversified, board representatives must be balanced across the "product/service lines." Members must be committed to the synergy and not to programs; otherwise, "balkanization" of a cohesive organization could result.

14. *Aggressively pursue information regarding industry changes.* A final recommendation calls for stepping up the level of "intelligence data" to support decision making. The WCSC must have information on (a) who will be the key public and private school competitors of the future and what they are doing, (b) efficiency of operations such as billing and reimbursement (especially changes), (c) student referral streams, and (d) new business opportunities.

Reports such as this one can facilitate change, but there must be a follow-up process. Beginning with open discussions—executive committee, full board, and all staff members—will initiate some lively debates about the next actions. As noted, all staff members, board members, and school representatives were open and helpful in the provision of information regarding the organization. Too infrequently do organizations attempt to be proactive, searching for ways of continuing their forward process in a rapidly changing environment. With a combination of continuous improvement, some reengineering, and an expanded vision, the WCSC will be as successful in the future as it has been in its short past.

Note

1. From F. E. Kast & J. E. Rosenzweig, *Organization and management: A Systems and Contingency Approach.* Copyright © 1985 by The McGraw-Hill Companies. Reprinted with permission.

6

Solving Cultural System Problems

*Dust as we are, the immortal spirit grows like harmony in music;
there is a dark inscrutable workmanship that reconciles discordant
elements, makes them cling together in one society.*
—William Wordsworth

In each chapter, we have talked about the Internal Revenue Service (IRS) case as a way of understanding this organizational model and whole approach to problem solving and consulting. To this point, we have identified a series of problems at the IRS including *technical/product* concerns about computer capability, *structural* questions about business unit alignment, *psychological* issues related to IRS agent behavior, and *management* actions regarding planning for and making decisions about technology modernization. This final system target has us asking about the overall culture including the core goals and values of the IRS. Just "how do they do things at the IRS?" Are "customer friendly"

263

and "equitable treatment" the fundamental shared assumptions that drive the IRS's executive and staff behavior?

The Nature of the Cultural System

The final system, another source of organizational problems, is the culture of the organization—the goals, values, philosophy, and more. Kast and Rosenzweig (1985) defined this system by focusing on organizational goals in their original presentation of the model:

> Simply stated, goals represent the desired future conditions that individuals, groups, or organizations strive to achieve. In this sense, goals include missions, purposes, objectives, targets, quotas, and deadlines. However, the concept of a goal has acquired a variety of meanings, depending on the perspective of the writer. . . . One of the major problems in the analysis of organizational goals is that distinction between official goals and actual operational goals. Official goals are often stated in broad, ambiguous terms to justify the activities of the organization. (p. 179)

Whereas goals are a part of a total system of values, assumptions, and beliefs, there are other contributions to what we have come to think of as culture. In a widely used text, Hellriegel et al. (2001) cited the following dimensions of culture (Martin, 1992), an enriched view of this last of the five subsystems in our model:

> The culture of an organization represents a complex pattern of beliefs and expectations shared by its members. More specifically, organizational culture is defined as shared philosophies, ideologies, values, beliefs, assumptions, expectations, attitudes, and norms. It includes the following dimensions:
>
> - Observed behavioral regularities when people interact, such as organizational rituals and ceremonies and the language commonly used
> - The norms shared by working groups throughout the organization, such as "a fair day's work for a fair day's pay"
> - The dominant values held by an organization such as "product quality" or "price leadership"
> - The philosophy that guides an organization's policy toward employees and customers
> - The rules of the game for getting along in the organization, or the "ropes" that a newcomer must learn in order to become an accepted member

- The feeling or climate conveyed in an organization by the physical layout and the way in which its members interact with customers or other outsiders

None of these dimensions individually represents the culture of the organization. Taken together, however, they reflect and give meaning to the concept of organizational culture. (Hellriegel et al., 2001, p. 512)

This cultural dimension has been defined and elaborated by Schein's work. Schein (1993a, 1993b, 1996a, 1996b, 1997) has described the formation and maintenance of culture as problems of *external* adaptation to a changing business environment and *internal* integration of technology, climate, and structure. He indicated that culture is formed as the organization acts on and responds to environmental trends and pressures. This external adaptation merges with the internal integration of social-psychological and technical dimensions to form corporate culture.

Schein's formative characteristics of culture include the following. In our model, his points provide both clues to potential problems and points of intervention.

■ *Problems of External Adaptation and Survival*

- *Mission and strategy:* Determining the organization's primary mission and main tasks; selecting the means to be used in pursuing this mission
- *Goals:* Setting specific goals; achieving agreement on goals
- *Means:* Methods to use in achieving the goals; getting agreement on methods to be used; deciding what the organizational structure, division of labor, reward system, authority system, and so on will be
- *Measurement:* Establishing criteria to use to measure how well individuals and groups are fulfilling their goals; determining the appropriate information and control systems
- *Correction:* Types of actions needed if individuals and groups do not achieve goals

■ *Problems of Internal Integration*

- *Common language and conceptual categories:* Identifying methods of communication; defining the meaning of the jargon and concepts to be used
- *Group boundaries and criteria for inclusion and exclusion:* Establishing criteria for membership in the organization and its groups

- *Power and status:* Addressing the issue of rules for acquiring, maintaining, or losing power; determining and distributing status
- *Intimacy, friendship, and love:* Setting rules for social relationships and for handling relationships between the sexes; determining the level of openness and intimacy appropriate in the work setting
- *Rewards and punishments:* Identifying desirable and undesirable behavior

Culture characteristics are "hard to see"; thus, a casual review will not dig deeply enough to reveal cultural understanding. Because these are hard to discover without personal contact and multiple sources of information, culture is best examined through the use of diverse data collection tools including the following:

- Personal interviews
- Attitude surveys
- Focus groups
- Critical incident analysis
- Official meeting minutes
- Official records and physical objects

When a problem is diagnosed as "cultural," the issues to be addressed are wide-ranging. For example, about 10 to 15 years ago, the hospital industry became very competitive, moving from a community service paradigm to one of economic competition. Catholic hospitals developed from a set of values and traditions that did *not* include "cutthroat competition." Their "culture" was not defined by the language of war strategy, market position, customers, and the death of competitors. Ensuring that Catholic hospitals had a viable future meant paying attention to a wide range of service, structural, and managerial actions—an accommodation of culture to a changing environment. This meant confronting the question "Do we want to be in the hospital business?" The changing environment forced Catholic leaders to reevaluate their core goals and values—the very culture of their institutions.

Like Catholic hospitals, the IRS is in a similar "cultural warp." Long accustomed to acting as "tough-minded inspectors of forms and citizens," they are now asked to improve their customer friendliness. To hardened agents with long experience in chasing tax evaders, this seems like a turnabout—to put it mildly. To redefine the ways in which they behave toward citizens, they will need to engage in deep discussions of who they are and what mission they have.

Leaders, managers, and their consultants sometimes find themselves confronting problems of "corporate culture." Several cases are included here: a company's sports experience, a national research laboratory's inquiry about its culture, an auto manufacturer building innovation, a health system's failure to merge cultures, and a fund-raising dilemma for a hospital.

Case 6.1   The Softball Game

Corporate athletics is by now a regular part of the business and industry scene. But the playing field may reveal something about the corporate culture that would surprise both executives and technical personnel. If you found the following "softball game problem" in your corporation, what would you do?

The case questions are presented in three sets:

I. Diagnosis
    What is the presenting problem?
    What systems are involved?
    Who are the stakeholders?

II. Approach
    What is your plan for action?
    What personnel are needed?
    How much time is required, and who has responsibility for the solution?

III. Impact
    What systems changes are expected?
    What happens to the problem?
    What additional data are needed?

Along with the case analysis questions, consider the following:

1. How do you characterize corporate culture?
2. Is this a silly and harmless issue?
3. How do organizational ethics and staff development come into play?
4. Should an inside problem solver or outside consultant handle this case?

Table 6.1 Case Facts: Manufacturing Company

1. Business: Food industry
2. History: Established during 1920s, it has expanded greatly over the years in size and in range of products manufactured
3. Location: Northeast United States
4. Products/Services: Cookies, cakes, and flour
5. Territory: Entire United States and foreign countries
6. Customers/Clients: Public at large and corporations
7. Employees: 25,000
8. Ownership: Publicly owned
9. Revenues: $3 billion during recent years
10. Reason for consultation: Questions regarding role of sports in the organization

The case facts that were available are provided in Table 6.1.

A dispute in the company's recreational program was surfaced when participants started an argument over a *Wall Street Journal* article titled "Marathon Gossip Session? Just Say You're Training for the Olympics" (Fountain, 1989). They filed a complaint.

The article made corporate sports seem fun and entertaining. The argument started when one staffer suggested that the "O-Wimpics" (as opposed to Olympics) in the article would be better than the cutthroat softball league at their company. A colleague argued that "fight to the finish—no-holds-barred softball" was good practice for their business. Four other employees walked off wondering about that.

The Softball Game

The next day, several employees were heard to complain that the softball umpires for the company tournament had been asked to favor one division team over the others. Each umpire was promised two cases of imported beer if he favored the marketing group. Divisional business competition was at a high level, and it carried over into the sports activity. Engineering, marketing, and finance were the leading competitors in the finals of the tournament.

The corporation's "ombudsman" (the employee service manager) was presented with the complaint after two employees decided it was too "risky" to surface the problem directly with their divisional boss. He was known to strongly support the competition.

The individual actions and methods of "complaint handlers" vary from company to company. Five steps are somewhat generic to complaint handling. The employee service manager (ombudsman) in this case acted as an internal problem solver, attacking what he first thought was a simple problem. His five-step procedure was as follows:

- *Step 1:* He identified the complaint, considered the facts and context, and then reduced the complaint to a specific issue (softball umpires were bribed).
- *Step 2:* He investigated the complaint by clarifying the problem, outlining a procedure for the investigation, and (for presentation of the results) including relevant and specific recommendations.
- *Step 3:* He reported the investigation findings to the employees using a written report and a face-to-face meeting with the complainants.
- *Step 4:* He developed his recommendations by collaborating with the employees and independently suggesting alternatives.
- *Step 5:* He monitored the response plans to ensure follow-through according to the proposed time schedule.

In this case, the employee services manager began by collecting the facts. How was the one team favored by the umpires (calling strikes and balls, close calls on the baselines, etc.)? Which umpires were involved? What were the days and specific examples? Who could corroborate the statements? Throwing the game to one division would be an unfair act, but it might be symbolic of additional issues.

A secondary problem related to the negative aspects of the intensity of the competition. Was this an organizationwide phenomenon condoned by the culture "as the way we do business"?

The facts were gathered by talking to the umpires, players, and divisional managers. The allegation was found to be true. It turned out that many of the games had been "influenced." Several staff believed that this was harmless. Others suggested that it reflected poorly on their company culture. The employee services manager asked for suggestions on how to resolve it. There was rather quick agreement on a replay of the game, with consensus on downplaying the reasons. The employee services manager suggested a meeting of the two teams to clarify the problem and to reduce the negative aspects.

Some employees believed that this was a common problem in other sports activities. The employee services manager and the recreation department director decided to address the "level of competition" issue in a series of light memoranda and team discussions. Subsequent softball games and other activities were monitored over the next 3 months.

Other corporate complaints are more serious than this—sexual harassment, discrimination, dangerous physical conditions, and so on. But this recreational activity is an important part of the corporate culture that is maintained and supported by leaders (a symbol of core values). Seemingly less significant complaints often include clues to serious concerns. Here the deeper issues were as follows. Is this the way we "do business" in foreign cultures? Does this behavior match our espoused values and expected behavior? In this case, the corporation eventually addressed the problem of what level of competitive intensity is desirable.

Case 6.2 Applied Research Labs

This research and development laboratory intends to further support and increase its already successful track record of applied research. An organizational survey was used to collect data to support quality of working life and culture improvements. The case is based on an actual survey in another type of company. The results are changed to protect anonymity. Three memoranda and some sample data are included here.

The case questions are presented in three sets:

I. Diagnosis
   What is the presenting problem?
   What systems are involved?
   Who are the stakeholders?

II. Approach
   What is your plan for action?
   What personnel are needed?
   How much time is required, and who has responsibility for the solution?

III. Impact
   What systems changes are expected?
   What happens to the problem?
   What additional data are needed?

Table 6.2 Case Facts: Applied Research Labs

1. Business: Research and development
2. History: Founded in 1910, it is the oldest and largest applied laboratory
3. Location: Four lab sites (Washington, Atlanta, Boston, and Los Angeles)
4. Products/Services: Programs in space, transportation, environment, energy, health, communication, military, and oceanography
5. Territory: 60% of work is U.S. supported; projects come from all 50 states and various foreign nations
6. Customers/Clients: Public and private sector
7. Employees: 10,001 men and 3,602 women full-time
8. Ownership: Public
9. Revenues: $6.14 billion
10. Reason for consultation: Continue development of the labs and test culture

Along with the case analysis questions, consider the following:

1. Are the data topics relevant?
2. How would you use the data?
3. How would the data be fed back to departments?
4. Will this have any real effect on research?
5. Who should conduct and facilitate this project?

The case facts that were available are provided in Table 6.2.

Applied Research Labs (ARL) has been competing nationally and internationally, but leaders are aware that pressures are intensifying from the following:

- Globalization
- New technology
- Diversity in the workforce
- Strong economy
- Turnover of existing staff
- Competition for new staff

To continue to recruit and retain the best people, the culture and policies that represent it must be oriented toward high performance and high quality of working life. Believing that culture building is continuous, the leaders sought information.

ARL is focused on and organized around its eight product fields: space, transportation, environment, energy, health, communication, oceanography, and military. Use of a matrix structure groups the scientists by product and by discipline (e.g., engineering, biology, and medicine). To analyze this case, we have some information collected from scientists and staff members to review. And we have the series of memoranda written by the chief executive officer (CEO) of ARL and distributed to all members. On reading the memos and considering the data, what do we know about the culture of this lab and the purpose of this survey and follow-up work?

MEMORANDUM 1

FROM: Johnathan Morehead, M.D., Ph.D., M.Eng.
               Chief Executive

TO: Applied Research Labs

ARL has retained Welham Warrick Hopkins of Chicago to conduct an opinion survey among all our regular full-time scientists, project directors, and staff in all classifications and at all locations. The purpose of the survey is to obtain your thoughts about a variety of corporate culture, values, career, and work-related subjects. Your answers, and those of your colleagues and co-workers, will provide insight into how we might further improve ARL as a place to work. We have chosen an outside organization to do the survey in order to ensure *impartial* and *confidential* analysis.

Prior to the survey, during the months of April and May, a sample of scientists, directors, and staff representing a cross section of ARL will be asked to participate in exploratory interviews. These sessions will enable Welham to design a comprehensive questionnaire for ARL. The actual survey will be distributed to all scientists and staff members in the fall. As plans for the survey progress, articles will be published in *ARL Weekly*.

This survey is a result of ARL's strategic planning process during which we agreed to identify scientist and staff needs and concerns that would guide human resources-related programs in the years to come. In short, we want to collect valid, reliable data on the lab's culture and on career- and work-related issues from our employees.

MEMORANDUM 2

FROM: Johnathan Morehead, M.D., Ph.D., M.Eng.
                   Chief Executive

TO: ARL Scientists and Staff Members

I previously announced our annual employee survey of all regular full-time scientists and staff in all classifications at all locations. To ensure an impartial, confidential, and professional analysis of responses to the survey, an outside organization will be used to conduct it. Several organizations were considered; Welham Warrick Hopkins was selected.

Welham conducted exploratory interviews with a sampling of scientists, project directors, and staff and used this information in developing the survey questionnaire. This questionnaire will be distributed on or about October 18. Please complete it and mail it back to Welham in the postage-paid envelope provided no later than October 29.

We are very interested in identifying scientist, director, and staff career- and work-related issues, particularly as they affect our working life quality here at ARL. Your responses should be candid so that we have honest information to guide us. Both Welham and I assure you that you will not be identified by anything you say. We will only use summary data.

We hope to have the results of the survey in late spring of this year. These findings will be shared with all scientists, project directors, and staff and will be used to help guide our management philosophy and our human resources programs in the years to come.

MEMORANDUM 3

FROM: Johnathan Morehead, M.D., Ph.D., M.Eng.
                   Chief Executive

TO: Applied Research Laboratories

(Continued)

Last October, Welham Warrick Hopkins, a Chicago consulting firm, conducted a written questionnaire survey of ARL scientists, project directors, and staff. Welham is an independent, internationally known organization that has conducted comparable surveys for a number of employers throughout the world.

The survey included full-time scientists, project directors, and staff appointed prior to the end of spring. The response rate was encouraging, with an approximately 60% return, well above the 40% to 50% that we were advised was common for a mail survey.

Welham has submitted its summary of results from the questionnaire, and I am enclosing a copy of it for your information.

We also are receiving individual reports detailing survey data for each of our major product divisions. This information will be in units large enough to ensure confidentiality of the survey responses but small enough to allow these divisions to study their own situations for planning purposes. These detailed breakdowns will be disseminated to division vice presidents.

Again, I wish to express my appreciation to all who responded to the survey. This information will help ARL develop program and resource allocations for the future.

Enclosure

Annual Employee Survey: Applied Research Labs

INTRODUCTION

This report presents the major findings of a survey of ARL scientists, project directors, and staff members conducted by Welham Warrick Hopkins during late October. Welham began the project by conducting a series of group and individual interviews with a broad range of members of ARL. These included interviews with scientists, project directors, and staff in the Washington, Atlanta, Boston, and Los Angeles locations.

Using material gathered in these interviews, Welham developed two versions of a questionnaire. One addressed issues unique to the staff, whereas the other focused on issues of importance to scientists and project directors. The two versions of the questionnaire also had a number of questions in common.

Questionnaires were sent to all scientists, project directors, and staff through e-mail. Respondents returned completed questionnaires directly to Welham by "snail mail."

In all, 6,260 employees completed surveys. This represents about a 61% response rate. Because of this high response rate, Welham has a great deal of confidence in the survey results.

Some of the issues are specific to particular locations, divisions, administrative units, or job classifications. In this report, we focus on survey results for ARL as a whole.

SCIENTIST AND PROJECT DIRECTOR RESULTS

View of the ARL. Without high-quality people, ARL will not be able to compete. When asked to rate ARL as a place to work, half of the scientists and directors (50%) rate ARL as "one of the best" or "above average," whereas 27% rate it as "average." Only 8% rate ARL below the average for research and development labs.

ARL goals. The CEO has spent much time talking about ARL's mission and vision. The survey asked scientists and directors to indicate up to four strategic goals that they believe are most important to ARL. Of the goals presented, those chosen most frequently are increasing private sector projects (82%) and increasing revenue from public grants and contracts (71%). When asked what *should* be most important to ARL, scientists and directors choose professional development (80%), increasing private sector projects (51%), and increasing revenue from public research grants and contracts (39%).

Diversity. Few leaders are unaware of the diversity in the future workforce. A majority of respondents (57%) agree or strongly agree that "ARL is committed to diversity," whereas 20% disagree or strongly disagree. Among minority scientists and directors, 43% agree and 26% disagree. About half of the scientists and directors (51%) agree or strongly agree that "ARL is committed to diversity," whereas 21% disagree or strongly disagree with this statement. Recruiting female scientists has been a key objective. Among female respondents, however, 26% agree and 51% disagree.

Equipment, research support, and clerical support. Ratings of the availability of state-of-the-art equipment and supplies tend to be average (40%), whereas 35% give favorable ratings and 16% give unfavorable ratings. Speed of replacement was often written in as a problem.

Ratings of research support are mixed, with 36% rating it as good or very good, 30% rating it as average, and 34% rating it as poor or very poor. More than half (57%) say that ARL clerical support is good or very good, whereas only 18% rate it as poor or very poor.

Promotion and recognition. Scientists and directors were asked what factors were most important in promotion and recognition decisions. Respondents were then asked to rank them according to how they think these factors *should* be weighted. The largest discrepancies occur for the relative weights given to patents and project contracts/awards. On average, respondents believe that patents receive the highest weight. A discrepancy occurs for project contracts/awards, which respondents, on average, believe receive a higher weight. But respondents *believe* that patents should receive the highest weight.

A total of 42% of respondents agree or strongly agree that assignments without patent or project development potential interfere with their chances for promotion.

Salary. Ratings of salary are mixed, with 26% of respondents giving good or very good ratings, 42% giving average ratings, and 30% giving poor or very poor ratings. The majority (46%) disagree or strongly disagree that their salaries are "competitive with other industry labs."

STAFF RESULTS

Commitment to the ARL. Scientists depend on reliable and loyal staff. A large majority of ARL staff (70%) agree or strongly agree that they are committed to ARL's growth and success. The survey asked, "If you were asked by a friend about ARL, how likely would you be to recommend ARL as an employer?" In response, 65% say that they "probably" or "definitely" would recommend ARL, whereas 14% say that they "probably" or "definitely" would suggest another lab.

Ratings of job security are quite high, with a large majority of ARL staff (72%) giving good or very good ratings and only 2% rating job security as poor or very poor.

Job satisfaction. Most of the staff (72%) say that they like their jobs, and 52% rate their jobs as good at providing challenging and interesting work.

Communication. Ratings of open communication are mixed, with 35% rating ARL as good or very good at keeping employees informed, 38% giving average ratings, and 20% giving poor or very poor ratings.

Management style. About one third of all staff (31%) give good or very good ratings to ARL on "participative management," whereas 41% give average ratings and 19% give poor or very poor ratings. Ratings are less favorable on "feedback," where 20% give good or very good ratings, 34% give average ratings, and 40% give poor or very poor ratings.

Diversity. About two thirds of all staff (64%) agree or strongly agree that ARL honors its public commitment to diversity, whereas 5% disagree or strongly disagree. Among minority staff, 51% agree and 16% disagree. About half of all staff (51%) agree or strongly agree that ARL is committed to supporting women, although 16% disagree or strongly disagree. Among female staff, 42% agree and 21% disagree.

Supervision. ARL staff positively rate their immediate supervisors on job knowledge (65% good or very good) and on interpersonal relations (62% good or very good). But some job activities receive mixed ratings. These include incentives (36% good or very good, 39% poor or very poor) and offering education and training (32% good or very good, 24% poor or very poor).

Advancement. Nearly one third (30%) of all staff say that they have good opportunities to advance at ARL, 25% say that their chances are average, and 20% rate career development prospects as poor or very poor.

Training. About one third (32%) of all staff give good or very good ratings to ARL on providing education, training, and development opportunities. But many (75%) agree or strongly agree that staff members need more management training.

Salary. Whereas 38% of all staff rate their salaries as good or very good compared to the competition, 24% rate them as poor or very poor. About half of all staff (49%) disagree or strongly disagree with the statement "Salary levels are in line with responsibilities." About one quarter (24%) agree or strongly agree with the statement.

ATTITUDES TOWARD BENEFITS

Interest in flexible benefits. The survey asked scientists and staff to comment on benefits—both existing benefits and new benefits not currently offered. In response, 42% of scientists and 46% of staff members say that they agree with current benefit designs.

The survey asked which benefits employees would like to improve or add. The most frequently chosen responses are expanded health care benefits (53%) and retirement benefits (40%). Many staff members (41%) would like to add tuition benefits.

This survey was one tool used to obtain feedback from the many scientists, directors, and staff. Their input helps direct future human resource changes, and it provides data on how the university culture is perceived, as indicated by human resource philosophy, policy, and practice. These data are necessary but not sufficient to make statements about the ARL culture. What other methods could be used to confirm or disconfirm the positions taken by scientists, directors, and staff members?

Case 6.3   Innovation in the
Culture at AutoPoint

The automobile industry has changed radically during the past 20 years, having become even more competitive. Many companies build minivans, sport utility vehicles, and sports cars, cutting into established markets. One auto company determined that to survive and be successful it would need to be more innovative. Only by offering truly new designs and services could AutoPoint survive the pressure of the marketplace. This case addresses two questions. First, does the company now support innovation? Second, what changes, if any, should the company make to support innovation? The organization used both internal and external teams.

The case questions are presented in three sets:

I. Diagnosis
   What is the presenting problem?
   What systems are involved?
   Who are the stakeholders?

II. Approach
   What is your plan for action?
   What personnel are needed?
   How much time is required, and who has responsibility for the solution?

III. Impact
   What systems changes are expected?
   What happens to the problem?
   What additional data are needed?

The case facts that were available are provided in Table 6.3.

AutoPoint executives recognize the increasingly competitive nature of their industry. They believe that the company's survival rests on an ability to be adaptive to a changing environment. Importantly, this means innovation in auto design products and services and in organizational structure. How could leaders encourage innovation organizationwide—from design to manufacturing to management? AutoPoint executives organized a task force of senior managers and an outside consulting team to approach this question.

Innovation at AutoPoint

Responding to what is widely recognized as a hotly competitive auto industry environment, company leaders determined that an increase in the level of innovation would be critical to the company's success and survival. A task force was organized to address the broad question of how the company would gener-

Table 6.3 Case Facts: AutoPoint

1. Business: Design and manufacture automobiles
2. History: 85 years of service
3. Location: Northeastern United States
4. Products/Services: Auto design and manufacture
5. Territory: International
6. Customers/Clients: Drivers, lease companies, and corporate owners
7. Employees: 70,000 personnel
8. Ownership: Public
9. Revenues: $18 billion
10. Reason for consultation: Develop an innovative culture for success in a high-competition environment

ate increased innovation in all areas of corporate activity, particularly design and manufacture.

The task force was charged by the president of AutoPoint to address innovation in regard to the following:

- Design
- Safety
- Comfort
- Convenience
- Reliability
- Cost

Attention to each of these characteristics was long believed to be a fundamental element of the company's product success. The group was to address these characteristics while crossing all product lines—from minivans to sports cars to trucks to sport utility vehicles.

The task force was composed of 15 persons representing the diverse stakeholders in the company—engineers, production managers, marketing professionals, design engineers, and board members. A consultant team was engaged to assist in designing the study process and in facilitating the discussions of the group. The following methodology was developed and presented to the task force by the consulting team.

Method

The method of approach to the group's task was based on the "idealized design" concepts of R. L. Ackoff, a Wharton School professor. Briefly described, the idealized design approach has four steps, here adapted to the innovation problem.

- *Step 1:* Develop a reference scenario. Describe AutoPoint's current organizational environment with regard to its ability to encourage and maintain innovative effort. Assess the level of innovation in the auto product line.
- *Step 2:* Develop an ideal redesign. Define the characteristics of the ideal innovation-rich organization if you could redesign AutoPoint in any way you wanted.
- *Step 3:* Compare the reference scenario (Step 1, AutoPoint now) to the ideal (Step 2, AutoPoint future), developing an analysis of the gaps between them, that is, between the current design and an organization that is perfectly suited to innovation—from vehicle design to manufacture to service.
- *Step 4:* Invent ways of filling or closing the gaps, and propose the actions/activities to move toward the ideal—an innovation-supportive AutoPoint culture.

Following the presentation of this approach, the task force divided into two smaller groups. The first group took as its task the review of existing methods for identifying, evaluating, and managing innovative ideas in public and private companies (across industries). It was to design a system for collecting and evaluating new ideas.

The second group's task was to identify the total organization change needed to support increased innovation. Each group first constructed a reference scenario of the organization's current state—one on innovative idea processing methods and one on culture—and then created an ideal future and a set of actions.

Process and Discussion

The members of each group included the business environment and internal AutoPoint structure. Topics within the AutoPoint company were categorized as product/technology, goals and values, managerial climate, psychological climate, and structural incentives.

During the process, the task force used a variety of resources for reference and direction, including the following:

- Current industry literature on innovation in the auto industry in the form of texts, abstracts, journal articles, and video material (e.g., literature on car design, safety, and applied science)

- AutoPoint mission, vision, values, and strategies documents

- Consultant team input regarding other national and international projects (e.g., creativity training and idea processing)

- Information from a local university's Center for Innovation program attended by several task force members

- Employee interviews and opinion gathering (e.g., employee opinions on how innovative AutoPoint is now)

- Group member experience (e.g., with ideas in their department)

- The results of prior work on creativity by design engineers

The task force met for about 1 hour approximately three times per month, with work assignments given in between. The discussions produced several insights. First, it was apparent that the nature of what encourages and sustains organizational innovation is a complex subject and, moreover, that the many facets of it are not very well understood. Actions to enhance organizational innovation would call for initiatives along several lines, and there would be little in the way of tested and true methods to draw on both within and outside the auto industry.

Group 1's task was to develop an idea processing system and an awards/rewards program. The group began with a review of the existing suggestion program, rapidly expanding discussion to a more general program of idea processing. The flow of ideas in design engineering was mapped out, with the engineering group and marketing group taking joint responsibility for idea processing. The team used retro sports car design and minivan continuous improvement as study examples. Concern was expressed that ideas should be reviewed quickly, with minimum bureaucracy and with immediate reward for the idea presented, regardless of eventual use. Quick thank-you's were in the form of dinners. Larger awards (e.g., European vacations) would be made on a drawing basis from a pool of significant suggestions.

Group 2 mapped the current organizational climate and culture (finding minimal support for innovation) and then moved to create a description of the ideal innovation-supporting culture (as illustrated in Table 6.4). This provided the group with the design, manufacturing, and service data to match its current culture against what it believed would be the best culture for innovation (if a redesign could be effected).

Table 6.4 An Ideal Innovation-Supporting Culture at AutoPoint

The descriptors of the ideal culture for innovation, as expressed by group consensus, are as follows:

- A climate in which innovation is prized and failure is not fatal
- A corporate culture characterized by cooperation and collaboration across department and subsidiary lines; a continuing emphasis on the corporate vision, which would ensure that staff at every level understand the vision
- Working relationships of design and manufacturing engineers, department managers, and supervisors that would be characterized by (a) encouragement of new ideas, (b) autonomy in decision making (i.e., latitude for employees in deciding how to accomplish agreed-on tasks), and (c) managers offering time for employees to pursue new ideas
- A commitment of resources for innovation including, at a minimum, an effective and credible mechanism for evaluating and developing ideas, a budgeted amount of discretionary monies for the development of new ideas, and a reasonable and fair innovation reward/recognition system

---

The final step was to establish a set of strategies and action steps that would make the current culture more like the desired future. This final step produced the planned actions presented in Table 6.5.

Outcomes

How did the two groups do relative to their objectives? First, they educated themselves about the nature of innovation and processes needed to support innovative ideas. Taking a long-term view to changing the culture of AutoPoint, the task forces identified adversity to risk and some interdepartmental distrust as current problems. Recognizing seed money needs, they identified the usefulness of a pool of funds to support innovation. Interdepartmental communication barriers and value conflicts over diversification also were noted. Last, processes and procedures for managing innovative ideas were created; that is, an idea processing system was designed, developed, and tested. The system was created for the whole company—from design engineers and staff to support technicians to secretaries.

The group suggested strategies that would affect each dimension of the organization, illustrating systems thinking in action:

Product/Technical: Provide resources to maintain and encourage innovation and quick review of presented ideas (e.g., during new model development for all cars and trucks).

Table 6.5 Strategy and Actions

Seven actions comprised the defining strategies:
- To instill in the culture of AutoPoint the notion that innovation is desired and prized
- To ensure that the vision of an innovative AutoPoint is understood and valued throughout the organization
- To enhance the abilities of managers and supervisors to encourage innovation, protect creative employees, provide freedom in decision making, and develop trust
- To develop mechanisms to bridge functional barriers, engender trust, and attain a general climate of cooperation and collaboration in service of innovation
- To provide the necessary resources to encourage and sustain innovative effort
- To develop and maintain the procedures and mechanisms necessary to process ideas
- To recognize and reward innovative contributions from employees at all levels of the company

Structural: Create cross-functional bridges (between departments) using additional task forces (e.g., interdisciplinary terms of engineers; safety and environmental scientists and marketing and service professional in the sport utility vehicle redesign project).

Psychosocial: Encourage innovation and increase freedom through team building and management-employee dialogue sessions (e.g., managers led "meaning of innovation in the car industry" sessions with all employees).

Managerial: Provide a significant level of innovation funds for development and praise innovation with recognition and rewards (e.g., design and market innovation awards for in-house ideas, a $10 million innovation seed money pool).

Cultural: Instill understanding of vision and value of innovation using dialogue sessions and planning (e.g., the CEO and senior managers personally led sessions on the contribution of innovation to AutoPoint's car culture).

The set of actions to accompany this list was long and varied. For example, to enhance managerial ability to support new ideas, a seminar series was to be created for mid-level managers.

AutoPoint's effort to increase innovation indicates the multidimensional *nature* of the problem and the *necessary responses.* The identification and use of a change strategy to increase innovation that affects only one part of the organizational architecture is unlikely to be successful.

There are several implications of this AutoPoint case. First, an integrated perspective of the organizational innovation problem needs to be more widely disseminated. Second, "packages of interventions" for increasing innovation need to be created and used (e.g., ones with product/technology, structural, psychosocial, managerial, and cultural implications). Third, expectations of widespread success from single initiatives need to be diminished or eliminated. Fourth, the nature and resolution of the organizational innovation problem itself—large, complex, and widespread—needs to be considered in terms of years, not months.

How would you address innovation in your company?

Case 6.4   Culture Clash Undercuts Merger

Hospital and health systems and academic medical centers are searching for ways of surviving an increasingly tight economic and political environment. This was the reason why Pennsylvania State's Milton S. Hershey Medical Center and the Geisinger Health System merged. But after 3 years, the linkage was undone in part because of a failure to merge the two distinct cultures. Two newspaper articles (McGaw, 1999a, 1999b) summarize this real case. Using the Web sites for Penn State's medical center (www.hmc.psu.edu) and the Geisinger Health System (www.geisingerhealthsystem.com), identify the reason for the culture clash.

Article 1: "Add PSU Geisinger Flop to Industry's
Growing List of Medical Mergers" (McGraw, 1999a)

Thursday was a bittersweet day for Dr. C. McCollister Evarts, and it's not hard to understand why.

All day long, employees of the Milton S. Hershey Medical Center, an institution to which he has devoted himself for 12 years, applauded the demise of the Penn State Geisinger Health Plan that he helped create two years ago.

In 1997, merging the medical center with the Geisinger Health System in Danville seemed right. Last week, said Evarts—Hershey's chief executive officer—the opposite seemed true.

At a meeting in Wilkes-Barre on Thursday morning, the 18 men and women of the Penn State Geisinger Health System Board of Trustees voted unanimously to break up the health system.

The official time of death was 12:30 p.m. The cause was listed as incompatible corporate cultures.

Both partners in the merger were dedicated to quality patient care. However, the $1 billion-plus health care machine—three hospitals, 13,000 employees, 90 clinics, 1,000 doctors—struggled to reconcile Hershey's primarily academic and research-oriented culture with Geisinger's more market-driven culture, said Geisinger Health System CEO Stuart Heydt.

The Penn State Geisinger Health System is not the only merged health care organization with problems.

On November 1, the leaders of UCSF-Stanford Health Care, the four-hospital system formed by the merger of the academic medical centers of the University of California San Francisco and Stanford University, was undone after two years. The merged system posted $34 million in losses in two years.

"With great anguish I have concluded that, in our efforts to find bold solutions to the problems of academic medical centers, we have taken on too much," Stanford University President Gerhard Casper said.

Architects of that merger predicted $65 million in profits in its first two years. Instead, the system incurred $86 million in operating losses and a loss of $73 million on operating revenue of $1.5 billion.

Merger-related costs totaled $19 million in two years, according to California State Auditor Kurt Sjoberg. Rather than cutting staff, the system added nearly 1,000 employees—most of them to handle merging the technology of the system. The cost of doing that job jumped from an estimated $25 million to $126 million.

Not long after the UCSF-Stanford deal breakup was announced, Irving-based Texas Health Resources and Baylor Health System in Dallas decided against a long talked about merger that would have created an 18-hospital system.

Officials from the systems felt the integration process would have taken too long and diverted too much attention from system operations.

Closer to home, Allegheny Health System, a nonprofit, Pittsburgh-based health care giant, aggressively expanded its empire to include nine Philadelphia-area hospitals and a multifaceted medical school program as the University of the Health Sciences.

In doing so, it stretched its funding sources too thin and began building debt that reached $1.5 billion by the summer of 1998, when it filed for bankruptcy.

All of its nine hospitals—Hahnemann, Medical College of Pennsylvania, Graduate, St. Christopher's, City Avenue, Parkview, Elkins Park, and Bucks County in Pennsylvania and Rancocas Hospital in New Jersey— were put up for sale.

A year later, the Western Pennsylvania Healthcare System in Pittsburgh bought Allegheny's four remaining hospitals. In October, the University of Pennsylvania Health System announced it would cut 975 positions in November, with 750 more to come later in the fiscal year as part of a cost-cutting campaign designed to improve financial results by $250 million. The system lost $198 million on $1.9 billion for the fiscal year ended June 30. By the end of fiscal year 2000, the system said, it will have eliminated 2,800 positions, or 20 percent of its workforce.

Unlike many of those mergers, the Penn State Geisinger Health System, with its low debt, ready cans and assets, and good reputation, was on solid financial footing. It was the culture clash disease that ultimately claimed the organization. It is a disease known well in merger circles.

Hill and Knowlton, the giant New York public relations firm, studied mergers and issued a 1998 report in which it concluded that one third of failed mergers fail due to nonfinancial reasons; furthermore, researchers wrote, "culture differences" are the major nonfinancial reason for a deal's failure. About 10.2 percent of deals founder due to the problem.

The clashes are not always fatal.

A merger between Yew York University and Mount Sinai Medical Center was completed In August 1998 after months of delays due to lawsuits filed by NYU faculty.

In the summer of 1998, Baptist Health Systems of South Florida Coral Gables and Mercy Health System in Miami called off a full-asset merger because Baptist performs abortions at one of its hospitals.

Dr. Roger Bulger, president of the Association of Academic Health Centers and who keeps tabs on health care mergers, said he was surprised by the breakup of Penn State Geisinger Health System.

"I felt this was a merger made in heaven," he said. "It seemed almost perfect. They were not competitors. Both were not-for-profit. . . . I thought they would be culturally close enough to pull this off."

Robert Dickler, senior vice president for health care affairs for the Association of American Medical College, said "cultures are difficult to change and difficult to meld."

"You take well-established businesses that have their style of doing business, different value systems, different perspectives on the world," he said, "and say let's put them together and have it all work efficiently and effectively. . . . That's very hard to do, not only in health care but in all economic sectors."

In a 1995 *Business Week* magazine article, Toronto consultant Kenneth W. Smith said one reason for culture-related failures is that the players "often stack the odds against success by rushing headlong into mergers and acquisitions for the wrong reasons in search of synergies that don't exist."

"Finally," Smith said, "and this is the real deal killer, they fail to effectively integrate the two companies after the toasts have been exchanged. Good post-integration rarely makes a bad deal work. Bad execution almost always wrecks one that might have had a shot."[1]

Article 2: "PSU Geisinger Split: Patient Care
Unaffected at Hershey, Danville" (McGraw, 1999b)

They were described as the perfect couple, and their marriage was considered a match made in health care heaven.

Yesterday, however, 28 months after Penn State's Milton S. Hershey Medical Center and Geisinger Health System in Danville merged to create the Penn State Geisinger Health System, those partners officially filed for divorce.

Citing a clash of cultures between the two institutions, the 18 members of the board of directors voted unanimously to dissolve the 1997 merger. The motion to dissolve came from Edward Junker, III, president of Penn State's board of trustees.

Starting today, Hershey Medical Center is once again under the management of Penn State University, and Geisinger Medical Center in Danville is under Geisinger Health System. Lawyers hope to officially untangle the merged assets by June 30.

The state attorney general's office, meanwhile, will work to ensure that some $30 million in charitable trusts are directed to the causes for which they were originally intended.

It was an amicable parting, officials from both organizations said.

"I think both partners believe we can better serve future patients and better achieve our goals on our own," said Penn State President Graham Spanier.

Patient care will not be affected, officials say. Treatment for patients now in the hospital will not be interrupted.

When plans for the merger were announced on January 17, 1997, officials gushed about how right the organizations were for each other.

Both were formed by the generosity of rich benefactors—Milton S. Hershey and Abigail Geisinger—and were led by physicians. Both were homegrown Pennsylvania institutions that shared the values of academic excellence and research, complementary geography, and economic strength.

At the time, architects of the merger, such as Dr. C. McCollister Evarts and Dr. Stuart Heydt, the chief executive officers of the Hershey and Geisinger organizations, respectively, agreed that merging would allow both institutions to survive in the increasingly competitive health care environment.

"Penn State Geisinger Health System will be at the forefront," Evarts said in 1997.

In fact, the merged organization was formidable, comprising more than 13,000 employees; 77 clinics; three major hospitals, including the Wyoming Valley Medical Center in Wilkes-Barre; a drug-and-alcohol rehabilitation facility; access to about 1,000 physicians; net revenues of more than $1 billion annually; and nearly 1,2000 licensed hospital beds.

With academic medical centers under tighter and tighter financial constraints, including an increased load of uncompensated indigent care, and given the fact that Penn State's College of Medicine gets less money from its home state than any of the nation's 75 public medical schools, there was a strong feeling that bigger was better.

"What we were looking for three years ago was a broader financial base," said Spanier at a press conference at Hershey Medical Center last night.

The merger accomplished that to some degree.

Despite well publicized operating losses of $21 million in its first year of business and $31 million last year, and despite the recent announcement that up to 600 jobs would be eliminated and several rural clinics closed, officials say the breakup was not about money.

To the contrary, the organization was on solid financial footing, according t independent financial analysts. Health system officials said the organization even posted operating profits in the first three months of the current fiscal year.

The cause of this breakup was closer to newlyweds fighting over the television remote.

Many at Hershey Medical Center referred to it as a culture clash pitting Hershey, an academic institution with a heavy emphasis on research, against Geisinger's more market-driven approach.

Specifically, many doctors at Hershey Medical Center said they came to Hershey to do research but that since the merger they had been pressured—as a result of Geisinger's influence, they believed— to spend more time in the clinic and less time in the laboratory and classroom.

"At a time when there are external forces that are really pushing us to make very difficult choices, Penn State understandably looked at their first priority as education. And we inevitably looked at our first priority as patient care," said Heydt during a news conference at the Wyoming Valley Medical Center in Wilkes-Barre yesterday.

"In our circumstances, bigger was not better," added Heydt, who will stay on indefinitely as CEO of Geisinger Health System.

Spanier said the College of Medicine "will survive and thrive. . . . We will have to do that now with a smaller base. It's now completely up to us to make it happen within our value system."

They were other concerns about the merger.

Hershey workers, once employed by Penn State University, lost benefits—including the cherished 75 percent Penn State tuition benefit—when they went to work for the new health system.

Spanier announced yesterday that the tuition reimbursement will be restored.

As for Evarts, who labored long and hard in support of the merger, there was a touch of sadness.

"This is a bittersweet moment for me," Evarts said. "I would proudly defend the merit of it when we did it. I think right now, given the circumstances and given the way our environment has changed so rapidly, that this is the right decision."

"It wasn't a case of when it went wrong," said Frank Henry, chairman of the Penn State Geisinger Foundation board. "It was when we saw it could go better. And I think that's what drove the decision for both Penn State and ourselves."[1]

Many mergers do not work. Driven by expected financial returns, the consolidation of two companies frequently is undercut by neglect of the cultures.

Case 6.5   Diversity in the Corporate Culture: Office Logistics and Supply

Maria Juarez talked to her friend Donna about equity in her office. Her company, Office Logistics and Supply, sold office supplies and equipment to a wide range of private companies and public agencies. Her district included Maryland, the District of Columbia, and northern Virginia. She was a marketing representative with a strong career drive. The district supervisor had been very nice to her on hiring and remarked at the time that it was "great to have a woman and a Hispanic, no less, in the business." Maria had long grown accustomed to snide comments about her gender and race, and she just sloughed it off.

Three sales manager positions had come open during the past 2 years. She was eligible and applied for each one, but she did not get any of the jobs. After the third selection was made, she went to the district manager and asked directly what the problem was.

Although he made no direct references, he did suggest that it was important to have a good match between the personnel coordinating the team and the makeup of the team. He did not offer to explain this, and Maria did not follow up with additional questions.

She remarked to her friend that, in part, she was afraid that she already knew the answer. She was unsure about how the company felt with regard to race and gender diversity, and she wanted first to know what the official positions were as well as what informal actions have been taken in the past. She also wanted advice on how to handle the problem.

At the same time, she remarked that her husband was an attorney who was active in civil rights. If she did not get satisfaction within the company, then she intended to take it further and expected to receive full support at home.

How would your team solve this problem?

Case 6.6 *Cultural Ethics and Values in a Nonprofit*

Who should be allowed to contribute funds to a nonprofit organization? Almost anyone, given the needs of sick patients, students, citizens, and the poor and disabled. This is an easy question to answer. But the following case illustrates that the question can be complex. What would be the policy at your university (or hospital or other nonprofit)—a policy consistent with your organization's culture and values?

At the opening of the university's board of trustees meeting, one member mentioned an article from the *New York Times* regarding corporate ethics. In a column titled "Goodfella's Good Works" (Cohen, 2001), the following was used to present the problem: "I am on the board of a health facility raising funds for a necessary extension. A local businessman with known ties to organized crime has offered a substantial donation. Should we take the money?"

The university board member said, "We have an almost identical problem. It seems that the state agency for environmental protection has caught one of our energy corporations—drilling, digging, and refining—in a blatant case of pollution, ignoring both state and federal regulations regarding disposal of waste. The fine, $15 million, is intended to send a message. But this has become *our* problem."

Other board members looked puzzled. "Why is it our problem?" one asked.

"Well, the chairman of the board of the energy company came to me to ask if we would be interested in a donation. I said, 'Of course—we always are.' And you know he has been one of our high-profile alumni with quite a strong track record of supporting our engineering programs in past years."

"I still don't understand the problem," said another board member impatiently.

"I'm getting to it. It seems that the CEO would like to propose to the state agency for environmental protection, and to the governor, that his company's $15 million fine be used to endow a school of pollution control in the engineering college. His company would receive some good public relations and perhaps a tax write-off, although his attorneys were not sure. He wants to know before he negotiates this settlement—will we take the money?"

So, if this were the board of your nonprofit university (or hospital or other nonprofit if another type of donation was involved), would you take the money? If so, would there be constraints? If not, why not?

Notes

1. From J. McGraw, "PSU Geisinger flop to industry's growing list," *Sunday Patriot News 11/21/99*. Copyright © The Patriot-News. Reprinted with permission.

2. From J. McGraw, *"PSU Geisinger flop to industry's growing list," Sunday Patriot News 11/19/99*. Copyright © The Patriot-News. Reprinted with permission.

References

Ackoff, R. L. (1981). *Creating the corporate future: Plan or be planned for.* New York: John Wiley.

Ackoff, R. L. (1987). *The art of problem solving.* New York: John Wiley.

Ackoff, R. L. (1993). Rethinking education. *Journal of Management Consulting, 7*(4), 3-8.

Badaracco, J. L. (1998, March-April). The discipline of building character. *Harvard Business Review,* pp. 115-125.

Bates, D. L., & Dillard, J. E., Jr. (1993). Strategy implementation hurdles: A diagnostic paradigm. *Journal of Management Consulting, 7*(3), 18-21.

Bergholz, H. (1999). Do more than fix my company. *Journal of Management Consulting, 10*(4), 29-34.

Berry, J. (1999). Does management consulting really have a "behavioral side"? *Journal of Management Consulting, 10*(3), 22-24.

Biebuyck, J., & Ziegenfuss, J. T. (1992). How physicians can create their future. *Physician Executive, 18*(4), 31-36.

Bigelow, M. S. (1994, Spring). Customer focus: An internal revenue service priority. *Tapping the Network Journal,* pp. 20-21.

Birnbaum, J. H. (1998, April 13). Unbelievable! The mess at the IRS is worse than you think. *Fortune,* pp. 98-110.

Blake, R. W., & Mouton, J. S. (1982). *Consultation.* Englewood Cliffs, NJ: Prentice Hall.

Bovard, J. (1998, April 14). How the IRS repays a citizen's taunt. *The Wall Street Journal,* p. 1.

Bowers, W. B., & Degler, W. P. (1999). Engaging engagement. *Journal of Management Consulting, 10*(4), 23-28.

Brown, F. W. (1998). An approach to organizational intervention. *Journal of Management Consulting, 10*(1), 46-40.

Burrington, D. D. (1985). Development of management consulting capability in the Utah Division of Personnel Management. *Public Personnel Management, 14*(2), 139-151.

Cahoon, A. R. (1993). The search conference technique: An organizational development tool for strategic planning. In R. T. Golembiewski (Ed.), *Handbook of organizational consultation.* New York: Marcel Dekker.

Canback, S. (1999). The logic of management consulting (Part 2). *Journal of Management Consulting, 10*(3), 3-12.

Champy, J. (1995). *Reengineering management.* New York: HarperBusiness.

Cherns, A. B. (1975). *The quality of working life* (Vol. 2). New York: Free Press.

Chisholm, R., & Ziegenfuss, J. T. (1986a, Spring). *An overview of community-wide labor-management committees* [Newsletter]. Center for the Quality of Working Life.

Chisholm, R. F., & Ziegenfuss, J. T. (1986b). A review of applications of the sociotechnical systems approach to health care organizations. *Journal of Applied Behavior Science, 22,* 315-327.

Coates, N. (1997). A model for consulting to help effect change in organizations. *Nonprofit Management and Leadership, 8,* 157-169.

Cohen, R. (2001, February 11). Goodfella's good works. *New York Times Magazine,* pp. 33-36.

Collins, J. (1999, July-August). Turning goals into results: The power of catalytic mechanisms. *Harvard Business Review,* pp. 70-82.

Cook, T. D., & Campbell, D. T. (1979). *Quasi-experimentation: Design and analysis issues for field settings.* Boston: Houghton Mifflin.

Cooper, O. (1992). Technically based management consulting. *Journal of Management Consulting, 7*(2), 62-63.

Covin, T. J., & Fisher, T. V. (1991). Consultant and client must work together. *Journal of Management Consulting, 6*(4), 11-19.

Cowan, D. A. (1993). An executive map of organizational problems. In R. T. Golembiewski (Ed.), *Handbook of organizational consultation.* New York: Marcel Dekker.

Cummings, T. G. (1993). Sociotechnical systems consultation. In R. T. Golembiewski (Ed.), *Handbook of organizational consultation.* New York: Marcel Dekker.

Cummings, T. G., & Srivastva, S. (1977). *Management of work.* Kent, OH: Kent State Press.

Cummings, T. G., & Worley, C. G. (2001). *Organization development and change.* Cincinnati, OH: South-Western.

Daft, R. L. (1998). *Essentials of organization theory and design.* Cincinnati, OH: South-Western.

Davidson, K. L. (1997, November-December). When consultants and clients clash. *Harvard Business Review, 75*(6), 22.

Dennis, A. (1999). Consulting to lawyers and families. *Journal of Accountancy, 187*(3), 68-72.

Drozodow, N. (1997). Consulting in a constellation of advice-givers. *Journal of Management Consulting, 9*(4), 48-52.

Fishman, R. G., & Moses, S. A. (1999, Winter). An incremental process of software implementation. *Sloan Management Review,* pp. 39-52.

Fountain, J. W. (1989, June 16). Marathon gossip session? Just say you're training for the Olympics. *Wall Street Journal,* p. 1.

Fox, W. (1995). Sociotechnical systems principles and guidelines. *Journal of Applied Behavioral Science, 31*(1), 91-106.

French, J., & Raven, B. (1968). The bases of social power. In D. Cartright & A. Zarder (Eds.), *Group dynamics.* New York: Harper & Row.

French, W. L., & Bell, C. H. (1990). *Organization development: Behavioral science interventions for organization improvement* (4th ed.). Englewood Cliffs, NJ: Prentice Hall.

Fuqua, D. (1993). Conceptual models in organizational consultation. *Journal of Counseling and Development, 71,* 607-619.

Galbraith, J. (1973). *Designing complex organizations.* Reading, MA: Addison-Wesley.

Garvin, D. A. (1998, Summer). The process of organization management. *Sloan Management Review,* pp. 33-50.

Gebelein, S. H. (1989). Profile of an internal consultant: Roles and skills for building client confidence. *Training and Development Journal, 43*(3), 52-59.

Gilmore, T. N. (1993). Issues in ending consultancies. In R. T. Golembiewski (Ed.), *Handbook of organizational consultation.* New York: Marcel Dekker.

Golembiewski, R. T. (1993). Giving effective feedback: Stakeholders in consultation. In R. T. Golembiewski (Ed.), *Handbook of organizational consultation.* New York: Marcel Dekker.

Goodall, H. L., Jr. (1984). The status of communication studies in organizational contexts: One rhetorician's lament after a year-long odyssey. *Communications Quarterly, 32,* 133-147.

Gose, B. (1999, May 7). Colleges turn to consultants to shape the freshman class. *Chronicle of Higher Education,* pp. A49-A52.

Greenbaum, T. L. (1987). *The practical handbook and guide to focus group research.* Lexington, MA: Lexington Books.

Greenwood, D. J., & Levin, M. (1998). *Introduction to action research.* Thousand Oaks, CA: Sage.

Greiner, L. E., & Metzger, R. O. (1983). *Consulting to management.* Englewood Cliffs, NJ: Prentice Hall.

Hambrick, R. S., Jr., & McMillan, J. H. (1989). Using focus groups in the public sector: A tool for academics and practitioners. *Journal of Management Science and Policy Analysis, 6*(4), 44-53.

Hamel, G., & Prahalad, C. K. (1993). *Competing for the future.* Boston: Harvard Business School Press.

Hammer, M., & Champy, J. (1993). *Reengineering the corporation.* New York: HarperBusiness.

Hammer, M., & Stanton, S. (1999, November-December). How process enterprises really work. *Harvard Business Review,* pp. 108-118.

Hannabus, S. (1987). The importance of user studies. *Library Review, 36,* 122-125.

Harrison, M. I. (1994). *Diagnosing organizations.* Thousand Oaks, CA: Sage.

Hayes, P., & Setton, D. (1998, May 14). McKinsey 101. *Forbes,* pp. 130-136.

Hellriegel, D., Slocum, J. W., & Woodman, R. W. (1998). *Organizational behavior* (8th ed.). Cincinnati, OH: South-Western.

Hellriegel, D., Slocum, J. W., & Woodman, R. W. (2001). *Organizational behavior* (9th ed.). Cincinnati, OH: South-Western.

Herbst, P. G. (1970). *Behavior Worlds.* London: Tavistock Institute.

Heyssel, R. M. (1989). Changing environment and the academic medical center: The Johns Hopkins Hospital. *Academic Medicine, 64*(1), 7-11.

Hiscock, J. E. (1986). Does library usage affect academic performance? *Australian Academic and Research Libraries, 17,* 207-214.

International Council of Management Consulting Institutes. (1994). *The management consulting future.* Washington, DC: Author.

Jackson, M. C. (1995). Beyond the fads: Systems thinking for managers. *Systems Research, 12,* 25.

Jacobsen, I. C. (1990). What makes PPC succeed. *Journal of Management Consulting, 6*(1), 24-28.

Jacques, C. H. M., Bauer, L. C., & Ziegenfuss, J. T. (1993). Characteristics of strong departments of family medicine: Results of a Delphi survey. *Family Medicine, 25,* 256-261.

Jang, Y. (1998). Factors influencing the success of management consulting projects. *International Journal of Project Management, 16*(2), 67-72.

Kampmier, C. (1997). High impact consulting: How clients and consultants can leverage rapid results into long-term gains. *Journal of Management Consulting, 9*(4).

Kast, F. E., & Rosenzweig, J. E. (1970). General systems theory: Applications for organization and management. *Academy of Management Journal, 15,* 452-456.

Kast, F. E., & Rosenzweig, J. E. (1985). *Organization and management: A systems and contingency approach* (4th ed.). New York: McGraw-Hill.

Katz, D., Gutek, B., Kahn, R., & Barton, E. (1975). *Bureaucratic encounters.* Ann Arbor: University of Michigan, Institute for Social Research.

Katz, D., & Kahn, R. L. (1978). *The social psychology of organizations* (2nd ed.). New York: John Wiley.

Kelley, J. (1995, November-December). Lockheed flies into action to assuage urgent ergonomic issues. *Journal of Business Strategy, 16*(6), 11-13.

Kerr, S. (1995). On the folly of rewarding A while hoping for B: More on the folly. *Academy of Management Executive, 9*(1), 7-16.

Kesner, I. F., & Fowler, S. (1997, November-December). When consultants and clients clash. *Harvard Business Review,* pp. 22-38.

Kipping, M. (1999). American management consulting companies in Western Europe, 1920-1990: Products, reputation, and relationships. *Business History Review, 73,* 190-220.

Kolenko, T. A. (1994). Academic consulting teams: A case example and team management guidelines. *Journal of Education for Business, 70*(1), 38-41.

Krueger, R. A. (1988). *Focus groups: A practical guide for applied research.* Newbury Park, CA: Sage.

Kuhnert, K. W. (1993). Survey/Feedback as art and science. In R. T. Golembiewski (Ed.), *Handbook of organizational consultation.* New York: Marcel Dekker.

Lacey, M., & Samuels, N. (2000). Why quality professionals clash with other consultants. *Journal for Quality and Participation, 23*(3), 57-60.

Laffie, L. S. (1997). The National Commission on Restructuring the Internal Revenue Service. *Tax Adviser, 28*(8), 473.

Lear, J. A. (1993, November). Reinventing the Internal Revenue Service: IRS and the National Performance Review. *National Public Accountant,* pp. 8, 16.

Lear, J. A. (1996, November). The Internal Revenue Service: Bash it or better it? *National Public Accountant,* p. 8.

Lightbown, T. H. (1993). Fostering international reciprocity through a uniform body of knowledge. *Journal of Management Consulting, 7*(3), 52-60.

Lippitt, G. L. (1975). The trainer's role as an internal consultant. *Journal of European Training, 4,* 237-246.

Lippitt, R., & Lippitt, G. L. (1975). Phases in the consulting process. *Journal of European Training, 4,* 263-273.

Lipton, M. (1996). When clients resist change. *Journal of Management Consulting, 9*(2), 16-21.

Long, C. (1999). To create value, first understand your client. *Journal of Management Consulting, 10*(4), 12-19.

Lundberg, C. C. (1993). Knowing and surfacing organizational culture: A consultant's guide. In R. T. Golembiewski (Ed.), *Handbook of organizational consultation.* New York: Marcel Dekker.

Lundberg, C. C. (1994). Transactions and games in consultant-client relations. *Journal of Management Consulting, 8*(1), 3-7.

Martin, J. (1992). *Cultures in organizations.* New York: Oxford University Press.

Massie Mara, C., & Ziegenfuss, J. T. (2000). Creating the strategic future of long-term care organizations. *Care Management Journal, 2*(2), 116-124.

McConkie, M. L., & Boss, R. W. (1994). Using stories as an aid to consultation. *Public Administration Quarterly, 17,* 377-395.

McGraw, J. (1999a, November 21). Add PSU Geisinger flop to industry's growing list of medical mergers. *Sunday Patriot News,* p. A1. (Harrisburg, PA)

McGraw, J. (1999b, November 19). PSU Geisinger split: Patient care unaffected at Hershey, Danville. *Harrisburg Patriot,* p. A1. (Harrisburg, PA)

McGrath, J. E. (1982). Introduction. In J. E. McGrath, J. Martin, & R. A. Kulka (Eds.), *Judgment calls in research.* Beverly Hills, CA: Sage.

McKenna, C. K. (1990). Using focus groups to understand library utilization: An open systems perspective. *Journal of Management Science and Policy Analysis, 7,* 316-329.

McLean, G. N., & Sullivan, R. L. (1993). Essential competencies for internal and external OD consultants. In R. T. Golembiewski (Ed.), *Handbook of organizational consultation.* New York: Marcel Dekker.

Mick, C. K. (1980). Toward usable user studies. *Journal of the American Society for Information Science, 10,* 345-356.

Miller, J. B., & Brown, P. B. (1995). The corporate coach: How to build a team of loyal customers and happy employees. *Journal of Management Consulting, 8*(3), 64.

Minto, B. (1998). Think your way to clear writing (Part 2). *Journal of Management Consulting, 10*(2), 45-54.

Mintzberg, H. (1975, July-August). The manager's job: Folklore and fact. *Harvard Business Review,* pp. 49-61.

Mintzberg, H. (1994, Fall). Rounding out the manager's job. *Sloan Management Review,* pp. 11-27.

Mitchell, R. K., Agle, B. R., & Wood, D. J. (1997). Toward a theory of stakeholder identification and salience: Defining the principle of who and what really counts. *Academy of Management Review, 22,* 853-886.

Mitroff, I. (1983). *Stakeholders of the organizational mind.* San Francisco: Jossey-Bass.

Moline, T. (1990). Upgrading the consultant. *Journal of Management Consulting, 6*(2), 17-22.

Morrell, K., & Simonetto, M. (1999, May). Managing retention at Deloitte Consulting. *Journal of Management Consulting, 10*(3), 55-61.

Nadler, D. A., Gerstein, M. S., Shaw, R. B., & Associates. (1992). *Organizational architecture.* San Francisco: Jossey-Bass.

Nadler, D., & Tushman, M. (1980). A model for diagnosing organizational behavior. *Organizational Dynamics, 9*(2), 35-51.

National Commission on Restructuring the IRS. (1997). *Reforming the IRS.* Washington, DC: Author.

Norris, D. B. (1994). Agreements help make the practice. *Journal of Management Consulting, 8*(2), 33-38.

Oakley, K. (1994). Consultancies need a "brains" approach. *Journal of Management Consulting, 8*(2), 3-6.

Old, D. R. (1995). Consulting for real transformation, sustainability, and organic form. *Journal of Organizational Change Management, 8*(3), 6-17.

Organization Development Institute. (1981). *Improving profits through organization development* [Brochure]. Cleveland, OH: Author.

Ott, J. S. (1989). *The organizational culture perspective.* Pacific Grove, CA: Brooks/Cole.

Paisley, W. J. (1968). Information needs and uses. In *Annual review of information science and technology.* Chicago: Encyclopedia Britannica.

Palmer, P. J. (1998). *The courage to teach.* San Francisco: Jossey-Bass.

Pasmore, W. A. (1988). *Designing effective organizations: The sociotechnical systems perspective.* New York: John Wiley.

Phillips, B. (1999, March-April). Are the IRS districts being eliminated? *National Public Accountant,* p. 6.

Pick, P. J. (1992). Relationships: The critical success factor in building a management consulting practice. *Journal of Management Consulting, 7*(2), 3-5.

Prager, K. P. (1992). Ethical decisions: Recognizing right and wrong. *Journal of Management Consulting, 7*(2), 15-29.

Pringle, E. G. (1998). Do proprietary tools lead to cookie cutter consulting? *Journal of Management Consulting, 10*(1), 3-8.

Puri, S. (1997, Fall). Dangerous company: The consulting powerhouses and the business they save and ruin. *Sloan Management Review,* pp. 103-105.

Quick, J. C., & Kets de Vries, M. F. R. (2000, February). The next frontier: Edgar Schein on organizational therapy—Commentary on the Schein interview. *Academy of Management Executive,* pp. 31-49.

Radin, B. A. (1988). New directions in research. *Journal of Management Science and Policy Analysis, 6*(1), 6-13.

Reason, P., & Bradbury, H. (Eds.). (2001). *Handbook of action research.* Thousand Oaks, CA: Sage.

Rice, S. A. (1931). *Methods in social science.* Chicago: University of Chicago Press.

Ridley, C. (1993). Putting organizational effectiveness into practice: The preeminent consultation task. *Journal of Counseling and Development, 2,* 72.

Ross, R. S., & Johns, M. E. (1989). Changing environment and the academic medical center: The Johns Hopkins School of Medicine. *Academic Medicine, 64*(1), 1-6.

Sabath, R. E. (1992). Establishing alliances. *Journal of Management Consulting, 7*(2), 10-14.

Sartain, L. (1998). Why and how Southwest Airlines uses consultants. *Journal of Management Consulting, 10*(2), 12-17.

Schaffer, R. H. (1995). Consulting for results. *Journal of Management Consulting, 8*(4), 44-52.

Schaffer, R. H. (1997). Looking at the 5 fatal flaws of management consulting. *Journal for Quality and Participation, 20*(3), 44-51.

Schaffer, R. H., & Thomson, H. A. (1992, January-February). Successful change programs begin with results. *Harvard Business Review,* pp. 80-90.

Schein, E. H. (1987). *Process consultation* (Vol. 2). Upper Saddle River, NJ: Pearson.

Schein, E. H. (1990). Organizational culture. *American Psychologist, 45,* 109-119.

Schein, E. H. (1993a). Models of consultation: What do organizations of the 1990s need? In R. T. Golembiewski (Ed.), *Handbook of organizational consultation.* New York: Marcel Dekker.

Schein, E. H. (1993b). On dialogue, culture, and organizational learning. *Organizational Dynamics, 22*(2), 40-51.

Schein, E. H. (1995). Process consultation, action research, and clinical inquiry: Are they the same? *Journal of Managerial Psychology, 10*(6), 14-19.

Schein, E. H. (1996a). Culture: The missing concept in organizational studies. *Administrative Science Quarterly, 11,* 229-240.

Schein, E. H. (1996b, Fall). Three cultures of management: The key to organization. *Sloan Management Review,* pp. 9-20.

Schein, E. H. (1997). *Organizational culture and leadership* (2nd ed.). San Francisco: Jossey-Bass.

Scott, W. G. (1961). Organization theory. *Journal of the Academy of Management, 4*(1), 7-26.

Senge, P. M. (1990, Fall). The leaders' new work: Building learning organizations. *Sloan Management Review,* pp. 7-24.

Shafritz, J. M., & Ott, J. S. (1996). *Classics of organization theory* (4th ed.). Belmont, CA: Wadsworth.

Shapiro, B. J., & Marcus, P. M. (1987). Library use, library instruction, and user success. *Research Strategies, 5*(2), 60-69.

Shapiro, E. C., Eccles, R. G., & Soske, T. L. (1993, Summer). Consulting: Has the solution become part of the problem? *Sloan Management Review,* pp. 89-97.

Shimkus, J. (2000). Rethinking systems. *Business and Management Principles, 9*(4).

Smircich, L. (1983). Concepts of culture and organizational analysis. *Administrative Science Quarterly, 28,* 339-358.

Stringer, E. T. (1999). *Action research* (2nd ed.). Thousand Oaks, CA: Sage.

Sull, D. N. (1999, July-August). Why good companies go bad. *Harvard Business Review,* pp. 42-52.

Susman, G. I. (1979). *Autonomy at work: A sociotechnical analysis of participative management.* New York: Praeger.

Tagiuri, R. (1992). The training and managing of consultants. *Journal of Management Consulting, 7*(1), 3-8.

Trist, E. L., & Bamforth, K. W. (1951). Some social and psychological consequences of the Longwall method of coal getting. *Human Relations, 4,* 3-38.

Trist, E. L., & Murray, H. (Eds.). (1993). *The social engagement of social science: A Tavistock anthology.* Vol. 2: *The socio-technical perspective.* Philadelphia: University of Pennsylvania Press.

Trist, E. L., Higgins, G. W., Murray, L., & Pollack, A. R. (1963). *Organizational choice: Capabilities of groups at the coal face under changing technologies: The loss, rediscovery, and transformation of a work tradition.* London: Tavistock.

Tschirhart, M. (1996). *Artful leadership.* Bloomington: Indiana University Press.

Turner, A. N. (1982, September-October). Consulting is more than giving advice. *Harvard Business Review,* pp. 120-129.

Van Maanen, J. (1982). Introduction. In J. Van Maanen, J. P. Dabbs, Jr., & R. R. Faulkner (Eds.), *Varieties of qualitative research.* Beverly Hills, CA: Sage.

Vicira, W. E. (1997). Consulting on change management in South Asia. *Journal of Management Consulting, 9*(3), 46-48.

Washburn, S. A. (1995). Coaching the client: Another role for management consultants. *Journal of Management Consulting, 8*(3), 2, 62.

Webb, J. R. (1995). Sherlock Holmes on consulting. *Journal of Management Consulting, 8*(3), 34-36.

Weisbord, M. R. (1987). Toward third-wave managing and consulting. *Organizational Dynamics, 15*(3), 4-24.

Zabrosky, A. M. (1999). The art of writing an engagement letter. *Journal of Management Consulting, 10*(3), 34-38.

Ziegenfuss, J. T. (1985). *DRGs and hospital impact: An organizational systems analysis.* New York: McGraw-Hill.

Ziegenfuss, J. T. (1987a). Toward a definition of roles for physicians in quality assurance. *Quality Assurance and Utilization Review, 2*(2), 36-41.

Ziegenfuss, J. T. (1987b). Why hospital linkages are increasing: Sharing institutions and organizational environment. *Health Matrix, 5*(1), 38-45.

Ziegenfuss, J. T. (1988a). Increasing innovation organization-wide: A systems approach and case example. In *Sixth World Productivity Congress proceedings* (Vol. 2). Montreal: Canadian Council for Productivity and World Confederation of Productivity Science.

Ziegenfuss, J. T. (1988b). *Organizational troubleshooters.* San Francisco: Jossey-Bass.

Ziegenfuss, J. T. (1988c). Toward productivity in five giant steps: An integrated systems approach. In *Sixth World Productivity Congress proceedings* (Vol. 2). Montreal: Canadian Council for Productivity and World Confederation of Productivity Science.

Ziegenfuss, J. T. (1989). *Designing organizational futures: A systems approach with cases for public and non-profit organizations.* Springfield, IL: Charles C Thomas.

Ziegenfuss, J. T. (1991). Organizational barriers to quality improvement in medical and health care organizations. *Quality Assurance and Utilization Review, 6*(4), 115-122.

Ziegenfuss, J. T. (1992). Are you growing systems thinking managers? Use a systems model to teach and practice organizational analysis and planning, policy, and development. *Systems Practice, 5,* 509-527.

Ziegenfuss, J. T. (1993). *The organizational path to health care quality.* Ann Arbor, MI: Health Administration Press.

Ziegenfuss, J. T. (1996). A methodology for use of systems thinking and redesign in graduate health care management education. In W. W. Gasparski, M. K. Mlicki, & B. H. Banathy (Eds.), *Praxiology: International annual of practical philosophy and methodology* (Vol. 4). New Brunswick, NJ: Transaction Publishing.

Ziegenfuss, J. T., & Perlman, H. (1989). Decreasing medical malpractice: An organizational systems approach. *Health Care Management Review, 14*(4), 67-75.

Ziegenfuss, J. T., Munzenrider, R. F., & Lartin-Drake, J. (1998). Organization change in a university hospital: A six-year evaluation of the Horizons Project. *Systemic Practice and Action Research, 11,* 575-597.

Ziegenfuss, J. T., & Bentley, J. M. (2000). Implementing cost control in health care: Strategies driven by an organizational systems approach. *Systemic Practice and Action Research, 13*(4), 453-474.

Index

About the Author

James T. Ziegenfuss, Jr., Ph.D., is Professor of Management and Health Care Systems at Pennsylvania State University, Harrisburg. He joined the faculty in 1983 and now teaches courses in strategic planning, organization behavior, health care systems, and quality management. He holds a Ph.D. in social systems sciences from the Wharton School of the University of Pennsylvania as well as master's degrees in psychology (Temple University) and public administration (Penn State).

While attending graduate schools, he worked full-time from 1973 to 1983 in organization analysis and planning including consulting evaluations, planning at the single- and multi-organizational levels, organizational change projects, and research and development of health care systems.

At the Penn State Medical College, he is Adjunct Clinical Professor of Medicine. He has been evaluation coordinator for the 6-year Robert Wood Johnson/Pew Trust project on transforming organization and care delivery systems and for the medical education diversity project. His education, research, and consulting work have been supported by more than 70 organizations.

He has written more than 90 articles for journals and conferences and has authored 8 books including *Organizational Troubleshooters: Resolving Problems for Customers and Employees; Designing Organizational Futures;* and *The Organizational Path to Health Care Quality.* His most recent work is represented by two international prize winning monographs: "Country and Community Health Systems: The Futures and Systems Redesign Approach" and "Building Citizen Participation: The Purposes, Tools and Impact of Involvement." Both won recognition at the 12th and 14th meetings of the Latin American Countries convocation on the reform of public administration in 1998 and 2000. His current teaching, research, and consulting interests are in the fields of strategic planning, quality management, and organizational development, particularly design and facilitation of planning processes and corporate ombudsman programs. He is an active consultant to public and private organizations.